PRAISE FOR
FINTECH WARS

The principles mentioned in the book helped us build Nubank, and
they will help you too.
David Vélez, CEO and Founder of Nubank

A history—and much more—of the evolution of financial technology,
Fintech Wars provides strategic insights along with some amazing
stories of the characters and strategies that have built multi-billion
businesses. Insightful and accessible, this is *the* book for people
thinking about investing or working in fintech and also for those just
curious about what all of the hype is about.
**Jeffrey Pfeffer, Thomas D. Dee II Professor of Organizational
Behavior at Stanford Graduate School of Business and author of
*7 Rules of Power***

James da Costa has the inside scoop on billion-dollar companies you
know like PayPal as well as some you haven't heard of... yet. He takes
those stories and breaks them down into lessons that everyone can
use to start, or grow, their business.
**Nicole Lapin, *New York Times* bestselling author and host of
finance podcast *Money Rehab***

In one of the most extensive collections of fintech stories from across
the world, James da Costa examines the success factors and failure
modes of unicorn fintechs. A must-read for aspiring fintech
entrepreneurs and business students.
**Ali Tamaseb, bestselling author and Super Founders and General
Partner at DCVC**

An unmissable account of many of the most influential fintechs of our generation. James da Costa is a performance superstar and this book is just another example of his ability to get to absolutely everyone and find the story in everything.

Heidi Roizen, Partner at Threshold Ventures, Board Director at Planet Labs, Lecturer at Stanford, and Former VP of Worldwide Developer Relations at Apple

Fintech Wars

Tech Titans, Complex Crypto and
the Future of Money

James da Costa

KoganPage

First published in Great Britain and the United States in 2024 by Kogan Page Limited

2nd Floor, 45 Gee Street
London
EC1V 3RS
United Kingdom
www.koganpage.com

8 W 38th Street, Suite 902
New York, NY 10018
USA

© James da Costa, 2024

The right of James da Costa to be identified as the author of this work has been asserted by him in accordance with the Copyright, Designs and Patents Act 1988.

ISBNs
Hardback   978 1 3986 1704 9
Paperback   978 1 3986 1702 5
Ebook   978 1 3986 1703 2

British Library Cataloguing-in-Publication Data
A CIP record for this book is available from the British Library.

Library of Congress Control Number
2024038764

Typeset by Hong Kong FIVE Workshop, Hong Kong
Print production managed by Jellyfish
Printed and bound by CPI Group (UK) Ltd, Croydon CR0 4YY

CONTENTS

ACKNOWLEDGMENTS

Thank you to my Developmental Editor and trusted collaborator, Chiara Benn—without you this would not have been possible, nor nearly as good. Secondly, thank you to my family and friends for your encouragement and proofing: Laura-May Nardella, Bonnie Choi, Ryan Davies, Shaden Alsheik, Jack Hilton, Helena Gostelow, Akshita Joshi, Faith Meyer, and Kasia Chodurek.

Fintech Wars explores startup rivalries, conflicts, and success stories from the world of fintech across banking, real estate, e-commerce, and insurance. The companies in this book represent over one trillion dollars in market capitalization.

Shortlisted by the *Financial Times* Bracken Bower Prize 2022, the book distills over 100 interviews, including with the founders of Capital One (Nigel), Nubank (David, Cristina, and Edward), Zillow (Spencer), Ripple (Chris), Xoom and Eventbrite (Kevin), Venmo (Andrew and Iqram), Mercury (Immad), OpenSea (Devin), LastMinute.com (Martha), SoFi (Ian), Monzo (Tom), Libra (Christina, Morgan, and David), Oscar (Mario), Trulia (Pete), Jeeves (Dileep), Ethos (Peter), Wealthfront (Andy), Kiva (Jess), and Newfront (Spike), as well as seasoned investors and operators like Reid Hoffman (PayPal and LinkedIn), Alex Pall (The Chainsmokers), Maurice Werdegar (WTI), Keith Rabois (Square and PayPal), Fern Mandelbaum (Emerson Collective), Scott Sandell (NEA), Sam Lessin (Slow Ventures), Bill Ready (Braintree and Pinterest), Brian A. Wong (Alibaba), Sarah Smith (BCV and Quora), Hans Morris (Visa), Jeff Epstein (Oracle and Bessemer), Roelof Botha (PayPal and Sequoia), and leading Stanford scholars including Professor Ilya Strebulaev, Associate Professor Saumitra Jha, Professor Jeffrey Pfeffer, Assistant Professor Chenxi Xu, and Professor Erik Brynjolfsson.

I am exceedingly thankful to everyone who gave their time to make this book possible. Stanford University is a petri dish for innovation and the home, at one point, to many of the protagonists in this book. I am deeply grateful for the unwavering support I received from the University in writing this book. Thank you for fostering an environment where ideas flourish.

Finally, thank you to Nick Hungerford, founder of Nutmeg, who I was fortunate enough to spend time with before his passing. Nick encouraged me to finish penning this book and to give it my all. A percentage of all author profits will be donated to Elizabeth's Smile, a charity set up by Nick in his daughter's name with the aim of helping grieving children.

Introduction

The Very First Fintech

A global financial crisis saved Capital One.
It was the early 1990s. The Gulf War and ensuing oil price shock triggered global anti-inflationary measures. Following the Cold War's close, the Soviet Union was dismantled and defense spending shrank. The combination plunged the global economy into recession.

Civil unrest broke out in the UK and the prime minister resigned; shortly followed by Canada's leader. In Japan, the recession prompted the "Lost Decades" of economic stagnation, from which the country has yet to fully recover. Meanwhile, Nigel Morris and Rich Fairbank set off each morning on their daily commute—104 miles from Northern Virginia to Richmond—to the headquarters of the Signet Banking Corporation. One hour and 40 minutes of worrying.

"I could feel the walls closing in," Nigel recalls.

As management consultants, in 1988 the pair had pitched an idea for a data-driven personalized credit card to Signet Bank. Receptive, the bank suggested that Nigel and Rich lead the operation; now on the other side of the table, they began building out the tech, hiring talent, and testing initial frameworks, a process that took longer than initially planned. Having promised tremendous returns, Signet Bank's credit card division still had little traction. The pair began to fear for their jobs.

Just as the pressure reached breaking point, Signet was knocked by the real estate crisis. Overbuilding in the 1980s led property values to drop by as much as 50 percent. As loan portfolios deteriorated, a slew of banks collapsed.

On 17 December 1991, the *Washington Post* reported: "Signet Banking Corp. announced that it intends to sell off $845 million in bad loans and foreclosed real estate." Macroeconomic pressures and a toppled US housing market had turned Signet's real estate loan portfolio red, slashing profit by 66 percent that quarter.

Enough management attention was diverted for Nigel and Richard to avoid premature termination. Relieved of pressure, Signet Bank's card division had its first success through a mass personalized postal mailing effort offering to transfer customers' existing credit to Signet Bank for a lower teaser rate. By 1994, Signet Bank had spun out its credit card division in an IPO, with Rich as CEO and Nigel as COO and President. Capital One overtook their high hopes, as a company with one product: Credit cards.

At Capital One's lowest moment, Nigel had confided in a friend, who consoled him with the proverb: "The darkest time is just before the dawn."

And when they reached dawn, Capital One created an industry—fintech.

Fintech is a portmanteau of the words "financial" and "technology." As defined by McKinsey, fintech companies use technology to deliver or enable the delivery of financial services. Fintech impacts how we store, save, borrow, invest, move, pay, and protect money. There is no typical fintech company—they include startups, banks, insurers, brokers, and credit providers.

Neobanks, neobrokers, crypto collapses, IPOs, bank insolvencies, SEC lawsuits, FTX, decentralization, tokenomics, 99.99 percent market wipeouts, 10,000x returns, and tech platforms you have never heard of processing more transaction volume in one day than entire countries do in one year—all these followed Capital One. Financial technology unicorns, with rare valuations of over $1 billion, have changed the world.

For founders, investors, and the interested bystander, this raises a critical question: How were these fintech unicorns built and what do they have in common? The following pages trace the rise of some of the most influential fintechs of our generation.

What follows are the blueprints for billion-dollar growth.

But First, Why Fintech is Important (and Affects Us All)

Money makes the world go round, but how does this actually happen? And who is behind it all? Fintech. It's how money moves around the globe.

Capital One's Nigel Morris fell into the industry and stayed because across the world fintech and finance account for "20 to 25 percent of GDP, depending on the country." Fintech has "massive economic rents and a huge disparity between the incumbent and the individual in terms of intellectual power, visibility, and confidence... If you know where to look. But if you ask the average American 'What's an APR, and how does it work? What's the Federal funds rate? What's a discount rate? How do I think about savings for my retirement?' The lack of financial sophistication and education is frightening," Nigel laments.

"Schooling doesn't help the average American or Brit."

Meanwhile, fintech is shaping everyday life and is behind almost everything we do. There are straightforward applications like checking your bank statement online or tapping Apple Pay to board the bus. And then ones you'd never imagine: Inventing money from nothing with new cryptocurrencies; getting a credit card from your favorite retail store; and even financing and insuring space exploration. The packages that arrive at your doorstep do so because of complex webs of interconnected economies and technologies that enable the rapid movement of goods and services. Fintech is a fundamental enabler in many of the world's biggest companies.

Even in remote areas of the world, fintech powers everyday services. There are 2.6 billion people offline today—that's one-third of the global population. And yet some are still beneficiaries of this wave of fintech disruption. M-PESA, a mobile phone-based fintech, processes over 50 percent of Kenya's GDP, much of which happens offline with users sending money in text messages (powered by telephone networks on old feature phones).

A recent report by Boston Consulting Group (BCG) and QED Investors predicts fintech revenues will grow to $1.5 trillion by 2030. We are just at the start of the journey.

Peeking behind this curtain into a world of heated rivalries, all-out wars, and market crashes, it's clear that fintech is everywhere.

Every Company is a Fintech Company

Andreessen Horowitz (a16z) General Partner Angela Strange famously stated, "Every company is a fintech company." QED's Nigel Morris agrees: "In the long run, everything is finance."

Fintech products are becoming a sustainable revenue stream for any software company. To Nigel, Toast is a perfect example. Toast is a leading restaurant and food delivery operating system in the United States which manages orders, inventory, and payroll. "Five years from now, Toast is not going to make as much money out of its SaaS (software as a service) subscription model. It's going to make money out of bill payments, insurance, and lending." Leveraging user data, Toast will be able to create financial products tailored to each customer.

Software startups will be able to expand into profitable financial services; Nigel continues, "We'll see AI and machine learning layering on top of that." This transition to embedded finance (the integration of financial services into non-financial applications) is expected to grow into a $320 billion market by 2030.

Another example is Twitch, the world's largest video streaming platform (think YouTube, but mainly for live-streaming video games). It was acquired by Amazon for close to $1 billion in 2014 and is now independently valued at $45 billion. Although rooted in video game streaming, Twitch became a unicorn because of a fintech realization: Gamers want to spend all day gaming and to do this they need to make money. Twitch enabled gamers to unlock monetization through affiliate links and payouts based on views.

The result was an explosion in the quality and quantity of content—the viewers followed.

Since the founding of Capital One, fintech has moved markets; we've seen the crashes of the Terra-LUNA cryptocurrencies, the FTX exchange, and Silicon Valley Bank (SVB). We've also seen fintech achieve decentralization, enable money to be sent from the device in our pockets, and engage with a large portion of the financially marginalized. And yet today, almost 25 percent of adults globally are still either underbanked or unbanked; fintech is ripe with opportunity.

But with opportunity comes war—between founders, governments, and rival startups.

Fintech: Born Out of Conflicts And Crashes

Finance is rooted in friction. The Bank of England was created to fund wars. In the United States, Founding Fathers Alexander Hamilton and Aaron Burr created two banks, known today as BNY Mellon and J.P. Morgan Chase. Alexander Hamilton's Bank of New York, operating today as BNY Mellon, would not lend money to Jefferson's Democratic-Republican faction. Aaron Burr responded, founding the Bank of the Manhattan Company, operating today as J.P. Morgan Chase, to break Hamilton's monopoly.

One of the earliest rivalries in fintech was Visa vs. Mastercard. Frenemies of a convenient duopoly, the pair control over 80 percent of the global card payment market. The two payment processors compete fiercely for bank partnerships, yet cooperate on industry standards and lobbying efforts.

The other Morris in fintech, Hans Morris, oversaw Capital One's IPO in 1994 and PayPal's at the turn of the century; Hans then took Visa public as its President in the late 2000s (aside from sharing a surname and an industry, Hans and Nigel also share a love of punk rock). Hans recalls, "Every investor meeting talked about [the duopoly]. I still have the notebook with a detailed competitive analysis: Mastercard—Visa. What they did better and what we did better. Competition is a good thing." It pushed each company to innovate.

Visa (and Mastercard) earn royalties on consumer and business spending. Visa has stitched together thousands of distribution agreements across banks and vendors to ensure you can use your card just about anywhere in the world. In exchange, Visa receives a percent of all processed volume in fees. Today, Visa is valued at more than any bank in the world, including the banks that helped to create the network.

Hans continues, "Visa was the best business model ever created. The basic idea boils down to authorizing and settling transactions; then they issue enterprise agreements with banks for distribution. You don't choose whether you get a Chase Visa card or a Mastercard. You get the debit card that Chase [bank] has selected." Visa and Mastercard's profits lie in their distribution agreements.

Historically in the United States, you could only send cash and cheques. Banks settled up with other merchants and banks at the end of each month. Visa, Mastercard, and a handful of other card issuers worked hard to build payment networks between them and now reap the rewards—Visa generated $34 billion in profit in the 2024 financial year, with a market capitalization of over $500 billion.

Today, Visa and Mastercard are so embedded in consumer spending that their revenues correlate with US GDP. Fintech wars have proved profitable.

Unexpectedly, global recessions have also accelerated financial innovation. In 2008 the global financial crisis decimated consumer faith in banks. This coincided with major developments in cloud computing and smartphones. With a supercomputer in everyone's pocket, the infrastructure costs for providing credible financial services plummeted. Hans recalls, "People started trusting application software in an unprecedented way... Disillusionment with traditional financial structures created a receptive environment for fintech."

Central banks across the world implemented new regulations and financial institutions slashed expenses, notably eliminating innovation groups. As a result, banks failed to adapt to the revolutionary technologies, leaving the door ajar for Silicon Valley entrepreneurs to disrupt the market. In the United States, fintech is the coming together of New York's finance and Silicon Valley's tech. These colliding forces lend their name to Hans's more recent endeavor, the venture capital firm Nyca (New York-California) Partners. Although some startups exploited this opportunity effectively, Hans reflects that other newcomers "just didn't understand how [finance] worked, so a lot of money got wasted."

After this cycle of disruption, the incumbents are now beginning to fight back with technology, whilst the disruptors have sharpened their financial acumen. Fintech wars rage on—and billion-dollar companies grow out of them.

Building a Company is Hard; It's Even Harder in Fintech

Fintech is one of the most difficult sectors in which to build a company. Having helped build Capital One and invested in over 225 startups at his VC fund QED, Nigel Morris shares that "Fintech is different... You have to understand credit, fraud, compliance, tech and treasury risk—assets and liabilities and how they come together—and if you don't understand, you end up being SVB or FTX."

Nigel calls this the 0.9^6 problem, "A 90 percent chance of success across six issues will lead to an overall chance of success of just 50 percent. Even if the best leaders have a 90 percent chance of overcoming early challenges, they are contingent on each other." Fintech founders must "understand the unit economics at an atomic level [and] understand the regulatory climate."

These complexities compound the typical struggles of entrepreneurship, namely rapid growth, which Nigel suggests is as vital for a startup's survival as food and water are to humans. Founders should also be prepared for the worst-case scenario. Nigel explains that Houdini, the famous magician who captivated audiences with his daring escapes, "died when somebody punched him in the stomach, even though he had the most incredible physique. Why? Because he hadn't tensed his stomach. Be prepared for something bad to happen."

Despite the challenges, Nigel built Capital One "out of this little rinky-dink but very authentic, traditional, orthodox Signet Bank... into a juggernaut." Since Capital One, a new wave of fintechs has disrupted the status quo.

Fintech is complex. But those who break through create generational companies. Although just 1 percent of VC-backed startups reach unicorn status, a large proportion of them—according to Stanford, 21 percent—hail from fintech.

Deconstructing success

This book offers a series of independent stories and case studies, tied together by their influential standing within the world of fintech. Each story offers unique learnings and "tips from the trenches;" when combined, they provide us some thematic insights into the key ingredients of success in starting and scaling successful fintech companies. It's a book that can be enjoyed as a whole or chapter by chapter.

In my own journey, I have always been intrigued by fintech. I grew up in the North of England, with mixed roots from India and Kenya, and became fascinated with how money works in different places around the world. I was surprised to find how differently it flows in each region.

Experiencing first-hand the innovation of mobile banking through companies like Monzo as a student in the UK, I decided to start my own digital bank (Fingo), aiming to provide financial services to underbanked youth in Africa, backed by Y Combinator and several unicorn founders. Today the bank has over 150,000 customers and was launched by the President of Kenya.

Somewhere in between, I had the chance to serve large incumbent banks and insurance companies at McKinsey in the UK, build my own mini-programs on top of super apps like WeChat, and dabble in the world of crypto. In fact, I purchased my first cryptocurrency (Bitcoin) as a physical coin, with its digital key (a string of letters and numbers) on the back, in cash, for $500 at a tech conference in 2016.

The book covers issues of talent and people, tactics for navigating cycles of booms and busts, the underlying technology and business models behind fintech, and the role of competition and conflict in building outlier companies. Conflict and competition, in particular, are powerful engines for innovation and a useful lens for understanding the world around us.

How do great co-founders navigate the toughest of times and conversations? How do you build an unstoppable team around you to execute on your vision? What do you do when you are hit with a crisis or you have to overcome the seemingly impossible? Should you fight competition or let your customer focus do the talking? What different business models and technology stacks are unique to fintech, and how might they accelerate or hinder your growth?

It's a book for aspiring fintech entrepreneurs, students, and curious industry bystanders. My hope is that it leaves you more excited and informed about an industry than when you started.

Capital One is a wonderful place to start, as arguably the first fintech company, and certainly the first to leverage customer-level data to truly tailor products for their end customers.

Let's dive in.

Capital One: Founding the First Fintech

The Watergate Building housed a scandal that toppled a US President, but it also seeded one of the 10 largest banks in the United States—and the first fintech.

Capital One ushered in a new era of credit cards based on data and grew into a systemically important bank. Grounded in history, America's nine other largest banks have weathered Ponzi schemes, global warfare, stock market crashes, and the Great Depression. How did Capital One, a newcomer, infiltrate?

Nigel Morris and Rich Fairbank sat in a strategy consultancy office at the Watergate Building. Nigel had grown up in Wales. With his father serving in the army, he had spent his formative years across 11 different schools. He was always an outsider: "I had come out of a non-business background, I had no idea about stocks and shares and assets and liabilities and revenues. Business was an anathema." Yet as a consultant, Nigel found that he was a pretty good talker: "People would ask me questions that they seemed to want to pay me to give them answers to that I had no right giving answers to." Nigel had "this massive imposter syndrome." To tackle this, Nigel wanted to try operating himself.

Signet Bank at the time ranked among the 50 largest banks in the United States but boasted one of the largest credit card portfolios. Signet had already shown progressive tendencies in student lending, aggressively cross-selling to their customers, and building a decent credit card portfolio. However, they faced a strategic dilemma about their future direction, prompting them to hire management consultants.

Back in 1988, many banks ignored their credit card divisions. But Nigel and Rich believed there was huge untapped potential there. Close to 50 percent of the US banking population didn't have access to consumer credit, and for the most part, banks charged the same rates and offered the same product to every customer. Nigel and Rich proposed a bold idea to Signet Bank: Using data to customize credit card offers to individuals. Their pitch was so compelling that Signet invited them to implement the plans. In Nigel's words, they planned to "price people according to [their] underlying risk." Doing so would allow them to achieve a similar profit margin for each customer, regardless of their risk level.

Capital One was realized as a branch of Signet Bank. Each morning began with Nigel and Rich driving what looked like a police car, a Ford Crown Victoria, to Signet Bank's headquarters, with a bagel stop in Fredericksburg. Yet as Capital One's personalized credit card offerings failed to gain uptake, on these long commutes, instead of biting into bagels the pair worried they had bitten off more than they could chew.

That global recession in the early 1990s lifted the pressure from their division for just long enough for the business to start gaining momentum.

Lowell L. Bryan's book *Breaking Up the Bank* put forward the case to break down banks into their component parts and drive revenue and profitability within each. As consultants, Nigel and Rich advised building on this, and their team's research discovered "a consistent pattern of where economic value was created [in banks]. We found that it was either investment banking and trading FX [foreign exchange], but that had a great cyclicality, or unsecured consumer lending. Virtually everything else destroyed value. So [at banks] there's massive cross-subsidization [across their services]." Nigel and Rich decided to go after unsecured credit in a new way: an information-based strategy, using customer data to offer better rates or higher rates to those previously unable to access credit.

But then, the regulators caught wind.

Guilty by Association

In 2002, regulators launched an investigation into Capital One.

By this time, the credit card landscape had become crowded with other players using information-based strategies; these newcomers borrowed terms from Capital One's playbook such as "closed loop" decision making and "test and learn analytical models," despite not always actually putting these terms into practice.

Many of these companies were less robust than Capital One. Some even engaged in malpractice. NextCard, for instance, had launched a credit card with Amazon.com, but regulators found it had insufficient funds to cover credit losses. NextCard had also been misreporting credit losses as fraud losses. The investigation triggered consumer mistrust and NextCard's stock price fell from its high of $53.12 to just $0.14 per share. The company was ultimately taken over by the FDIC.

Skeptical of Capital One's similar "information-based strategy," the regulators assumed guilt by association and launched an inquest.

Nigel and his team entered into a Memorandum of Understanding with bank regulatory authorities, "the first volley of regulatory intervention," with respect to Capital One's systems and controls. The market reacted harshly; Capital One's stock price plunged by half with the announcement.

With this jolt, Nigel realized he was running out of steam: "By 2002, I had been [co-running Capital One] for nearly 10 years. I could feel the regulatory environment becoming more difficult. The bloom was beginning to come off the rose, in terms of how innovative and creative Capital One was at that point. Becoming a big company is part of growing up, [but] I'm a disruptor, I'm an iconoclast."

But he was also loyal. "I could not leave a ship that looked like it was sinking," he continues, so he stayed on until the regulatory interest settled. "I spent the year handing over pieces of my job to others and watching them grow into it."

The most important lesson he taught them? Resilience. Nigel explains, "It's not just the people who've got an IQ of 145 that win, it's the people that know how to get it done." In the toughest moments, when "your heart, your stomach sinks" and "your dream" is shattering, "What do you do? You have to get up." Rally around the team, "The opportunity is there."

Once Capital One had stabilized after its regulatory setback, Nigel stepped away. After recuperating, he began exploring new horizons with his venture fund QED. Rich Fairbank, with whom

Nigel shared all of those long commutes, is still at Capital One. All these years later, he is the second longest-serving chairman and CEO of a financial company in the United States, close on the heels of renowned investor Warren Buffett, who chairs Berkshire Hathaway.

"In many ways, Rich was my soulmate, strategically," Nigel said. "Individually, we were polar opposites—he was an economics undergrad, a free spirit, and the son of a famous physicist, and I came from a working-class background in the UK, but we both held a fanatical shared vision to leverage data to create value. At Capital One, we divided the responsibilities so that Rich focused more on brand and customer origination and I spent most of my time on processes, tech, and people. I learned so much from my dear friend Rich, including many things that I still carry with me today. He has a world-class strategic mind. The odds of me turning Signet Bank into Capital One would have been considerably less if we weren't in it together."

One of the greatest challenges in Rich's tenure, he would have to face without his co-founder.

Boom and Bust

On 15 September 2008, Lehman Brothers filed for bankruptcy, the largest in US history. From there unfolded what the Federal Reserve Chairman deemed "the worst financial crisis in global history, including the Great Depression." Primarily triggered by the collapse of the US subprime mortgage market, when borrowers with poor credit histories began defaulting en masse, the chain reaction brought down financial institutions and crashed markets across the globe.

As a credit provider to the underbanked, Capital One was especially exposed to the market shock.

In the fourth quarter of 2008 alone, Capital One recorded a net loss of $1.4 billion. They suffered charge-offs—credit card users with debts so unlikely to be repaid that they were written off as losses—driven by increasing unemployment and declining home prices.

Under Rich Fairbank's leadership, the company pre-emptively allocated $1 billion toward an anticipated rise in charge-offs. This cushioned the impact of defaults. Capital One also implemented efficiency measures, adapted to new regulations and, to drive recovery, focused on its core business offerings: Credit cards and consumer banking.

Despite the 2008 scare, Capital One had been planning for the worst since its inception. Frank Rotman—Nigel's co-founder at QED and Capital One's first Chief Credit Officer, before that was even a role—was responsible for building the entire analytic infrastructure of Capital One from the ground up. Frank "collapsed everything to the atomic units, and built it back up using holistic frameworks that the different business units could apply to their customer and product segments. Everything is integrated. And if you can't make an integrated decision, you're going to make a poor decision."

Under Frank, Capital One was one of the first credit card companies to build a worsening credit risk environment and a recession into its risk model, even though there were no signs of it happening. To Frank, "It meant that the customer would be resilient. It's very easy to give out money, the hard part is getting it back."

Yet Capital One did exactly that. In the late 90s and early 2000s, while other banks lost billions, Capital One never made a loss as an overall business. That said, "Just because you don't cross below zero, [in recession] you're not making money, you're missing earnings... It was stressful, trust me," Frank says.

"The most stressful day of my career was having to say we've had five months in a row with the [profit] forecast getting a little worse." This gave Frank a difficult task. "We announced that we were going to miss earnings [targets] for the first time in the history of Capital One." After several months of missing internal projections, Frank learnt an important lesson. "We finally took it on the chin." Sometimes it doesn't pay to fight the situation but instead accept its difficulty and communicate candidly. By resetting expectations, Capital One went on to outperform its new benchmarks.

Inherent in founding a company are cycles of booms and busts. What do you do when you are hit with a crisis? Or when your stock price halves? Or when you have to overcome the impossible?

Nigel shares the "amplitude, the size of the wave in venture [capital] is pretty extraordinary." He reminisces on the fintech boom that grew out of a global pandemic: "With Covid, there was a big shift to digital. When that happened, the CAC [consumer acquisition cost] fell dramatically. LTVs [lifetime value] went up. The old school started to lose ground. And there was an inherent acceleration in all fintechs everywhere around the globe." Publicly listed fintech valuations "went from four times revenue to 20 times [revenue] in one year."

"These companies were worth all this money, and then down it came. Putin invaded [Ukraine], supply chains were disrupted, interest rates went up 500 basis points and everybody was worried about a deep recession. Valuations fell back to four or five times revenue." Although the market took a hit, there have been silver linings, Nigel continues, "We're seeing our companies now starting to perform much better than they did a year ago. And the ones that survived this little ice age [will] come out of the blocks fast and do well." But it is worth noting that for every survivor there are many startups that don't make it. The nature of entrepreneurship is navigating times of abundance as well as famine.

Warren Buffett, Chairperson of Berkshire Hathaway (a diversified holding company with interests in railways, energy companies, manufacturing, retail, real estate, and investments) offers sage advice on navigating volatility. In a 1987 letter to shareholders, Warren popularized the concept of Mr Market:

> Without fail, Mr. Market appears daily and names a price at which he
> will either buy your interest or sell you his. For, sad to say, the poor
> fellow has incurable emotional problems. At times, he feels euphoric
> and can see only the favorable factors affecting the business. When in
> that mood, he names a very high buy-sell price because he fears that

you will snap up his interest and rob him of imminent gains. At other times he is depressed and can see nothing but trouble ahead for both the business and the world. On these occasions, he will name a very low price, since he is terrified that you will unload your interest on him.

Mr Market is a metaphor to explain the stock market's erratic behavior and cyclical shifts. The private markets that founders navigate experience secondary effects of this volatility. Warren advocates for remaining calm: "Insulate [your] thoughts and behavior from the super-contagious emotions that swirl about the marketplace." Berkshire Hathaway's late vice chairman, Charlie Munger, lays out the remedy in a collection of his talks republished by Stripe Press (the publishing house of fintech Stripe): ignore yesterday's valuation—you must make decisions based on what is happening right now.

Just as history is not an indicator of future performance, Capital One's Nigel Morris takes the same approach to hiring. "By the time you have the experience, often, it's obsolete, because the world is changing so fast... Go long on talent and short on experience, because experience doesn't predict the future."

Capital One's pioneering approach included giving stock options to all employees. This move motivated the workforce, contributing to Capital One's reputation as an innovative and employee-focused company. To Nigel, "It's about alignment, it's about believing in a common view of what you're trying to do and how you are going to do it... It's about working hard and marshaling around you talented people."

After Capital One, Nigel founded the venture fund QED with Frank Rotman, a long-time key colleague. "Frank is, of course, brilliant, and he's a wonderful co-pilot with me. We worked together at Capital One and QED, so for 31 years now. Poor soul," Nigel quips. "These are people that I've grown up with. They know me and I know them, and we have a common view of the world. We use similar frameworks. When in doubt [we] go to the facts, not to supposition. Life is about the journey, [and] the people that you get to grow up with and build with."

Today, QED has reached threshold scale in terms of size and brand. One of the few global fintech specialists, QED has invested in more than 225 companies across 19 countries, with $4 billion of assets under management. The firm has offices in Northern Virginia, New York City, and London and a stable of worldwide unicorns including Nubank, Credit Karma, Remitly, SoFi, AvidXchange, Creditas, Flywire, and OneCard, many of which QED first invested in at the Series A stage or earlier.

Prior to QED, Nigel and Frank grew Capital One's revenue 1,000-fold since 1991, and it now hovers at over $36 billion. Buffeted by market turmoil in the global financial crashes in 1991 and 2008, Capital One has emerged stronger, joining the ranks of legacy banks. Capital One outlasted its creator, spinning out in 1994 as an independent bank before Signet was absorbed into First Union Corporation (now part of Wells Fargo) in 1997.

Today, Capital One has a market capitalization of over $50 billion.

Even now, as a behemoth, Capital One still suffers market shocks. In 2019, it was the victim of one of the most significant data breaches in history, affecting over 100 million customers. The compromised data included customer incomes, credit scores, limits, and payment histories, allowing hackers to pinpoint individuals to defraud. The hacker served jail time and Capital One reinforced its cloud safety measures.

In the early days of Capital One, managing fraud, Frank "almost wanted to applaud how smart the fraudsters were, but at the same time, I hated them. Many fraudsters are better customers of technology," and are often more adept at utilizing technology, "than the companies are that are trying to fight the fraudsters." Frank recalls "just how smart and quick they were to adopt new tools and new methodologies of doing things. They were so creative." Fraudsters operated with the efficiency of businesses.

One fraudster cracked every single rule in Capital One's system around authorizations and pre-authorizations, having worked for another bank. That fraudster would take regular trips internationally, knowing how to stay at hotels, book travel, and how long it would take for his card to show up in a fraud book in any given country. Despite Capital One never extending a credit line beyond $500 to him, by the time Capital One caught the fraudster, through a private investigator, he had managed to spend $500,000 on the card.

The path to success is often turbulent. Yet by harnessing user data and technology, Capital One set a precedent—opening the floodgates for others to follow.

The First of Many Fintechs

How can fintech help solve the global environmental crisis? Why was Facebook (now Meta) looking into digital currencies? Can fintech solutions bridge the gap for the unbanked and underbanked populations globally? Why are JPEGS selling for millions of dollars online?

Pondering some of these questions, I started writing this book. I continued because my outline became a powerful prediction for the next 12 months, with the collapse of FTX, SVB, and rising costs of living across the world.

Breaking down the jargon, *Fintech Wars* peeks into the future of money: The business models, underlying technologies, and talent driving forward these changes. This book chronicles the watershed moments that defined fintech, and serves as a compass for building billion-dollar fintechs.

01

PayPal vs. No One

The Fintech Unicorn That Spawned a Mafia

It's 2000 and you're struggling with rent. You're at an interview to join Peter Thiel at PayPal. You *need* this job. Peter asks: "You have a round table of arbitrary size. You and your opponent have an infinite number of quarters (25-cent coins). You take turns placing a coin on the table. The coins cannot overlap and must be placed flat. When no more can be placed without falling off, the person with the most quarters on the table wins. To win, should you go first or second? And what is your strategy for placing your coins?"

The correct answer: Go first. In one extreme yet logical scenario, the table could be the size of just one coin. The strategy for larger tables: First, put your coin at the center of the table. On subsequent turns, place your quarter opposite your opponent's coin; on a round table, if they have found space, so will you. That way, you are always one coin ahead.

PayPal's co-founder, Peter Thiel, posed this question to Stanford student Roelof Botha. Originally from South Africa, Roelof's savings were in Rand. At the turn of the century, the volatile currency devalued against the US dollar by 30 percent in just one month, eroding what he'd planned to live on. Whilst he studied the history of finance and capital management at Stanford, he was experiencing in real time an emerging market's currency crisis. Roelof needed income. So when fellow South African Elon Musk suggested for a third time that Roelof apply to join PayPal in March 2000, Roelof jumped at the chance. The pair had met through a mutual friend.

Roelof passed his PayPal interview and, despite his precarious financial situation, made an unconventional move. Roelof negotiated his salary down from $100,000 to $85,000, in exchange for more stock options in the company. This decision left him in debt. However, Roelof's learnings from scaling PayPal would prove invaluable and his increased stake in the company ultimately paid off. PayPal grew into the world's most valuable digital payment platform and within two years, Roelof climbed the ranks to become its Chief Financial Officer.

In doing so, Roelof joined the so-called "PayPal mafia"—a network of founders and early employees who have started many generational companies over the past two decades, and have been compared to a mafia because of their tight-knit nature and outsized influence on the startup ecosystem. PayPal spearheaded the creation of digital payments. The PayPal mafia has since built Tesla, SpaceX, OpenAI, Palantir, LinkedIn, YouTube, and Yelp, to name just a few.

A constellation of successful investments also orbits the PayPal mafia. Peter Thiel was the first investor in Facebook, with his $500,000 stake netting him $1 billion by 2012. Had Peter held onto the shares, they would be worth close to $15 billion today. Leading Silicon Valley's most prestigious venture capital funds, the PayPal mafia has backed the likes of Airbnb, Stripe, Quora, Uber, and Lyft, propelling the group's net worth to an estimated $310 billion.

PayPal's journey began at the dawn of the internet era, in 1998, as two companies: Peter Thiel's Confinity with their product PayPal, and Elon Musk's X.com, with co-founders hailing from Germany, the Soviet Union, and South Africa.

The dotcom crash triggered a wave of bankruptcies across the tech industry. Meanwhile, Confinity and X.com were burning through cash in ruinous attempts to become the market leader. The fierce rivals opted to merge, as equal partners, with Elon Musk as CEO. The merger dissipated any competitors.

Together as PayPal, the pair could take on a bigger adversary: eBay.

Fending Off eBay

Not long after the merger, Roelof joined PayPal. It was not plain sailing: "At least three times I thought we were going to die. I was thinking: okay, so I'm going to have to make my way back to South Africa. I'm going to lose my work visa. This is all going to be over."

The first of these challenges was eBay. PayPal had found product-market fit by enabling sellers on the e-marketplace giant. Though the two were not integrated, PayPal COO David Sacks noticed that 54 eBay sellers were manually entering their PayPal payment details on their listings. A growing number of merchants on eBay wanted to be paid by PayPal, especially after PayPal pioneered the use of email as a way to facilitate online transactions. PayPal was novel in using email addresses. Yet, despite the positive flywheel between the two platforms, eBay constantly tried to have PayPal shut down.

Roelof recalls, "Every now and again, we'd get word that eBay organized a new team [in] a war room trying to kill us. Or they cut off our scrapers. Then we'd just scramble. We'd have emergency meetings."

PayPal built tools called scrapers to monitor eBay auctions and auto-insert the PayPal logo and payment link. PayPal aimed to streamline the buyer experience; with a single click, successful auction bidders could seamlessly pay. eBay attempted to disable those links. Roelof recalls "We had to constantly 'badger mind' [come up with workarounds] against this onslaught."

PayPal overcame eBay's obstructions by building a network of loyal users. Roelof notes, "That peer-to-peer network is the reason we were able to beat eBay, even though they already had a payments company called Billpoint." The more buyers and sellers using PayPal, the greater the network effect and the more valuable its service became. eBay could not ignore its customers.

At the start of PayPal, Peter Thiel and Max Levchin each recruited a friend with experience in startups to their board. In Max's case that was Scott Banister (founder of IronPort, later acquired by Cisco), for Peter that was Reid Hoffman (co-founder of LinkedIn).

Later joining PayPal as its COO, Reid entered war mode: "As long as we were allowed to play, [and] eBay didn't drive us off the system, we could win." According to Reid, he took a defensive, "full-court press strategy," converting government officials and eBay employees to the PayPal cause, whilst through dialogue and shared wins keeping the prospect open that eBay may, one day, buy PayPal.

The PayPal team didn't anticipate that the startup's next encounter with death would come from inside the company...

Dotcom Fraud

When Roelof joined in 2000 as PayPal's Head of Financial Planning and Analysis (FP&A), he found "a canary in the coal mine."

Roelof was in a unique position to spot the problem. Back in South Africa, he had studied to become an actuary—managing risk for insurance companies using statistical modeling—one of the country's highest-paid professions. An insurance company even sponsored his education, offering a post-graduate job, which Roelof ultimately declined in favor of management consulting at McKinsey. This decision came at a significant cost, paying half of an actuary's salary, but gave Roelof the means to leave South Africa.

Roelof's appetite for personal risk and short-term sacrifice was already evident. After graduating from Stanford, instead of returning to McKinsey, Roelof joined PayPal where he could put these actuarial models to use.

Constructing a financial model for PayPal based on cost accounting, each month Roelof would compare predicted costs with actuals. He applied a technique called a 'chain ladder,' commonly used in short-term insurance to predict cash outflow based on historical cost patterns. Doing so unraveled a fundamental error in PayPal's fraud loss rate calculations—they were based on vastly outdated figures.

PayPal calculated its loss rate by dividing the losses reported on a given day by the payment volume on that same day. However, Roelof recalls, "I started to realize the fraud we were reporting was generally related to transactions 10–12 weeks ago." In a rapidly growing company like PayPal, this created a dramatic discrepancy between the numerator and denominator. Roelof's findings revealed that the actual loss rate was not 40 basis points, as previously believed, but over 100 basis points. PayPal had been underestimating fraud by 60 percent.

Roelof realized the error in June of 2000. Were it not for Roelof's discovery, the escalating fraud rate could have crippled PayPal. Roelof reflects: "We had seven months of runway and the Nasdaq had crashed already." At the height of the dotcom recession, PayPal was not going to be able to raise more money, so they had to make do. "If we'd caught the fraud problem a little bit later, we would have died." Roelof brought the fraud issue to PayPal co-founder Max Levchin, who then took action to address the problem, gathering a number of PayPal's most talented engineers: Jawed Karim (co-founder, YouTube); Nathan Gettings and intern Joe Lonsdale (co-founders, Palantir). Their solution accidentally developed another industry entirely: fraud detection.

To combat fraud, PayPal launched a CAPTCHA test, which uses human reason to prove users are not bots.

Levchin would later build Affirm—the buy now, pay later unicorn that instantly assesses users for loan eligibility. In particular, the insight that data can track down bad actors inspired Joe and Nathan to go on to build Palantir (PLTR), the data analytics decacorn.

Despite overcoming major obstacles, Roelof Botha cautions against overconfidence: "Peter had a great phrase—when somebody shoots at you and you don't get hit, you might think you're bulletproof. But it might just be that they're a bad shot. Eventually, a stray bullet might kill you." This mindset of vigilance served PayPal well as it navigated a cut-throat landscape.

In the wake of the underestimated fraud, acting in the best interests of PayPal, Confinity's founders convinced the board to replace Elon Musk with Peter Thiel as CEO. Elon was informed whilst on his honeymoon.

The coup, however, was not the last hurdle for PayPal. As it clawed its way back from the brink and readied for an IPO, a new threat loomed...

IPO: PYPL

Now PayPal's Chief Financial Officer, Roelof Botha, led the company's public listing; eBay sought to undermine that too. Back then, Roelof lived "in fear that eBay was constantly trying to kill us." During PayPal's IPO roadshow, eBay representatives spoke negatively of the startup. This antagonistic stance from a powerful player in the e-commerce space—one that PayPal relied on for many of its transactions—made investors reluctant to buy into PayPal's IPO. "That's why [leading underwriter] Morgan Stanley refused to take us public."

At just 27, Roelof recalls having to look older to justify his position. "I wore these little metal-framed spectacles, in a very conservative style, because I needed to look older. Peter [Thiel] used to tease me that my accent, a Commonwealth English accent, gave a little bit of credibility. [That it made people think] we can trust that kind of person."

Roelof's efforts paid off. In February 2002, PayPal floated on the Nasdaq exchange under the ticker symbol "PYPL." On its first day of trading, PYPL's stock soared 50 percent.

Steering PayPal through an IPO in his late 20s showcased Roelof's remarkable business acumen. However, Roelof humbly attributes this achievement to being part of an extraordinary team, united by a common goal. Zooming out further, Roelof reminds us that PayPal is not unique; there is a history in Silicon Valley of companies that have spawned other so-called mafias including Sun Microsystems, Facebook, Stripe, Square, and Salesforce. PayPal was just another one of these petri dishes for innovation.

Comparing today's climate to the dawn of the internet era, Roelof explains, "At PayPal, we had an unnatural concentration of talent post [dotcom] crash, whereas in the last couple of years, talent has been spread." On the other hand, in those days, "You had a very high rate of equity dilution." Taking PayPal public, even with his increased share due to his salary sacrifice, Roelof made just a few million dollars. Although a huge sum of money for a young person, it was not quite so large that Roelof would never have to work again. And he was certainly not done with his ambitions.

"PayPal had to fight incredibly hard to win," Roelof recalls. This competitiveness was channeled into subsequent companies that the PayPal mafia invested in, started, or joined, including LinkedIn, YouTube, Yelp, and Palantir—and on the VC side at Founders Fund, Greylock, Sequoia, and more. Roelof marvels, "The 'PayPal effect' infused into companies" throughout Silicon Valley.

Except one.

PYPL to eBay, and Back Again

Just months after listing publicly in 2002, PayPal was taken private by eBay for $1.5 billion, after several prior attempts at lower offers.

Having battled eBay for years, PayPal experienced a mass exodus of its founding team after the acquisition. Typically, such departures following mergers and acquisitions (M&A) are more gradual, reflecting the clash between entrepreneurial spirits and rigid corporate structures. But for PayPal, the animosity ran deeper; the team had been fighting eBay for years. As Roelof recalls, "the acquisition created a cliff date" so the subsequent string of startups founded by former PayPal employees and founders "were all concentrated in time." In the lead-up to 2005, "the browser [became] more powerful" so there was "an explosion of technology and a bunch of talented people" launching innovative products.

Just over a decade after the acquisition, eBay spun out PayPal as a far more valuable company than eBay itself.

The two rivals could not be contained beneath one umbrella. PayPal returned to the stock market as PYPL. The split meant PayPal and eBay could become more nimble at innovating their respective industries, without being constrained by the other entity's priorities. Where eBay sellers had once accounted for a significant portion of PayPal's revenue, this had withered and with it the synergies between the two companies. The spin-off would unlock value: PayPal's dynamic growth had long been overshadowed by eBay's lagging pace.

What was once a struggling payments startup had grown into a Silicon Valley institution. The legendary story of PayPal has been well documented, including in Eric M. Jackson's book *The PayPal Wars*, *The Founders* by Jimmy Soni, and Walter Isaacson's recent biography of Elon Musk.

PayPal's founding story brings light to a set of key founders, operators, and investors who would go on and shape Silicon Valley as we know it today. PayPal's former Vice President, Keith Rabois, maps out PayPal's culture and how it taught him to negotiate with Silicon Valley's leaders.

The Secrets of Negotiating

Keith Rabois, an early PayPal employee—who has founded, funded or helped start 23 unicorns in 23 years, including Opendoor, Square (now Block) and as Managing Director at Khosla Ventures—distills PayPal's distinctive character down to three key points:

1. Combining People with Key Attributes

PayPal's founders hired intellectual, competitive, and multilingual individuals who excelled in math. In Max Levchin's words, "they think like me, they're just as geeky. Great hire! We'll get along perfectly."

Keith adds, the team also shared a "dedication to individual accomplishment—most great innovations at PayPal were driven by one person who then conscripted others to support, adopt, implement the new idea." Reinforcing this, Peter required everyone to be tasked with one priority and would refuse to discuss virtually anything else with you except what was currently assigned as your number one initiative.

2. Culture, a Way of Doing Work That Was Differentiated

PayPal's culture was unusual, at the time.

PayPal had a ruthless knack for efficiency. PayPal's first COO David Sacks enforced a rule of no unnecessary meetings—if he could not see its value in three minutes, it was wrapped up. Management team meetings on Saturdays and Sunday afternoons were held in the office. PowerPoint, arriving late, and praising eBay were all considered cultural missteps.

But company culture isn't built in isolation. Keith shares, "Each successful company has its own specific cult and cocktail of ideas you've learned from different places, different people." Culture also varies "depending upon what kind of challenge you're trying to solve, [for] what market? What are the laws of physics that serve in those markets? What's the best composition of the team? What's the best style of decision-making?" Whatever the intended culture, Keith advocates for founders to lead by example, as "company controllers typically take on many of the traits of the founders or the founding team."

3. The Challenge of Surviving Was a Good Predictor for People Who Would Thrive in the Future

Keith's time at PayPal allowed him to predict who would be successful. Through all of PayPal's near-death encounters, he observed colleagues under intense pressure and resource constraints. After a company is already successful, you don't get a good strong, high-fidelity read on people's abilities."

The relentless pressure of PayPal's environment weeded out all but the most resilient team members, and their perseverance laid the foundation for future achievements. In Keith's experience, "Some people perform better in challenges and pressure, and some people don't. When you're starting a company, you typically want founders who thrive with ambiguity and with pressure." PayPal had an abundance of both.

PayPal's executive team—Peter Thiel, David Sacks, Reid Hoffman, Max Levchin, and Roelof Botha—all sat in close proximity to each other, with the engineering team close at hand. Keith reminisces, "We had very vigorous debates. Conflict is a good thing. We wanted the sharpest, best ideas to prevail—we were trying to solve difficult problems. Typically the edges of the debate are where you find insights," where opposing viewpoints clash.

When there were disagreements, Roelof recalls "it was intellectual." Unlike typical debates where individuals suffer from an escalation of commitment and "most people are loath to change their position in public," Roelof continues, "Peter [Thiel] was not. Peter would say we're turning left. And then you do analysis, the data suggests otherwise and you present it to Peter. Peter would look at it and go 'Yeah, you're right. We're going to turn right.' "

Delving into Keith Rabois' experience working with Silicon Valley's most influential CEOs, we discover his dynamic strategies for approaching debate, an essential skill for any founder. Keith reveals five secrets to negotiating learned over his time at PayPal, LinkedIn, OpenDoor, and Square:

- **Peter Thiel**
  Co-founder, PayPal, Palantir Technologies, and Founders Fund
  Dispute with data. "The best way to disagree is to have a data point that refutes his theory. He tends to extrapolate well from a single data point." Faced with a difference in opinion from

Peter, Keith would consider "What's the way to pierce [his] theory with an objective statement?"

- **Max Levchin**
  Co-founder, PayPal and Affirm
  Suggest an alternative path and demonstrate why it's better. Rather than contradicting Levchin's premise, show that if you follow those principles to their logical conclusion, another course of action is preferable to the one he has advocated for. For example, "If you take x, y and z as a given, [explain how an alternative] path navigates it better."

- **Reid Hoffman**
  Former COO, PayPal; Co-founder, LinkedIn; Partner, Greylock
  Use option values—explain the benefit of delaying an irreversible decision until more data is available and how this information will inexpensively validate or disprove your approach. "Articulate why there's an option value in your idea and that the option value can be validated or proven at fairly low investments of time or money." Essentially, Keith suggests making a case to Reid for preserving flexibility and gathering more data before committing to an irreversible decision.

- **Jack Dorsey**
  Co-founder, Twitter and Square (now Block)
  There are two ways to convince Jack Dorsey of your view, when Jack puts forward a proposal. At a detail level, identify specific limitations to the implementation of the proposal. Point out areas where his plan may face obstacles when put into practice. On a philosophical level, you should agree with the fundamental idea behind the proposal. Rabois would say, "The principles are right, the idea is right, we just need to sequence them slightly differently."

- **Keith Rabois**
  Co-founder, Opendoor; Former Vice President, PayPal; Former COO, Square; Managing Director, Khosla Ventures
  Keith attests to responding well to data-based arguments, like Peter Thiel. If someone highlights "a data point that's inconsistent

with a theory," he'll take note. That could be small indicators that upend a long-held assumption, "like Copernicus discovering the sun doesn't revolve around the earth with small observational errors. [Point out] the theory that the current paradigm doesn't account for." That leads to a discussion: "Either the data measurement is wrong or the paradigm is off."

Housing Tech Mafias

Why do tech mafias form in some places and not in others? Why were the founders and early employees of PayPal so prolific?

In part, it's the culture (or "cult") you build around the people.

"If you're going to build a cult, you need your own space," explains PayPal mafia member Keith Rabois, "because a cult, by definition, is a shared secret that the members believe, that the rest of the world doesn't understand or rejects. You need your own physical space because outsiders are antithetical." Keith Rabois has seeded a number of generational fintech companies such as Ramp, Stripe, and Affirm, and operated at many more, including PayPal and Square.

Converting people to believe in your startup and its culture, Keith attests, is not so different from a cult. Both need a headquarters. "That space should reinforce your key cultural principles. So for example, if your culture is very transparent, you need a transparent space; maybe all the conference rooms are glass, so people can see who's with me and why." If, however, "frugality" is the "company's cultural tenet, you want the space to represent discipline around cost." A working environment reinforces culture.

Keith continues, "Building companies is challenging and takes a lot of heroic effort. You want employees to spend more time working, so if you give them a space that they're excited about going to, that's energizing with quality lighting, furniture, food, they're more likely to spend incremental time working [at the office], versus half-working at home."

These need not be extravagant spaces. As this book will explore, Nubank can be traced back to a "casinha" in Brazil with toilet flushes so loud the team had to mute their calls; Venmo to its heavy-doored New York office and a stream of knocks from new hires that co-founder Iqram had met in saunas and other unusual sources; Monzo to a cordoned-off parcel of floorspace in a London office, where the team congratulated one another with high fives; and Alibaba to a dingy apartment in Hangzhou, to which the Alipay team returned to incubate their idea.

These spaces commanded almost mythic status once these startups transitioned to scale-ups and now form part of the legend of their resulting "tech mafias."

Lasting Impact

The foundational skills honed at PayPal—thriving under immense pressure, embracing conflict to sharpen ideas, and fighting for survival—enabled this group to repeatedly identify and capitalize on emerging opportunities. In doing so, they have become an all-powerful presence in Silicon Valley.

Although the term "PayPal Mafia" was coined in a 2007 *Fortune* cover story by Jeffrey M. O'Brien, which examined the outsized influence within the tech scene of a group of men who had launched PayPal almost a decade earlier, PayPal was a meritocracy, and there are numerous women who went on to conquer the tech world. Deborah Liu, an early product manager at PayPal, is now the CEO of Ancestry. Boa Cheung, Director of International and Cross-border, led other unicorns as Chief Experience Officer at Bill.com and is a board member of Remitly. Sarah Imbach, SVP of Customer Service Operations and Fraud, became COO at LinkedIn and a board member at Change.org. Denise Aptekar, Director of Product Management, became VP of Global Payments at UpWork.

Reid Hoffman shares his thoughts on the two factors behind creating a mafia or "people network." One factor was talent. PayPal had done "an unusually good job of recruiting very high energy, high talent, high IQ, young people." The second was that this talent was armed with resources. PayPal "had a great amount of success in a short period of time." Spurred on by the fact "the entrepreneurship part was over [having] sold to eBay" and "still young and energized and with money, [most decided] we'll go do something [new]. That combination created waves in many directions. Even [for] Elon because without the money that PayPal made for him, he wouldn't have been able to do Tesla [nor] SpaceX."

As Roelof Botha reflects, "PayPal had to fight incredibly hard to win." That shared struggle created an inseparable bond and "infused" an unstoppable drive into every subsequent venture the mafia launched. PayPal's treacherous route to success paved the way for an entire industry—digital payments.

TIPS FROM THE TRENCHES

1 Be contrarian (and right). PayPal was an environment of intellectual debate but also a place where data won. At every step, the team bet against the status quo, pursuing internet money before it was commonplace, merging X.com with Confinity despite their fierce rivalry, or solving fraud issues with novel technology approaches.

2 Hire young, exceptional talent. Reid Hoffman highlights the dichotomy of hiring: Do you choose someone with experience or "a young person [with] high talent, [who can] figure it out and learn it as they're doing it?" In his experience, young talent usually pays off—it did for PayPal.

3 Leverage network effects. PayPal's peer-to-peer network allowed it to fend off eBay's monopolistic moves. Building a loyal user base and positive network effects will make your product increasingly indispensable.

02
Venmo vs. Cash
"Money is Pure Fiction"

In 2009, an idea hatched that would *reinvent* US consumer banking. No more queuing to deposit checks at the bank, nor panicked delving in wallet folds and coat pockets, hoping to find a crumpled bill before a dash to the ATM.

You might expect the transformation of US banking to emanate from suited traders in the Gilded Age skyscrapers of Wall Street or trainer-donning programmers pitching for investment on Sand Hill Road, from the great university research labs or even the domed halls of Congress.

But this idea sparked between two friends in a sweaty Philadelphia music venue.

Andrew Kortina, known as Kortina, and Iqram Magdon-Ismail tapped their feet to an infectious funk beat. But they felt a pang of guilt. They were too lazy to descend from the balcony and wrestle through crowds to tip the performers. If only they could text the band money via their Blackberry phones. They jotted the idea down, the foundation of what became Venmo, and then forgot about it for a while. Little did they know that just over a decade later, in 2023, Venmo would process over $250 billion in payments for its 85 million active users and become a widely used verb in its own right.

The seeds of Venmo—a yearning for financial inclusion and a knack for finding clever solutions—were rooted in Kortina and Iqram's childhoods. Before the age of 14, Iqram had lived in Zimbabwe, Zambia, and Uganda. These formative childhood years gave Iqram the perspective of a wide world beyond the United States and an inherent desire to fight for equality.

Meanwhile, Kortina grew up in a modest New Jersey household. Toys were rare and reserved for occasions like birthdays and Christmas. They could have afforded more but abstained. Instead, Kortina made the most of what he had, namely Lego, merging pieces across Lego sets, strengthening his frugality and creativity.

Years later Kortina and Iqram were college roommates at the University of Pennsylvania (Penn). Immediate friends, they bonded over a shared love for the guitar and lifting weights. Iqram shares, "He would show me how to weightlift, I would show him how to play guitar. We would just exchange experiences and then one thing led to the next and that became Venmo. We were very much about working with friends and people we love." The two remain inseparable. As Iqram puts it, they are "salt and pepper." Upon graduation, the pair decided to build products and services together, in part so that they could continue listening to music, cracking jokes, and building things over all-night sessions.

Their first venture was a Craigslist-style website for Penn students. They also launched a music analytics website and a social music website. None of these took off. Facing dwindling savings, they began canvassing Philadelphia restaurants, offering to build their websites. Their most bitter rejection: A restaurant that declined to give Iqram and Kortina 100 chicken rolls in exchange for building them a website. The arduous process taught Kortina and Iqram to create products that solve a problem, rather than to simply use technology to bring their ideas to life.

Eventually, desperate for income, the founders changed tack. They could learn from startup founders as employees while they plotted their next move. Neither had past employers to list when applying for their first jobs, so put each other as references.

Iqram and Kortina both joined iminlikewithyou.com, a social dating site that had just finished the prestigious accelerator, Y Combinator. The startup later pivoted to build the viral game "Draw Something," and was acquired by Zynga. As iminlikewithyou pivoted, they decided to leave. Iqram joined TicketLeap, an events platform. Kortina joined Betaworks to work on bit.ly, a URL shortening service.

But Kortina and Iqram yearned to work together again. The two continued to riff on startup ideas. During this period, the pair made their first foray into payments software, helping a friend launch their yogurt chain, "Yogorino." Restaurant and payment systems were clunky, so Kortina and Iqram coded software that could convert any laptop into a till, complete with a USB swiper, for $50. Although the project didn't gain traction, they had identified the same tailwind that saw Toast, the restaurant fintech, grow into a multibillion-dollar giant. They were getting closer.

At the time, Kortina was based in New York and Iqram in Philly but they'd regularly travel up and down to see each other. On one such visit, the idea for Venmo was born. They didn't set out to reinvent banking. Originally a music startup, Venmo users could text a band to purchase an MP3. Venmo's name combined "vendere" (Latin for "to sell") and "mo" (mobile).

Unaware of Venmo's potential, Kortina and Iqram set this initial iteration aside and rushed on with their lives.

Venmo

A few weeks later, Iqram visited Kortina in New York and forgot his wallet back in Philly. Kortina paid for his drinks. If only there was a way to reimburse the other via text message. This time the idea stuck.

Kortina never got his money back for the drinks, but over a few sleepless nights the two fixated on coding a minimum viable product (MVP). They couldn't figure out why everyone still opted for cash and checkbooks to pay each other back. Why not use PayPal? But at the time PayPal didn't feel as user-friendly as other mobile-first tools. Having been acquired by eBay a decade earlier, PayPal's innovation had stagnated, mostly ignoring mobile.

So although mobile transfers had precedent, the market appeared ripe for disruption. Then came a blow: Nokia invested

$70 million into Obopay, a more or less identical idea. Kortina and Iqram felt crushed. But playing with Obopay's product, it fell short of its hype—they could do better.

Back then, mobile applications were still nascent and BlackBerry dominated the phone market. Their MVP operated over SMS. Kortina would send Venmo a text: "Pay Iqram $20 for Chinese food." Iqram would then be notified that "Kortina paid you $20 for Chinese food." The MVP was built upon a hacked Google Voice account.

As the pair onboarded friends onto the tool, they realized that the SMSs flowing through their newsfeed curated the best local events, restaurants, bars, and shows. "$3 to pick me up a cup of coffee on your way in," "$5 for Kirsty's shared birthday gift." Kortina and Iqram decided to make these spending updates public for users by default. Venmo was inherently social.

With an MVP, the pair enlisted the help of two friends-turned-mentors: Sam Lessin, the CEO of the file-sharing site Drop.io (later acquired by Facebook) and Chris Stanchak, CEO of TicketLeap, Iqram's previous employer.

One day Iqram told Chris, "Hey, I want to leave TicketLeap and start this thing with Kortina." As Iqram described Venmo, Chris's immediate reaction was, "Is anyone going to want to pay over the phone?" But Iqram's excitement convinced him and he offered to help get Venmo off the ground. Eventually, Chris chuckles, everyone from TicketLeap "ended up going over [to work at Venmo], including my wife."

Iqram recalls, "Venmo was built inside TicketLeap. We were fortunate to have a good support system when Venmo was getting off the ground. A lot of those discussions played a massive role in how we strategize. Eventually, Sam [Lessin] became one of our first investors and Chris [Stanchak] pushed us through fundraising meetings and deck after deck." In turn, Sam brought on his father and several friends as investors.

Together Venmo approached the venture capital market with their SMS prototype.

Venmo's key differentiator was that you could send money hassle-free and instantly to friends, instead of exchanging bank details for an ACH transfer that took three to five days to arrive. One investor rejected them, stating they were only looking for billion-dollar, home-run opportunities. Iqram responded, "This will be a trillion-dollar company." The investor passed.

The Automated Clearing House (ACH) is an electronic system used mainly in the United States for secure batch processing of financial transactions. It replaced checks and in 2022 processed over $72 trillion in payments. Around 94 percent of US workers receive their wages via ACH.

On top of their social features, Venmo was solving a valuable problem: The ability to send money instantly. But it wasn't obvious who the Venmo founders should target first. Venmo for charities? Venmo for food trucks? They landed on Venmo for friends, with the slogan "The original social payment company." You could log onto Venmo and see what your friends were up to, signaled by their money exchanges. Who went to that party? Who was borrowing from friends? Who was sneaking away for a holiday?

Initial user feedback for Venmo was lukewarm. According to Iqram, news and media platform Mashable referred to Venmo as "the most lackluster thing they had ever seen." It took two years and five logo switches to reach a product that resembles Venmo today.

By 2012, they had about 5,000 people regularly using the application. The business model for Venmo was simple: Subsidize peer-to-peer (P2P) transactions, losing 1 percent in fees to attract users, then profit by charging merchants a 3 percent processing fee, which had no base cost for Venmo. To make money the team needed to convince companies to join Venmo. Their first business customer was a Sri Lankan restaurant which still operates in New York today.

Kortina and Iqram gathered a team based on who was most excited about their product. Their strategy: Attend a university job fair without a booth and hire enthusiastic graduates. The team was insatiable. Standing up at a friend's birthday dinner, they encouraged everyone to pay the bill via Venmo. To onboard, users had to call a number and enter their credit card. After 30 minutes of chaos, everyone managed to onboard and pay. The Venmo team never lost an opportunity to use their product.

Their hard work paid off.

Venmo became known in New York circles. A famous beer pong tournament in the West Village collected team payments using Venmo. Applications, including virtual roulette, were built onto Venmo. You'd simply text "I bet $20 on red" and would get a text back announcing debits or winnings, to or from your Venmo account.

Slowly but surely, "Just Venmo me" became part of our vocabulary.

"Trust" Makes Money Meaningless

Growing up in Zimbabwe, "seeing how money works over there versus the United States," informed much of Iqram's thinking. "It got to the point where there was a trillion-dollar bill. Zimbabweans would make the best accountants because if you try to subtract 856,300,463 from a trillion in your head, it's complicated." Zimbabwe was suffering intense inflation, which almost rendered money futile to Iqram. "Part of the purpose of Venmo, of our early [feature] called 'Trust,' was to make money meaningless," so you can focus on relationships instead.

"Trust" was one of Venmo's first core features. It allowed users whom you "trusted" to take money from your account without your permission and was what got Sam Lessin excited to invest in the company. Having witnessed Facebook launch while at Harvard, Sam became fascinated with trust graphs between people.

"If you go to dinner with a bunch of people and someone puts a credit card down, people will repay them if the request comes, but they're not excited about it. How do we remove friction from the system? If I 'Trust' Kortina, he can just take the money. Then the byproduct becomes an interesting graph of who trusts who."

Sam does indeed "Trust" Kortina deeply, to the extent that they founded their next company, Fin, together.

In 2010, Sam, Iqram, and Kortina filed a patent for a "trust-based transaction system."

The "Trust" feature has been wound down over the years but it illuminates the mindset underpinning Venmo. Sam, Iqram, and Kortina maintain that "Trust" was one of Venmo's most disruptive ideas.

Iqram reflects, "A lot of people use Venmo to settle up small tabs and lunch, but my preferred version of Venmo is the 'I've got you, you've got me' sharing mentality present all over Africa. Venmo was just a ledger of people sending money back and forth. In the early days, we would send each other dollars here or there as a form of fun communication."

Andrew Staub led Venmo's initial growth with a defining product decision: "Prioritizing the [transaction] note over the actual amount." He continues, "It was not about the monetary exchange, it was about social interaction. The amount of the payment was almost secondary to what the note was for."

"'Trust' brought a lot of energy to Venmo. People would use Venmo without actually sending money, 'Trust' was like your LinkedIn network. You 'trust' people on Venmo that you want to have a joint account with and then your money flows freely between you," says Iqram.

Anyone who joined the Venmo team was immediately given "Trust" as a sign of assurance on their first day.

"Trust" was part of Venmo's culture.

Hiring in Saunas

As Venmo grew, Kortina and Iqram took an unconventional approach to hiring, growing the team organically, based on cultural fit. They struck up a conversation with a Columbia student over their Venmo-branded t-shirts. Iqram shot him an email the next day that read, "We'll give you $3k for every person you refer to us that we hire." The student referred six resumes. They hired all of them.

Sometimes, Iqram found employees in more peculiar places.

Early employee Dan Garfinkel recalls, "One day we were all in the office. It was morning. There was a knock and I opened the door. We had this massive steel door." A man stood there. "We're like, 'What's up?'" The man responded, "'Oh, I work here.' And I [thought], I don't think you do. 'Can you just sit tight? Let me see what's going on.' Nobody had ever met this guy. Finally, I asked, 'Who did you talk to?'" It was Iqram. They had met the day prior in the sauna.

I was fortunate to join the early Venmo team at Wall Street Baths, a Russian banya (sauna) in New York, to experience this first-hand, following an evening of Iqram singing funk beats at a New York gala.

Another early employee was hired from a Facebook post. Venmo was the first job of famed social media influencer Nas Daily. Head of Growth, Andrew Staub, describes Iqram as having "the strongest intuition for good-quality people." Iqram made final hiring decisions on personality, deploying the "Tiger Test"—he imagined them in a match with a tiger, and if he felt they would win, they were hired.

In the early days of Venmo, Kortina still lived in New York and Iqram lived in Philly, so they would commute between the cities to work on the product, sleeping at the office when necessary. Their first workspace in New York was above a Dunkin' Donuts and a massage parlor. It was a collection of standing desks and every hour the team would break for push-ups. Venmo's culture took its cues from Iqram and Kortina's friendship, which Iqram could "write a book" in appreciation of. For Kortina, it was the "same thing, salt and pepper."

Although the co-founders were best friends, Dan Garfinkel, who worked on Venmo's growth and marketing, reflects they were "so different... Iqram is in large part a loose cannon. Kortina is tactical, strategic, and logical. And so depending on what you needed to be done, you'd pick the right guy."

Whilst they possessed complementary strengths, unwavering determination united Iqram and Kortina. Andrew Staub, describes Venmo's founders as "Non-stop. Kortina is the hardest worker you know. He was at a standing desk from 8 am to 10 pm every night setting a great example. Iqram never takes no for an answer. He's persistent in whatever he does. If he wants to get someone to try something, they're going to try it."

Venmo investor Sam Lessin echoes the sentiment: "They're both crazy. They both work extremely hard and are deeply principled humans. Full of crazy ideas [but] they actually do the work."

Iqram attributes the camaraderie at Venmo to the bonding experience of pioneering. "There were a lot of firsts. I think that motivates people to rally together. One by one we just combated [them] as a team. That was fun."

One such first was when Jenny Stanchak (the spouse of Chris Stanchak, CEO of TicketLeap) joined Venmo as employee seven— she couldn't yet code but soon learned. Her first role was answering support tickets and responding to payment bugs. Jenny says, "I still recommend that as a great way to onboard into a new company. It'll make you investigate how things are supposed to work." After Jenny learned to code, she built Venmo's support system. From then on, starting in customer service became standard for new employees.

Venmo had built its financial rails on top of a startup called Braintree, needing an ACH pathway for users to withdraw money from the platform after depositing with their card. This meant it took users four or five days to cash out their balances. Expediting the process required a bank partnership and an anti-money laundering policy. Unused to entertaining guests, when the banking partner arrived coat-in-hand to approve the policy, the Venmo team realized they lacked a coat rack. Andrew Staub ran out to source one and carried it back four blocks to ensure a good impression.

Iqram and Kortina brought unconventional behavior out in their investors too. No one thought that having two founders in their early twenties on Venmo's licensing documents would aid their application. So the pair spent a full day in the city with their investor Sameer Gandhi—partner at the esteemed venture capital fund Accel—getting him fingerprinted to fulfill Venmo's licensing requirements.

The eccentric atmosphere was even sensed by the wider community. Philly, Iqram recalls, "was a playful office. It used to be a bookstore and we'd have a lot of barbecues in the back. There was a period of three months where someone was pranking us and always putting raw meat on our grill."

Despite all the fun, Iqram had a laser focus on their bigger mission: "If we didn't envision [Venmo] was going to be mainstream, it never would have [got there]. Nobody could tell us it wasn't going to work. We were blindly convinced. It became ingrained." Iqram wrote in one of his executive summaries at the time, "Sure we might run out of money, but Venmo will be something."

Iqram never quite worked out how to scale this atmosphere in the later iterations of Venmo. In a smaller startup, he reminisces, "There's a lot of excitement in one place. It's easy enough to include everyone on the team." When companies grow, he laments the difficulty of "maintaining excitement" and ensuring employees don't "feel left out of decisions."

As Venmo scaled, its growth took a turn for the worse.

Running Out of Money

Off the back of early traction, the team raised a $5 million Series A round. Then all of a sudden, they were running out of money again.

Venmo had misjudged their unit economics. To attract early users, they let anyone deposit or make payment with a credit card for free, waiving the standard 3 percent charge in the United States. This resulted in a steep cost: They were on track to spend $35 million in credit card fees for processing billions of dollars of transactions.

What's worse is that Venmo users had found a loophole to earn "free" credit card points. Since credit cards could be used on Venmo, users were transferring money back and forth to rack up points, without actually spending money. As such, most of that $5 million raised went straight to the credit card transaction fees Venmo was subsidizing.

In a way, the model worked because once users tried Venmo, they stayed for more than the credit card points. In 2012, Venmo had around 25,000 total users, 5,000 active users, and exponential growth. But in the short term, the costs were not sustainable or affordable. "The faster we were growing and the more transactions we did, the shorter our runway. We were the cause of our own demise at a certain point," explained Dan Garfinkel, who worked in growth and marketing.

By that summer, the situation turned critical. Venmo only had two weeks of runway left. Iqram and Kortina appealed to the board—including Sameer Gandhi of Accel and Ian Sigalow of Greycroft—to put in more money. Iqram reflects, "We had to find a solution to shutting down." The board of venture capitalists had just shelled up $5 million, which Venmo had digested within 12 months. Investing more was too great a risk.

Venmo would have to find another way.

Enter: Braintree (2.0)

Meanwhile, Bill Ready was entering his second year as CEO of Braintree, the full-stack solution that enables websites and apps to accept payments.

Growing up in a small town in Kentucky, Bill had worked from a young age. Starting in his father's shop aged 13, Bill progressed into mechanical roles. Whilst juggling two jobs to fund his science major, at the dawn of the internet, Bill discovered programming. Unable to afford a home computer, he wrote and compiled his first program in the university computer lab. When Bill met two founders building banking software, he saw an opportunity to consolidate his two current jobs into one and joined their fintech, Netzee.

That would not be his last.

Following an MBA at Harvard Business School, Bill served as President of iPay, a payments platform. iPay was formed via the purchase of a license to software that Bill had helped write at Netzee. The founders of iPay also purchased an existing book of business (a client list) along with the software which allowed iPay to scale faster than if it had started building from scratch.

Under Bill's leadership, iPay grew more than 6x in three years with their robust online payment infrastructure ultimately being used by more than half of US banks and credit unions. While the company was known primarily for its online banking and payment capabilities, it also provided peer-to-peer payment infrastructure to thousands of banks. Despite the traction, Bill and his team had not been able to convince banks to allow their peer-to-peer payment users to interoperate with users from other banks on the iPay platform (as would ultimately happen with Zelle many years later). At the time, banks saw other local banks as their primary competitors, not realizing that they were leaving an opening for fintech companies to provide this functionality. Bill recalls, "First National Bank of Tuscaloosa didn't want to interoperate with Second National Bank of Tuscaloosa," unable to see the bigger picture.

In 2010, iPay was acquired for $300 million.

One of iPay's board members joined Accel to create its growth fund and Bill followed him, as an Entrepreneur in Residence (EIR). Bill was driven by the thesis that the mobile payments space was ripe for innovation, even though the iPhone was still in its first generation and the largest volume of "mobile payments" at that time were ringtone purchases and $1 gaming downloads. Even in minor shifts in the market, Bill saw significant growth and innovation possibilities. On that first generation iPhone, Bill saw only one good buying experience for e-commerce, Amazon's one-click checkout, and saw an opportunity to make that buying experience available to other e-commerce companies on mobile. Learning from iPay, he wanted to get started with an existing "book of business."

A year later, Accel announced a $34 million Series A investment in a little known ISO (independent sales organization), Braintree, that operated primarily as a reseller of a payment gateway from NMI and payment processing from First Data. While Braintree had very little revenue from its own software and no payment processing capabilities, Bill saw a client list of startups that would be great candidates for the mobile buying experience he wanted to create. $27 million of Accel's investment went toward buying out the founder of the ISO and Bill took over as CEO.

With backing from Accel and Bill as CEO, Braintree quickly set about creating its own payment processing and the mobile payment capabilities that it would ultimately become known for. Having its own payment processing allowed Braintree to ease the signup process and reduce fees. They removed a $100 monthly charge for developers and slashed fees to 2.9 percent, plus 30 cents per transaction. Launching a mobile software development kit within months of taking over, Bill was able to tempt Airbnb and several other clients over to the new software and one-click mobile buying experience.

Another early user was, at the time, a little-known San Francisco startup: Uber.

Back then, Uber was not even a top 100 customer for Braintree. Travis Kalanick, the co-founder of Uber, worried regulators might shut the taxi marketplace down—as they had done with Wikileaks, by preventing payment providers from working with them. So Travis had a frequent dialogue with Bill. In one conversation, Travis pointed out that while the seamless buying experience Braintree enabled was great once users had signed up for Uber, Uber's biggest fall-off point in the acquisition funnel was getting customers to enter their payment information the first time. Travis challenged Bill, "What are you doing about that?"

Bill called up Braintree's larger clients, including Airbnb's co-founder Nate Blecharczyk. Each of Braintree's clients had "the same pain point, over and over again." The fact that Braintree's software stored the payment credentials allowed Bill and his team to see that much of the time it was the same user, on the same device, experiencing that same pain point with each new mobile app they downloaded. An idea clicked: Braintree should "build a consumer network."

PayPal had neglected mobile. Stripe was promoting the new mobile web format HTML5 over native mobile payments, making Braintree the only native mobile payment SDK for e-commerce payments in the market at the time. The market was wide open. Knowing the opportunity would be fleeting, Bill was looking for a way to move faster and set about looking for a potential consumer payment company to acquire.

Meanwhile, another little-known Accel-backed company was running out of money...

Saving Venmo

The Venmo team had one last opportunity to save the company: Sell it. Groupon offered $3 million, Facebook interviewed the team and passed, whilst Mastercard was interested but wanted a year to do due diligence. On Iqram's birthday in 2012, the team met with Braintree CEO, Bill Ready, and his team to discuss a potential acquisition. Bill had used and liked Venmo's new beta app and understood the broad potential of P2P (peer to peer payments) to form a consumer network from his time at iPay. Bill and his CFO, Amit Jhawar, had also both met and spent enough time with Iqram and Kortina to have conviction in their grasp of consumer mobile apps. According to Iqram, the conversation went a little like this:

> Bill: "What if we just did an acquisition?"
> Iqram: "Let's do it."
> Bill: "How much?"
> Iqram: "$26.6 million."
> Bill: "We're in."

Iqram recalls, "It was so close that I actually called Bill up and said 'We can't make payroll, so would you guys mind sending us this money right now?' [That was] before we actually signed everything, and they did it."

Bill, however, was not just interested in Venmo's product: "I wanted those guys and the handful of people that were there with them to come build with me." Almost all of the acquisition value was in equity, vested to incentivize the team to remain at the go-forward entity.

The deal was a unique moment in time. Venmo needed an acquirer. Braintree needed to kickstart its consumer network; the team had already been profiling potential startups across the United States with a target price in mind.

Braintree was a perfect home for Venmo. As a highly profitable business payments company, Braintree was looking to move into the consumer sphere. Both companies championed collaborative environments. Braintree paired programmers when delivering code to users (known as "shipping" in software development). Iqram and Kortina had been co-CEOs of Venmo. Both embodied a culture of doing things together.

"There was a lot of flow between the [companies]; each team had a lot to learn from the other." Iqram contrasts Venmo's "scrappy" and fast-moving approach to Braintree, which "was very methodical." Their differences didn't cause friction though, Iqram reveals: "Bill is just a delight to work with. He can relate to all kinds of people. He spent a lot of time talking to the team." In the acquisition meeting, a member of Venmo's early team, Julian Connor, stood up and asked, "How do we know we're not getting [screwed over]?" When Bill answered with grace, Iqram knew Braintree was the right home.

Braintree 1.0

Like Venmo's founders, Braintree's founder Bryan Johnson stumbled into the payments sector by accident. Returning from his Mormon Missionary Service in Ecuador, Bryan aimed to make his fortune in his twenties, freeing him to dedicate his future to causes that benefit humanity. To get started, he sourced a list of the 50 richest people in Utah and emailed them for advice and a job. Not one replied, so he felt he had to make his own way.

By the time Bryan founded Braintree, he was deep in debt. He had made a few attempts at building companies including a VOIP (voice over internet protocol) business, a foray into real estate, and selling phones. But Bryan maintained his conviction: "Those who show initiative reap the reward from those who won't." Bryan credits much of his learning to reading over 100 biographies.

While he worked on various startups, he got a part-time job as a door-to-door salesman. The product: Credit card processing software for businesses, selling on the software as part of an ISO (Independent Sales Organization). Taking a systematic approach to problem-solving, Bryan gleaned both how antiquated credit card fees were and a formula for getting to a sale each time. His approach? Simply explaining how credit card fees *actually* work and promising a great service. Bryan generated a staggering $60,000 per month in contributing revenue and became the number one salesman of 400 agents nationwide. Before long, Bryan wondered, why not do it for himself? So he founded Braintree, named after the town in Massachusetts where founding father John Adams was born.

Bryan began to build an ISO himself: Braintree 1.0 was an independent sales organization reselling a payment gateway, with better customer service. Even without its own technology, Braintree scaled to a few million dollars of revenue and even acquired a few Y Combinator companies as customers before Bryan exited the business at the time of Braintree's Series A in 2011.

Venmo's initial cash-out ACH system was built upon software that Braintree was reselling in its early days. Iqram recalls, "[Bryan] actually had to send us an email saying that he was shutting Venmo down since Braintree's payment rails were not intended to enable a peer-peer payment service. We were pleading with him to let us figure it out. Little did I know that [a few] years later we would end up merging with them." It turned out Braintree didn't have the power to continue processing Venmo payments as an ISO, so Venmo was forced to switch over to Wells Fargo. When Bill Ready took over Braintree, he made the company into a mobile payment pioneer and technology powerhouse with its own full stack payment capabilities that could power apps like Venmo, Uber, Airbnb and many of the largest mobile commerce companies.

In an individual capacity, Bryan has built multiple companies since, including around his new life mission: To age backwards. Bryan has been described as "the most measured person in history," monitored by a team of doctors seeking an "algorithm" for longevity. As part of Bryan's Blueprint project, each day he swallows over 100 supplements, adheres to a rigorous diet and sleep routine, and has received experimental treatments including blood transfusions from his teenage son. Bryan's inflammation levels are 85 percent below the average 18-year-old.

Venmo As We Know It

Many mourn how Braintree managed to acquire Venmo for just $26.6 million dollars, forgetting that at the time the company had less than 5,000 active users and significant fraud issues.

Braintree's CEO Bill Ready recalls, "We then built together what became Venmo. Kortina and Iqram stuck around until Venmo hit velocity. We were trying to build a consumer merchant flywheel. PayPal was the only [competition]."

In 2013, the team launched "Venmo Touch," a one-click buying experience that Apple Pay and others have since replicated. "Then PayPal started paying attention. PayPal had missed out on mobile." Next, the CEO of eBay, PayPal's parent company at the time, became interested. With Uber, Airbnb, Facebook and "all the mobile winners as our clients… we got all this buzz." Circumstances were looking up.

Until Bill realized that, even with the cash generation of Braintree, they would need to "burn $100 million to build a consumer network of Venmo." While some investors were ready to sell, Bill contemplated—he wasn't willing to forgo the opportunity but who would write the check?

Then late one Friday night, Bill received a phone call from an unknown number.

It was John Donahoe, the former CEO of eBay which owned PayPal (now CEO of Nike). He said, "I can write the check," Bill recalls. eBay (and PayPal) would purchase Braintree (and Venmo). Together, Braintree and Venmo represented a platform that could eclipse PayPal in mobile payments. Venmo's tight consumer engine with Braintree's merchant payment stack powered some of the US's fastest-growing companies.

PayPal had to act.

Enter: PayPal

In 2013, Braintree was acquired by PayPal for $800 million. Braintree had bought Venmo a year prior for just $26.6 million.

eBay's CEO and PayPal's president, David Marcus, saw Braintree-Venmo as the mobile incarnation of PayPal and initially asked Bill to continue leading Braintree and Venmo as separate businesses inside the eBay Inc corporate structure.

When David Marcus left PayPal to lead Facebook Messenger, a few months after the acquisition of Braintree, Bill was asked to lead Product and Engineering for PayPal in addition to running Braintree and Venmo. Bill oversaw the growth of Braintree and Venmo and translated the one-click payment feature to create 'PayPal One Touch,' "which outpaced Apple Pay for all those years." In fact, when Apple Pay launched, more than half the apps featured by Apple were powered by Braintree's mobile payments.

Two years after the acquisition, PayPal spun out of eBay and became one of the top stocks in the S&P 500 for several years running. Bill was made COO of PayPal, with profit and loss responsibility for the company. By the time Bill Ready left PayPal in 2019, Braintree, Venmo and the mobile payment experiences they created accounted for over half of PayPal's revenue.

Ironically, Iqram and Kortina had entertained the idea of being acquired by PayPal for some time. Periodically, Venmo met with a PayPal representative and Iqram recalls asking, "Hey, do you want Venmo? You guys can buy us right now. Just look at it."

The Venmo team saw the acquisition by PayPal as the end of an era. Iqram felt Venmo was operating "under the guise of this new bureaucracy." The greatest signal: The arrival of a photocopier. "[PayPal] sent a Xerox machine to the office." Over the years the team would depart one by one, but not without a last marketing hurrah.

Putting Money Behind Venmo

Venmo's creativity, backed by PayPal's resources, led to a number of memorable marketing campaigns. If you were around New York in 2014, you may have seen the "Lucas uses Venmo" advertisements. You may also be wondering where on earth that came from…

PayPal was about to pour hundreds of thousands of dollars into an advertising campaign for Venmo on the popular media platform Buzzfeed, but Iqram recalls it just didn't feel right. Iqram, Kortina, and Venmo's chief marketing officer Neil Shah, huddled in the office to discuss. Out of the blue, Neil asked, "What about Lucas?" He leapt up and grabbed a photo of one of Venmo's software engineers, Lucas, exclaiming "Lucas uses Venmo!" Pointing at the real Lucas across the room, Neil declared, "And Lucas makes coffee." Lucas was their *everyman*.

"We presented this to the whole team in a town-hall-style meeting. And it was just radio silence. But somehow we kept running with it." Neil and Iqram took Lucas out to dinner to convince him to star in Venmo's ads. "We had a couple of cocktails with Lucas. Next thing, he was in a Christmas hat in our office and Neil hired one of his friends to come shoot this massive ad campaign."

The team went on to run advertising across the United States, with a key focus on New York. On the billboards: everyday guy Lucas doing different activities—"Lucas rides the subway," "Lucas takes the stairs," "Lucas has dreams"—with zero context but for the Venmo logo. This unleashed questions all over Reddit, Twitter, and Facebook. People were asking, "What the hell is Venmo and who the heck is Lucas?" Engagement erupted. Memes featuring

Lucas flooded the internet, there were subreddits devoted to him, and fan sites like LucasLoves.com sprang up.

Lucas even became a fun dinner table conversation: "Have you seen that new Venmo advert?"

In Iqram's eyes, Venmo's competition was dollar bills and Facebook. They worked 24x7 for years to change consumer financial behavior. Iqram and Kortina ate, slept, drank, worked, and sweated with Venmo in mind, from sunrise to sunset. When they saw someone using cash, the team would convert a new user, taking the dollar bills and paying them back on Venmo. Life orbited Venmo. That's what it took to build a new payment mechanism.

Yet competition was brewing.

Foot Race

"I think there are few gifts better than a worthy competitor," Braintree's former CEO Bill Ready reflects. Back then, Braintree was "a little company," as were its competitors Stripe, Adyen, and Square. Each company went after different spaces. Square for in-store merchants, Adyen for international and enterprise e-commerce, Braintree and Stripe would collide head-on but with different flavors: Braintree for mobile developers, Stripe for web and app programmers.

This fight for market share prompted the question: "How do we differentiate?" Bill was determined for Braintree to "be more than just a feature function foot race with Stripe." That thinking led them to build a consumer network, unlike Stripe and Adyen.

Bill reflects, "It was a great moment. Dominated by a bunch of large legacy players, the industry [was] ripe for disruption." Vying to do so were Braintree, Stripe, Square, and Adyen. "We were all innovating around that same time and pushing each other, going out in different directions." The founders would come together and ponder whether to team up or fight each other. Bill uses the analogy of David and Goliath: "Back then, we were all Davids. Now those companies are all Goliaths." With this growth, each payment provider has since bled into the others' spaces.

Despite now standing at 85 million users, Venmo, in particular, butted heads with another social payment app...

Square's Cash App

In 2009, Jack Dorsey, co-founder of Twitter (now X) stepped down as CEO to focus on launching Square (now Block) to revolutionize merchant payments. In an unexpected twist of fate, Dorsey would later return to Twitter, standing as CEO of both companies simultaneously, but that's a story for another book. A company hackathon at Square sparked the creation of Square Cash (now Cash App), a peer-to-peer payment solution designed to simplify splitting bills. The year was 2013 and this was no longer a new concept.

In 2018, Square Cash was rebranded to Cash App and acquired 60 million customers within three years. To put that growth into perspective, J.P. Morgan Chase reached 60 million deposit account holders in the same year as Cash App, despite being founded centuries prior and having compounded customers through a series of acquisitions.

Cash App recognized early on that people either used their product or Venmo. Not both.

Venmo had conquered California and big cities like New York—the Democrat-voting "blue" states. Cash App identified an opportunity to serve underbanked populations across the country. Launching in Atlanta, they catered to demographics often overlooked by financial services including young adults, rural residents, Hispanic and African American communities, predominantly in southern Republican-voting "red" states. With a user-friendly interface similar to Venmo, Cash App distinguished itself by embedding itself in youth culture.

Cash App recruited major figures in pop and rap as ambassadors who resonated with the younger generation. During the pandemic, Kim Kardashian sent $500 to 1,000 people with her medium of choice: Cash App. Miley Cyrus ran a stock giveaway worth $1 million, paid out to entrants' $Cashtags, their corresponding identifier on Cash App. Cardi B partnered with Cash App to offer $1 million to powerful women.

These artists weren't just promoting the fintech; they used Cash App. The app offered a glimpse of a future where creators might monetize their audiences directly, eliminating the need for record labels and agents. This culture-led approach to financial services was underlined by Block's acquisition of Jay-Z's artist-first music streaming platform, Tidal, and the appointment of Jay-Z to Block's board in 2021. Cash App has even established a strong presence on Spotify—500 songs mention Cash App, including the chart-topping hit "The Box" by Roddy Rich, with 1.1 billion Spotify streams.

Cash App did what others wouldn't: They partnered with controversial right-wing podcaster Joe Rogan, sponsored esports competitions, launched a clothing line, "Cash by Cash App," and let users personalize their cards with poo emojis. Where Venmo dominated cities, Cash App won over the rural United States along political lines, building a loyal following in Texas and the South. It was a strategy that propelled Cash App to become the number one finance app in the App Store within five years, landing them among the eight most downloaded apps of all time in the United States, standing alongside social media giants Instagram, YouTube, and TikTok.

Money is inherently social.

Bugs and Business Models

Cash App's success was underpinned by more than just culture. It was built upon a top-notch product. Once Cash App got a peer-to-peer engine up and running, they aggressively introduced new features. Having initially trailed Venmo's feature set, Cash App soon overtook, letting users buy Bitcoin, receive rewards, conduct fractional stock trading, and even create a bank account, following the classic fintech model of finding a niche and rolling out additional products on top.

To acquire a new user, Cash App spends $10, aiming to recoup this cost and profit by monetizing active users. The more products users adopt within the app, the greater the incremental revenue generated. Cash App found that users had 31 percent more retention when they had four or more friends on the app, so they incentivized families with stock and Bitcoin gifting.

During the pandemic, however, Cash App was met with a hurdle.

The company encouraged users to deposit their stimulus checks in the app, making it simple and easy to request them from the government. However, criminals took advantage of the economic relief programs by using Cash App to launder illegally obtained funds from these programs. Following this, in 2023, Block and Cash App were hit by a Hindenburg Research report. The US investment research firm accused the company of having relaxed regulations that allow fraud and phishing. Hindenburg Research shorts the stocks of companies it publishes reports about, to profit from resulting stock price falls.

Block's stock price slumped more than 16 percent after the report was published, but has since recovered and continues to grow from strength to strength.

In addition to external forces, Cash App has been attacked by its own customers. In 2022, a bug enabled users to withdraw unlimited amounts from their accounts; taking out thousands of dollars they didn't have, users went viral on TikTok. Cash App followed up on negative balances by blocking users and threatening legal action if the money was not returned, but this didn't stop everyone.

Within three years of launching, Cash App overtook Venmo in payment volume. Yet in 2018, with the full force of PayPal's resources galvanizing behind it, Venmo passed Cash App again and now remains in the lead.

Common Ground: Social Money

Venmo and Cash App illustrate a 21st-century transformation of money. Dollar bills and credit cards now compete with social payment apps. Digital currencies are gaining traction globally. Elon Musk co-founded X.com to derail traditional money structures, before merging with Confinity to form PayPal. Now, as Elon steers Twitter—renamed X in a nod to his original payments startup—toward introducing a payments functionality, he has cast his vote. The future of finance is becoming ever more social.

While geographical divides color Venmo and Cash App's respective user bases Democrat "blue" and Republican "red," a common ground unites them—a shared belief in the value of digital currencies. Venmo co-founder Andrew Kortina explains, "Database transactions are only valuable because people believe [them]. This is true of art and of many other things people value." If you're curious to learn more about the Venmo story, check out Andrew Staub's upcoming book *Growing Venmo*.

TIPS FROM THE TRENCHES

1 Create a culture of curiosity. The founders of Venmo share a history of failed ventures and inquisitiveness. Iqram and Kortina continued iterating solutions to problems until one picked up steam and, after a long grind, became a generational product. For Iqram the journey was a haze: "It was easy and hard at the same time." But they did it as friends, "Salt and Pepper."

2 Have a thesis and envision how to get there. Bill Ready acquired a book of business, then scaled Braintree-Venmo into a juggernaut that reinvigorated PayPal. Don't rule out buying a business book or tech stack to start you off.

3 Go after the markets and geographies that have been neglected. Cash App encroached on Venmo's dominance in cities by going after underbanked populations.

03
Alibaba vs. Tencent
Red Envelope Wars and a Two-Horse Race

A day in the life of one of China's 1.4 billion consumers might look like this:

> Over breakfast, you scroll social media. An ad reminds you to send a virtual "red envelope" of money back home to your mother. Sending this has made you late. You rush across the intersection to the office. At your desk, you receive a notification: a fine for jaywalking (you were identified via facial recognition) has been automatically debited from your account (WeChat Pay). Your meeting runs over, so you scan a QR code for your lunch delivery. While eating, you book a doctor's appointment, check the inventory for your e-commerce side hustle, and browse flights or movies for your day off. Back to work. As you finish, there's a downpour, so you opt not to bikeshare. Instead, you order a cab. In the back seat, you play a game, pay your gas bill, or even file your taxes.
>
> All of this, you have done through a single app. A super app.

This functionality has existed for close to a decade in China. WeChat enables users and companies to build their own programs on top of their platform, called "mini programs." If your social media, medical records, cinema, eBay, Uber, Skyscanner, and bank accounts were all in one place—that's WeChat—you can do (almost) anything.

Tencent-owned WeChat is not the only super app jostling for the population's attention and transaction volume. Alibaba has long been its rival. Now, new tech powerhouses are emerging. ByteDance—TikTok's parent company—has integrated gaming, e-commerce, and live streaming within the social app. Pinduoduo—a group buying app worth over $200 billion—has now stepped into groceries and even job recruitment.

The underlying payment systems that allow users to socialize, buy products, and run businesses on these super apps are Tencent's WeChat Pay (40 percent market share) and Alibaba's spin-off AliPay (50 percent market share). Together, they dominate the payments market in China and are crawling out internationally.

Tencent is a key stakeholder in the fifth-largest social network in the United States, Discord. Alibaba powers the technology behind Paytm, India's largest payment company. Together, they are major shareholders in Didi, China's equivalent to Uber. Alibaba's founder Jack Ma and Tencent's founder Pony Ma (unrelated) have ruled China's tech sphere for over a decade. Since "Ma" translates from Mandarin as "horse," they are *literally* in a two-horse race.

Yet in the past few years, a new player has stepped into combat, one that they cannot ignore: China's regulator.

When AliPay spun out from Alibaba as an independent fin-tech—under the holding company Ant Financial (now Ant Group)—the world held its breath for the largest public listing in history. Ant Financial's IPO in October 2020, valued at over $300 billion, was halted by the Chinese government on the eve of listing. This slashed its valuation by more than $200 billion. A staggering loss—equivalent to 10 Snapchats.

The government regulator has since shrunk the fortunes of Alibaba's Jack Ma in half and Tencent's Pony Ma by a third, with both founders now rarely appearing in public.

How did Alibaba and Tencent rise to such heights? And what led the Chinese government to sabotage a national tech success story by derailing the country's most anticipated IPO?

Alibaba

Equal and opposite forces in China, Tencent stems from the shiny city of Shenzhen and Alibaba from ancient Hangzhou.

Hangzhou's prominence was established a millennium before Alibaba, as the southern terminus of the key trading canal to Beijing. These days, Alibaba has become synonymous with Hangzhou. Every shop uses Alipay (over WeChat Pay) and the community is biased towards any Alibaba-run sharing economy service. Neighboring "Cloud Valley" is even named after Alibaba's cloud services.

Jack Ma first launched Alibaba.com in 1999, with 17 other co-founders. As an English teacher in Hangzhou, he had seen the potential of the internet during trips to the United States. With a dial-up connection and a dream, Alibaba began as a China-based B2B marketplace connecting inexpensive Chinese manufacturers with global buyers. Alibaba wanted to empower local small and medium enterprises to export worldwide.

There were, however, already established players in this market. US multinational Global Sources dominated trade shows with print catalogs; their online presence was growing. To overcome this, upstart Alibaba built trust and market share through relentless on-the-ground efforts. Alibaba's 52nd employee, Vice President of Global Initiatives and former special assistant to the founder, Brian Wong, recalls they did this through "straight-up brute force." Which worked—Alibaba achieved international reach.

At least, until the dotcom crash.

In 2000, as cash flow ran low, the e-commerce platform was forced to prioritize core markets. Alibaba shut down its Hong Kong and international operations. Then the sinking ship was buoyed by an investment. Masayoshi Son, founder of growth-stage venture fund SoftBank, bought a 34 percent stake for $20 million. Considered one of the best investments of all time, those shares grew 2,500x to be worth $50 billion at the time of Alibaba's IPO. When SoftBank invested, Alibaba was not yet generating revenue and had no business plan. But Masayoshi Son was intrigued by Jack Ma's "shining eyes." Jack had a vision: For Alibaba to make it easy to do business anywhere and to build a company that would span three centuries. Alibaba emerged stronger from the market crash.

Then another lethal threat hit—the SARS epidemic of 2003. Risking losing its edge over its fierce competition, Alibaba prioritized employee safety. They closed offices and implemented a work-from-home policy to ensure uninterrupted customer service. Again they escaped unscathed.

Alibaba was battle-hardened by experience, in time for eBay— the well-funded US-based e-marketplace giant—to announce a launch in China. eBay was acquiring EachNet, China's most dominant auction player with over 2 million users and an 85 percent market share for $180 million. Where Alibaba focused on business-to-business (B2B) wholesale transactions, eBay enabled merchants to sell directly to end consumers with a higher markup. Fearing business users would be tempted away, Alibaba launched Taobao, a business-to-consumer (B2C) platform. But how could a small startup compete against a giant like eBay?

Alibaba employed guerrilla tactics. Vice President of Global Initiatives, Brian Wong, recalls that "[eBay] blocked us from exhibiting at eBay Live. So we set up outside the convention center and handed out [Alibaba-branded] orange bags that were so big, you could fit everything in there. With everyone carrying these orange bags, it looked like an Alibaba convention."

Alibaba was not daunted by being the underdog. Rather than worrying about the "three million people online that make purchases" being swayed, Brian explains that Alibaba went after "the 70 million internet users who did not use e-commerce" and "the 700 million consumers that had not yet discovered the internet." So it didn't matter that eBay had a dominant market share. According to Brian, Alibaba's founder had correctly predicted that "e-commerce would become so commonplace, it's going to be like a utility."

But Alibaba's founder had one concern.

To ensure buyer-seller trust, eBay had an escrow account which held the buyer's money until the seller mailed the item. Taobao was not licensed to do the same. But Jack Ma insisted. Consumer trust was essential and therefore worth the risk. In the end, Alibaba partnered with the Commercial Bank of China to legally facilitate escrow payments. Taobao had a master account at the bank, but each order form required manual processing. The inefficiency prompted Alibaba to move into the finance space—launching Alipay.

Thus, Alibaba's super app was born.

Over the coming decade, China's e-commerce sector boomed. Alipay facilitated trillions of dollars in transactions and its valuation mushroomed, laying the foundations for that botched IPO. Just as Amazon Web Services grew out of Amazon's cloud computing needs, Taobao and Alipay emerged as Alibaba fended off competition and vertically integrated. Today, Alibaba enables small businesses through five pillars—cloud, digital marketplaces, delivery, logistics, and entertainment.

In just a few years, Alibaba's Taobao rose from less than 5 percent market ownership to more than 50 percent. Meanwhile, led by Western executives, eBay focused on online advertising to a largely offline audience. Taobao knew the Chinese population watched TV and targeted them through commercials.

By 2006, eBay shut down its Chinese website and admitted defeat. Alibaba had staved off eBay and won the hearts of China's consumers.

In 2020, China's President Xi Jinping announced that national absolute poverty had been eradicated.

Alibaba's contribution was vital in lifting millions of Chinese citizens out of poverty. Alibaba's 'Rural Taobao Initiative' brought e-commerce to remote villages with limited digital literacy and banking access. At local delivery and pickup hubs, residents could order from Taobao vendors or sell their own products. Alibaba handled everything. Their initiative provided the logistical network and education for villagers to buy and sell online—enabling some to start million-dollar businesses.

At its peak, Alibaba's value surpassed $500 billion and when it listed in 2014 on the New York Stock Exchange, its IPO was and remains the largest in US history. But its significance has gone far beyond its financial worth: Alibaba has transformed Chinese citizens' lives. The tech giant has not acted in isolation. After a decade of fending off trade shows, pandemics, and eBay to become the number one tech company in China, in 2011 a new threat to Alibaba emerged—Tencent.

Tencent

South of Alibaba's Hangzhou and across the water from Hong Kong lies Shenzhen—the "maker" city of China. Home to DJI drones and ZTE phones, within 24 hours any electronic or knock-off can be manufactured.

It was here, in 1999, that Pony Ma founded Tencent.

Their initial product was QQ, a desktop-based messaging platform for gaming enthusiasts. Phone calls, games, and other internet services were embedded in QQ. The platform was monetized by selling virtual goods, like adding "energy" to make a game last longer. This product may sound familiar. Tencent excelled in building on borrowed concepts. In this case, Tencent was inspired by ICQ—the Israeli messaging service that was acquired by and became the foundation of AOL's Instant Messenger.

At the turn of the century, South African media giant Naspers made a life-changing investment in Tencent. Just as SoftBank struck gold investing in Alibaba, in 2001, Naspers acquired 46.5 percent of Tencent for $32 million. As the smartphone era flung Tencent to dominance, Naspers' stake skyrocketed in value, generating an immense 5,500x return—in percentage terms, more than double SoftBank's gain from Alibaba.

How did Tencent achieve this growth?

Forecasting a move away from desktops, Pony Ma launched an internal contest for teams to build a mobile app. Out of this came WeChat, China's primary social media and messaging platform. In

2012, just one year after launching, WeChat achieved 100 million daily active users—which pricked up the ears of Jack Ma at Alibaba. The following year Tencent introduced WeChat Pay, which allowed users to exchange money via QR codes. The move expanded WeChat from a social messaging app to facilitating business-to-consumer connections.

Back then, Alibaba's Alipay commanded 81 percent of the online payments market. But Tencent was closing in.

Spin-out

Alibaba, however, was distracted by a different adversary: The Chinese regulator. The People's Bank of China had issued regulations stating that foreign-owned payment companies would have to obtain licenses to continue operations. With American Yahoo and Japanese SoftBank backing Alibaba, subsidiary Alipay would fall under these new regulations. So in 2011, Alibaba spun out Alipay as a separate entity.

Founder Jack Ma didn't inform their major investor Yahoo for five weeks.

With the public announcement, Yahoo shares nose-dived by 12 percent. Alibaba and Alipay maintained their synergistic relationship after splitting up. A former staffer describes the transition as from "siblings to cousins." The spirit of Alibaba lives on in both companies and their affiliates.

Following the restructuring, Alipay launched Yu'E Bao—which translates as "leftover treasure"—allowing users to invest spare change (as little as ¥1) in money market funds and earn daily interest. Yu'E Bao offered a compelling alternative to traditional banks. Instant access allowed users to divest at any time, or even use funds to purchase on Alibaba. Yu'E Bao delivered high daily interest rates (around 6 percent, approximately 17 times higher than the typical bank offering of a meager 0.5 percent) by investing in foreign currency market funds.

This infuriated China's banks, who rely on consumer deposits to fund lending and interest income. Within months, Yu'E Bao ascended to China's top five money market managers, with $100 billion in assets. The banks implored regulators to place similar financial restrictions on Yu'E Bao as they faced. Some banks even prevented customers from transferring their deposits to Yu'E Bao.

In 2014, Alipay's parent company rebranded as Ant Financial. Aiming to serve 10 million small businesses within five years, they surpassed their goal, reaching 1.3 billion users. The name "Ant" reflects their mission of financial inclusion—one ant alone cannot go far, but collectively, ants can do almost anything.

Indeed, Ant has pioneered a revolutionary credit score system in China, leveraging over 1,000 data points to provide millions with access to credit for the first time. Farmers can access loans based on satellite data of their crops, or truck drivers based on trip productivity. However, in tying credit scores to everyday activities, those with low scores now cannot book flights, train tickets, or even rent a bike without a deposit.

With far-reaching access across China's population, Ant has been able to incentivize environmentally friendly behavior by helping users understand their carbon footprint. Eco-friendly choices like walking, public transport, and digital payments earn users "green energy" points. These points nurture virtual trees within the app and when enough are collected, Ant Group plants saplings in Inner Mongolia and Gansu. To encourage virality, Alipay gamified the program; leaderboards track friends' progress and users can "steal" energy, promoting friendly competition for a greener footprint.

Today, Ant Group is a giant of its own, grouped under several core product offerings, including Alipay, MyBank (a digital bank), Wealth (like Robinhood in the United States), and Insurance. Ant's sprawling reach, educational power, and friction with China's banks would snag the attention of the nation's regulators and lay the foundations for Ant's sabotaged IPO.

But for now, China's regulators orbited in the background. Alipay's split from Alibaba and Tencent's launch of WeChat had leveled the playing field—and these tensions erupted into war.

Red Envelope War

In 2014, Tencent laid down the gauntlet in a battle with Alibaba so ferocious that it garnered its own name— the "Red Envelope War" (红包大战 hóngbāo dàzhàn).

In Chinese culture, red envelopes symbolize good luck and prosperity, and are traditionally stuffed with cash and given during the Lunar New Year. Having just launched its wallet feature, Tencent sought creative ways to get money circulating on WeChat Pay. Tencent piloted virtual red envelopes containing digital Yuan. To gamify the tradition, WeChat Pay's "Lucky Money" feature split a pot of gifted money between recipients. Tencent's campaign went viral and cemented WeChat Pay as an alternative force to Alipay.

> **Red envelopes exchanged:** WeChat Pay: 20 million. Alipay: None.

In 2015, Tencent scaled up its attack, partnering with China Central Television (CCTV) on the eve of the Lunar New Year for its annual five-hour program. Viewers were invited to play red envelope-based games, vigorously shaking their phones to win WeChat prizes. On New Year's Eve alone, one billion red envelopes were sent via WeChat Pay.

This rocked Alibaba's Alipay to its core. Tencent had ambushed the digital payments market and Jack Ma likened the attack to Pearl Harbor.

The following year, Alipay retaliated, joining forces with Weibo, China's equivalent to Twitter, as the exclusive sponsor of the New Year's Eve broadcast. Alipay tempted users away from WeChat Pay with a red envelope giveaway and their own game: "Lucky Card Collection." Users who collected all five Alipay cards—earned by making three referrals and two transfers to friends—would share Alibaba's enormous grand prize. Alipay's social strategy deliberately invaded WeChat's home turf as a social media messaging platform. In spite of Alibaba's efforts,

WeChat Pay still dwarfed Alipay as the medium for sending New Year gifts.

Red envelopes exchanged: WeChat Pay: 1 billion. Alipay: 0.5 billion.

The innovation, numbers, and competition escalated. China's leading search engine, Baidu, even entered the fray, with users sending billions of red envelopes via "Baidu Wallet."

In 2017, inspired by Pokémon Go, Alipay shifted the Red Envelope War offline with augmented reality (AR) red envelopes that users could hide and collect around cities. WeChat Pay followed suit before Alipay could get much of a head start.

Red envelopes exchanged: WeChat Pay: 14.2 billion. Alipay: Unreported (conceding defeat).

Tencent emerged victorious in the red envelope war, cementing WeChat's position as the social home of China. Brian Wong, Alibaba's VP of Global Initiatives, recalls that Tencent "blindsided us in the same way we blindsided eBay." In some ways, the triumph was hollow. Tencent's WeChat and Alibaba's affiliate Alipay had invested far more in prizes and advertising than they had earned. However, the Red Envelope War had coaxed China's population into using mobile payments.

While Alipay remains the market leader (commanding 50 percent), during the Red Envelope Wars WeChat Pay captured a substantial share of the market (40 percent). Alipay has the edge with businesses and WeChat with consumers.

The war between China's two tech giants continued to rage, but the frontlines shifted—to mergers and acquisitions (M&A).

The M&A Frontlines

Tencent and Alibaba encircled one another.

Brian Wong, Alibaba's VP of Global Initiatives, explains it was a battle of "new platforms and functionalities." Tencent and Alibaba competed to collect user data. With this, they could build the largest super app ecosystem, retain users, and offer ancillary products.

To compete with Tencent's WeChat in the workplace communication market, Alibaba launched DingTalk, a corporate messaging app. When Tencent failed to enter Alibaba's realm of e-commerce, they partnered with JD.com in a move that Brian Wong explains "was [Tencent] supporting other businesses that would attack or weaken [Alibaba]."

The two tech giants have backed or acquired various competing Chinese startups across all industries. Each took a stake in China's leading bike-sharing startups, with investments that fueled growth at a rate that outpaced demand. Cities across China were overwhelmed by bicycles that blocked streets and began to stack up in "graveyards." The tech giants fueled unsustainable expansion—with startups just pawns in Tencent and Alibaba's rivalry.

In food delivery, Alibaba purchased Ele.me, while Tencent invested in Meituan-Dianping. Between them, they control 85 percent of the sector.

In the ride-hailing space, Tencent was an early backer of Didi Dache. Alibaba initially partnered with its rival, Kuaidi Dache, so Alipay was pre-installed as the app's payment method. In 2015, the two ride-hailing startups merged and Alibaba invested $1 billion, making Alibaba and Tencent fellow investors. A fierce battle ensued between WeChat Pay and Alipay to lead payments within the ride-hailing app. Both are now integrated and the app went on to acquire Uber's China operations.

On rare occasions, the two tech titans have even collaborated. Tencent and Alibaba invested alongside traditional insurance giant PingAn—whose CEO is also named Ma—in the insurtech disruptor ZhongAn.

Outside of China, Alibaba backed Grab, the Malaysian ride-hailing rival to Tencent's Go-Jek in Indonesia. In fintech, both companies have invested in Southeast Asia, with Tencent taking minority stakes and Alibaba's affiliate, Ant Financial, seeking to control. Purchasing a majority stake in Lazada, the Singaporean e-commerce giant, Ant Financial appointed Alibaba co-founder Lucy Peng as Lazada's key advisor.

The collateral damage of these investment sprees has been small businesses, moving away from Alibaba's core mission. Unable to compete with Tencent and Alibaba's cash injections, many have folded, sparking regulatory blowback. Though in 2019, when Ant Financial attempted to acquire peer-to-peer remittance startup MoneyGram, US regulators blocked the move for a different reason, citing national security concerns.

Whilst the firms do harvest data, Alibaba and Tencent have also induced positive change. Alibaba's affiliate Ant Financial has made significant technology transfers into startups across Asia, accelerating financial inclusion. In 2015, Ant Financial led a strategic investment into Paytm, India's largest mobile peer-to-peer payments service. Paytm pioneers digital wallets and QR code payments, which have been proven to increase earning opportunities and savings, particularly among women.

Paytm could not have succeeded in its mission without widespread mobile and internet adoption across India, orchestrated by Asia's richest man, Mukesh Ambani. His telecoms company Jio launched an unprecedented welcome offer of data at no cost for three months, which was extended multiple times. The JioPhone also flooded the market—an affordable medium to consume data—and sold for Rs999 (equivalent to US $12 at the time of writing). Facebook's previous bid to offer free internet in India was fiercely opposed. Their offering of "Free Basics," which provided zero-cost access to certain pre-selected websites, was banned by India's regulators. Subsequently, Facebook invested over $5 billion in Jio.

Alibaba and Tencent have accelerated digital literacy and opened up the opportunities brought by e-commerce through M&A.

Culture as Religion

How do you unite a company with a quarter of a million employees?

At Alibaba, company culture is based on the ancient Chinese religion of Taoism. Founder Jack Ma is a near-mythical figure within Alibaba. By instilling the company's philosophies with new employees—leading orientation classes even as Alibaba scaled—he was a teacher and founder. Jack saw culture as a vital cause to allocate his time to. It sustained employees through the crusades of startup building. Later, anyone who went on to lead spin-out companies would take that understanding of Alibaba's "Tao" with them. To ensure Alipay inherited Alibaba's core principles, its founding team incubated Alipay at the modest Hangzhou flat from which Jack Ma and his team launched Alibaba. The space has been preserved, a testament to the tech giant's humble beginnings.

To propagate Alibaba's "Tao" at its subsidiaries Jack Ma often placed loyal Alibaba-ists in charge. When promoting leaders, past experience wasn't as important as a deep understanding of the company's mission. A prime example is Jonathan Lu, Alipay's founding president. Before joining Alibaba, Jonathan had been a hotel manager. Some questioned Jack Ma's decision to hand Jonathan the reins, citing his lack of experience in finance. But Jack wanted to bypass the restrictive mindset that comes with experience. Jonathan's customer-oriented approach and ability to execute, honed from years in hospitality, made him a perfect leader for Alipay.

Another key apostle of Alibaba's "Tao" was VP of Global Initiatives, Brian Wong. Across Southeast Asia, South America, the US, and Europe, Brian sought to replicate the essence of Alibaba. In 2019, I travelled to Hangzhou to join Alibaba's eFounders Program under Brian, after launching a payments business for UK merchants to accept Alipay. There, I witnessed firsthand the philosophy that underpins Alibaba's success. It hinges on three core principles:

1. Mission

Alibaba's various business units work towards one overarching purpose—to help small businesses succeed.

Taobao Tmall e-commerce connects small businesses with global customers. Cloud provides big data and AI tools to increase productivity and digital functions. Local services enable food delivery and retail fulfillment. Alibaba International exports this mission of supporting small businesses to India, Vietnam, Kenya and others. As Brian Wong explains, "[Jack] was always encouraging us to do more for those who weren't being served, not just trying to consolidate and dominate."

By the end of 2009, Alipay had 270 million users and its daily transaction volume exceeded ¥1.2 billion. As with every widely adopted product, it had received some user complaints. But Jack Ma was not happy unless his customers were. At Alipay's annual holiday party, there were no festivities or performances. Instead, employees were greeted with booming recordings of infuriated customers: "You screwed up my livelihood! I'm never using Alipay again." Jack Ma addressed the audience with a grim expression: "Terrible, terrible, terrible to the extreme!" The party transformed into a conference on how to set things right.

2. Work Ethic

Alibaba's team worked long hours. To ensure dedication, Jack placed Alibaba's co-founders in the HR team to conduct final interviews and assess candidates' alignment with company values. Co-founder, Lucy Peng, in this role set up the "mom and pop" managing model in Alibaba teams, where a "mom" executive would be in charge of promoting teamwork and passion, while the "pop" executive assessed performance.

When studying the "China Model," VP of Global Initiatives Brian Wong identified the sales team as the workhorse behind much of Alibaba's success. Brian noted that one of Alibaba's co-founders, Trudy Dai, had been sent to Guangzhou for a year to set up the sales operation, leaving behind her family in Hangzhou. Brian marvels, "That was the level of sacrifice people made." Trudy, who later held the role of CEO at Taobao and President at Alibaba. com shares: "If the company requests that I do sales, I'll do sales. If it's customer service, I'll do that as well. No need to think too much, I'll just happily do the work." This work ethic was present from the very beginning. In 1999, "when the company was founded, each one of us was actually customer service staff." Working 16 to 18 hours a day, Dai and her colleagues answered emails so quickly customers began to doubt they were real people.

This extended to "996"—Alibaba's employees' habit of working from 9 am to 9 pm, 6 days a week. This was not a culture forced upon employees, but they enjoyed their roles and had joined Alibaba to work in a challenging professional environment, even before Alibaba was a household name.

Outside of China, many employees found the job too demanding and would quit. Elsewhere, in India especially, employees embraced the long hours, even outdoing China's 996 with 10107—10 am to 10 pm, 7 days a week.

Brian observes more of the sales team's methodologies—their continual planning, reviewing, and celebrating victories with enthusiasm—in detail in his book *The Tao of Alibaba*.

A defined mission and work ethic were a potent combination.

3. Harmony

As Alibaba grew from a small startup to a global enterprise, Jack Ma noticed the emergence of negative behaviors—office politics, gossip, and backstabbing. Recognizing the potential for these issues to spread and undermine the organization's unity and productivity, he took decisive action.

Jack gathered all the key managers together one evening and confronted individuals: "You're telling me about this person? You need to sit down and have a frank conversation with each other. Tell [them] exactly how you feel. Let's just get it all out on the table."

As the company grew, Jack continued applying these principles to manage conflicts within different business units. When leaders did not align with Alibaba's values—committing fraud or treating customers in an immoral manner—they were fired.

Brian Wong recalls that when Jack gave critical feedback, he was encouraging and supportive. He would say, "Look, I know you can do better. I believe that you are capable of this. However, here's where you disappointed me." Brian admits he couldn't bear "to let [Jack] down."

Under Jack Ma's leadership and governed by these principles, Alibaba experienced exponential growth, as did its subsidiaries. Alipay, under the umbrella of Ant Financial, had become the world's most valuable private unicorn, and was set to IPO at a valuation of approximately $300 billion...

Hijacked IPO

On 2 November 2020, just days before Ant Financial's IPO, Jack Ma and the Alibaba and Ant Financial leadership were summoned to Beijing.

The People's Bank of China presented them with a draft of new regulations. The rules would halt Ant Financial's IPO as its revenue model exploded: Their lending business would now face strict oversight, and online microloans would be limited, as would raising funds for consumer lending via asset-backed securities. Until now, fintechs in China could provide just 1 percent of a loan; overnight they had to provide 30 percent.

These restrictions were ordered by President Xi Jinping, who had been infuriated a few days prior when Jack Ma—on stage—condemned China's financial red tape as preventing innovation. Jack had proclaimed, "If banks don't change, we will change the banks." But China's regulator had the final word. That speech cost Jack Ma $200 billion and Tencent's Pony Ma approximately $50 billion. The collateral damage: almost 40,000 Alibaba employees lost their jobs in 2022 and 2023, as the company faced a more harsh regulatory environment.

The next day, local papers broke the news, with wording approved by the People's Bank of China: "If large internet companies develop financial services under the guise of being a technology company, it is not only evading regulation but also creating risks to consumers."

The narrative in Beijing was upended. For years, Ant Financial had been treading on the toes of traditional banks, chipping away at their primary source of income, consumer deposits, by tempting users to their Yu'E Bao money market fund with 17 times larger interest rates. Ant had been operating relatively free of regulation, unlike traditional banks. With mounting complaints from banks, the government was under pressure to react. Jack Ma's recent on-stage criticism was the tipping point.

Overnight, the value of Ant Financial collapsed by 80 percent. The market's reaction was exacerbated as the regulatory change came without warning. Chinese regulators' intentions are not necessarily different to those in the United States and the wider world, but the precision, power, and speed with which they altered policy set them apart and brought Ant's IPO crashing down. After receiving "input" from the People's Bank of China, Ant's money market Yu'E Bao cut its investment cap of ¥1 million, equivalent to around US $145,000, by more than half. Ant Financial rebranded to Ant Group.

Has China's regulatory crackdown been too harsh in decimating the valuations of Alibaba and Tencent? Perhaps. The move eroded half of Jack Ma's net worth and one-third of Pony Ma's in just three years. What is certain is that China's tech companies cannot be detangled from its governing Communist Party.

Elsewhere in Asia

Alibaba's success has set the bar for "super apps" across the rest of Asia. In South Korea, for instance, the instant messaging application KaKao Talk—used by 93 percent of the population—introduced KaKaoPay to enable users to transact. A rival payments service, Toss, followed shortly after.

Jin Oh, Partner at Goodwater Capital, was previously Head of Corporate Development at Toss. Over Jin's tenure, the company grew from a $50 million valuation to $7 billion. 30 percent of South Korea's population now uses Toss.

Toss's initial product was much like Venmo, but they fiercely shipped additional products. "In the first two years since I joined Toss, we probably launched over 120 MVPs," Jin shares. They also directed a lot of resources to eyeing competitors: "What is the best tech out there? What's Credit Karma doing? What's Revolut doing? What's Monzo doing? And then we started to integrate all those services into one platform." In the early days of Toss, the regulators had only just started to open up to the possibility of fintechs innovating the financial services space. This created a perfect storm for us to benchmark all successful fintechs out in the world and try to find product-market fit in Korea.

Toss founder Lee Seung-gun, now on his ninth startup, has been furnished with "eight lessons of failure." Jin believes that contributed to the success of Toss: "Because he's just failed so many times, [Lee] understands what needs to be right." And that is "top-of-wallet, top-of-mind user engagement."

Super Apps

Until the People's Bank of China's 2020 regulations, Tencent, Alibaba, and Ant Group held a combined valuation of $1.4 trillion—at the time, 10 percent of China's total GDP. Alibaba even created its own national holiday, "Singles Day," a 24-hour shopping event in November that generates more than double the sales of Black Friday and Cyber Monday combined. It is Alibaba's and Tencent's immense influence that the government has perhaps fought back against through regulation.

Digital payment services are not alone in being targeted by China's regulators and government. China's relationship with crypto has also been checkered. In late 2021, the People's Bank of China banned all cryptocurrency, citing fears of financial crime and economic instability. In fact, crypto was being used to facilitate capital flights to foreign markets. In 2019 and 2020, $50 billion in cryptocurrencies reportedly left China. Through crypto, many evaded the annual limit of $50,000 in foreign currency that an individual can buy or hold. And yet, China is pioneering among global governments to develop its own Central Bank Digital Currency—the electronic Chinese Yuan (e-CNY). In doing so, China perhaps aims to topple the dominance of the US dollar and clamp down on the capital flights previously enabled by crypto.

Beyond its borders, China has played a key geopolitical role in developing infrastructure and technology in Africa, and importing its residents' data. Chinese tech giant Huawei supported the technical development of M-PESA, a mobile money platform that facilitates 50 percent of Kenya's GDP, and the Chinese government funded an AI facial recognition program across Zimbabwe. The data centers, however, are based in China, sparking concerns over "digital colonization," as residents' data is taken—unrecompensed and for unspecified future uses. The same arguments prompted many countries' cautious stance on Huawei and its 5G infrastructure.

Nevertheless, China's mobile-first payment systems, which evolved into *super apps*, offer a glimpse into the future of global commerce. Super apps accelerate convenience and uplift small businesses, connecting them with the world. And yet the resulting lack of competition, implications for consumer data, and whims that China's government can enforce are worrying.

As Alibaba's Jack Ma and Tencent's Pony Ma vie to rule the tech sector, it's a two-horse race with not just the fate of China's tech sector riding on it, but much of South East Asia too.

TIPS FROM THE TRENCHES

1   Become a platform for others to build upon. Following China's example, we may see more vertically integrated business models creating a comprehensive "super app" ecosystem.

2   In the face of competition, consider the untapped market. Alibaba overcame established players like Global Sources and eBay by targeting those not yet on the internet or digital literates who weren't yet using e-commerce. This led to greater uptake than could ever have been achieved by tempting eBay loyalists to Alibaba.

3   Build a culturally relevant product. Digitizing cultural traditions or making these processes easier—like the gifting of red envelopes at China's Lunar New Year—is a recipe for virality.

Nubank vs. Regulatory Extinction

How a Presidential Decree Almost Killed Nubank

D avid Vélez woke up on a Friday morning to see the President had signed a decree changing how credit would work in Brazil.

After a quick calculation, David realized that his company, Nubank, would need to raise $1 billion Brazilian reals—equivalent to $200 million US dollars—almost overnight, just to keep operating. For a little-known company in Brazil that was barely past its Series A, this was not going to happen. David had moved heaven and earth to bring the company into existence and it was all about to be wiped away. What's worse, the company's annual end-of-year party was that evening.

Until the President's decree, credit worked differently in Brazil than in the rest of the world. When a Brazilian credit card was used, banks had 30 days to pay merchants, yet the bank received the customer's credit payment within seven days—this is known as negative working capital, as they received all funds before having to dispense them. Negative working capital decreases the funds required to provide credit cards, dismantling the barriers to entry; most credit providers have cash on hand to loan. This was a beautiful tailwind for Nubank, a new player in the market with limited existing funding, as they didn't need billions of dollars up-front to lend out. Following the President's decree, Nubank's working capital requirements would explode.

David Vélez, Nubank's CEO and Founder, debated what to do. Should he keep this to a smaller group or share the catastrophic news with the company? At the forefront of his mind was one of Nubank's core principles: We are owners, not renters. "When you treat employees like owners and expect them to work like owners, you must be transparent with them," David explains. So he did exactly that.

David took the company into war mode.

Over the next 72 hours, David galvanized his workforce with a single mission: Halt this regulation or it would be the end of Nubank. David and Cristina Junqueira (Cris), Nubank's COO and co-founder, marched out to the media. These rules were unfair. They would demolish the first competition that Brazil's banking sector had seen in decades, to the detriment of consumers. Only Brazil's five biggest banks, with huge balance sheets, could keep offering credit at scale if this regulatory change went through. Were the big banks colluding to bankrupt Nubank, the new cus-tomer-focused player on the block?

Cris quarterbacked the public relations process, lobbying regu-lators, rallying friends, and borrowing the ear of any journalist who would listen. A true shapeshifter, Cris has changed roles at Nubank more times than you can count, becoming what the com-pany needs at any given time. At this moment, she took off her COO hat and became Nubank's chief regulatory negotiator. It worked. Brazil's biggest newspaper grabbed onto the story.

The Nubank team harnessed their customers to take action too—a tactic that Uber has used over the years in the United States as they faced regulatory shutdown, adding an in-app feature for users to email their local congresspeople when Uber was at risk of shutting down in DC and New York. Thousands of customers flooded the Brazilian Central Bank's Twitter feed. After a bombardment of emails, messages, and phone calls from Nubank customers to the Central Bank, David received a call: They were stopping the regulation.

David is a wartime CEO. Even as he tells me about the greatest crisis in Nubank's history you can see his energy pick up, his focus sharpen. David has learned that "In peacetime, there are 100 priorities; in wartime, there is only one. You just focus on what can kill you and motivate everybody around a specific goal."

Whilst David and Cris scrambled to address the regulators, Edward Wible (Ed)—Nubank's CTO and co-founder—held the fort, processing hundreds of transactions per second through Nubank's seamless technology. Ed, the engineering mind of the trio, saw the silver lining to their predicament, "Having 30 days to pay merchants, while customers pay you in seven days? That was great luck. That wasn't the business plan that we pitched to [our lead investors] Sequoia. But in retrospect, negative working capital as we scaled was one of the most important aspects of the entire business."

Nubank was born and grew in challenging times, and has performed best with the odds stacked against it. Aside from overnight regulation changes, Nubank has survived scaling in one of the most unstable economic environments in the world, during civil unrest through several presidential elections, and rapid devaluation of the Brazilian Real. When Nubank entered crisis, David also called Capital One co-founder Nigel Morris, who had been in a similar predicament just a decade earlier. Nigel compares David's regulatory navigation to "Kissinger's ambassadorial skills."

Fittingly, when the team began preparations for its IPO in 2020, the Covid-19 pandemic hit. As David puts it, "When new challenges arise, we unite. Energy and motivation soar. When things are calm, I see the company become complacent, lose motivation, and become less excited. In a way, we are programmed to accelerate and to do better when times are hard."

Readers from outside of Latin America may not have heard of Nubank. Yet in Brazil, over half of the adult population bank with Nubank and the company cleared 100 million users in 2024. Their initial vision to distribute one million credit cards in five years was surpassed in just two. Nubank has always set lofty goals and exceeded expectations. At the time of writing, Nubank (NYSE: NU) is trading at over $50 billion.

Despite its meteoric success, Nubank is built on principles, not just profits. Nubank has harnessed its customers as evangelists; they have ditched the competition (Nubank is the primary banking partner of 50 percent of customers) and endorsed the digital bank (90 percent of Nubank's users join via word-of-mouth referrals and their NPS customer loyalty scores exceed 90).

Nubank has redefined the Brazilian tech ecosystem and banking for millions across Latin America. And yet, Nubank's visionary CEO, David Vélez, is not from Brazil. How did this outsider build a fintech unicorn and earn the loyalty of this Latin American nation?

Getting Started

David spent his childhood in Medellín, Colombia, among a troupe of entrepreneurs. His dad had 11 siblings and each ran their own business. For David's father, it was a button company. From a young age, David's father drilled into him the importance of owning your time and destiny, so David always wanted to be an entrepreneur.

Medellín, his hometown, was notorious for drug cartels and violence. A harrowing close escape from a shopping complex bombing and his uncle's abduction forced David's family to make a tough choice: Leave Colombia.

David enrolled at Stanford at 18. As an undergraduate, David never found the right time to pursue entrepreneurship and upon graduating, moved into finance. Years later, back at Stanford studying for an MBA, he promised things would be different.

David's classmate, David George (now a General Partner at a16z), mentioned that the renowned venture capital fund, Sequoia, was looking for someone to set up operations in Latin America. David George introduced him to Doug Leone, one of Sequoia's Managing Partners. They met and hit it off immediately. By the time David was back in his car, he already had an email from Michael Moritz (Sequoia's second Managing Partner) asking him to come back for a follow-up interview. David's interactions with Sequoia became key to how he would build and create the culture at Nubank. Sequoia's culture was idiosyncratic—both of the firm's Managing Partners were giving their time and attention to an interview with an intern. David had not seen this before.

David reflects, "Doug's superpower is his EQ. He has an uncanny ability to ask [deep] questions. [For example] Did you have a good relationship with your mother? How's your relationship with your father?"

David knew he wanted to embed this culture into whatever he built in the future. But for now, David was all-in on Sequoia. Throughout his MBA, on Tuesdays, David would fly out of San Francisco to Sao Paulo on Doug's private jet, take meetings all day with startups, and then return. On other days he would wake up at 4 am to work at Sequoia for six hours, followed by a full day at Stanford.

After his MBA, David formally joined Sequoia to finish setting up the office in Brazil. Then a day before his birthday, he received a frank phone call from Doug: "We're shutting down Sequoia's office in Brazil. It's not going to happen in South America." David was shattered. Sequoia offered him the opportunity to join their Menlo Park office, but David's heart was set on another idea, the seed for what would become Nubank, and began pitching to whoever would listen.

Life as a venture capitalist refined David's understanding of the type and scale of business he wanted to build. "The number one rule of investing is to look for big markets," David tells me. "Look at Latin America. Where are the largest markets? Five of the top 10 biggest companies in Brazil are banks. In Mexico they are banks; in Argentina, banks; in Colombia, banks. Even in the United States, banks. I was curious about the potential market size, about the continuous profitability of this industry through economic ups and downs."

And the biggest profit pool of these banks? Credit. Indeed, most transactions in Brazil are completed via credit card vs. other payment methods. Yet in the early 2010s, banks made it difficult for customers to get a credit card, as David had experienced firsthand. Entering a Brazilian bank branch resembled visiting a prison. Customers had to surrender their phones and undergo a series of airport-like security checks behind steel-barred windows, just to make it inside the bank building. Next, customers faced bureaucratic bank tellers and lengthy queues. In return, banks charged upwards of 10 percent interest per month, with many users paying upwards of 450 percent over the year. Moreover, at the time, the Brazilian banking space was incredibly consolidated; the big five players collectively owned 80 percent of the market (Caixa Econômica, Banco do Brasil, Itaú Unibanco, Bradesco, and Santander).

To validate his initial idea of a disruptive bank, David talked to over 30 experts across the banking space. Their responses were unanimous: It's not possible. David was not discouraged. Most of the reasons they gave for a new bank not working were either debatable or false; they were biases based on fear or hunches. Experts doubted the regulators would let David launch a new bank and questioned whether local consumers would be willing to trust a new player in the market. For David, these challenges were not unsurmountable. He listened to their concerns and evaluated each one for truth and assumptions as he socialized his idea. When the Brazilian Central Bank granted David an initial meeting and was optimistic about innovation and competition among Brazilian banks, all that was left to do was to test the idea.

"We knew it would be hard. Everyone was telling us so. But we wanted to do it. I was not going to [waste] more than 10 years of my career doing something easy. If it succeeded, it would be impactful; if it didn't, I'd fail, but I wanted to do something hard."

David was also building at an inflection point. The "Why now?" was clear: 60 million people in Brazil lived outside the banking infrastructure. A cloud bank wouldn't need branches and IBM mainframes to reach them. David could build a new type of first-principle bank in the cloud.

Consider the landscape back in 2012: Monzo in the UK was not yet born, Venmo had not reached prominence in the United States, and venture capital had yet to spread to Latin America (LatAm), not helped by Sequoia shutting down their Brazil office. There was no precedent for Nubank. But after weeks of hanging around the Sequoia office in San Francisco and pitching his idea, he wore them down. Sequoia co-led Nubank's $2 million seed round alongside Kaszek, one of LatAm's first venture capital funds. Kaszek was established by the founders of Mercado Libre, an e-commerce site and LatAm unicorn.

The Sequoia funding came with resistance. Roelof Botha, now Managing Partner at Sequoia and an early member of the PayPal mafia, was not so bullish. David recalls Roelof's stern South African tone warning about his lack of Portuguese, lack of technology capabilities, and lack of local knowledge...

David didn't take this as a critique. He saw it as useful feedback on the holes in his plan—a to-do list for the coming weeks. For David, this meant finding co-founders and an initial team who could plug these gaps.

Finding Co-Founders

David reframed Roelof's feedback as motivation. Roelof had identified two characteristics David needed to find in his co-founders: a Brazilian insider and someone technical.

David met dozens of candidates through a long, protracted process, but when he eventually struck gold, he struck big. "I met Cris, my co-founder, and we had a great coffee. I told her about Nubank and she loved it. Her first reaction was good and then 48 hours later she rang. She was in." David's other co-founder, Ed, had a similar reaction. Within 48 hours, Ed was on a plane to Sao Paulo without so much as a place to stay.

With hiring, David believes, "There's something [in] how quickly people got it. There were a lot of potential co-founders. I found myself enamored with their experience on paper, but it took five or six meetings for them to understand Nubank's concept. When I look back at [our] first team of 10 [or so] people, they were not necessarily perfect from a CV perspective," but they all immediately grasped what Nubank was trying to achieve. David saw it as a form of "self-selection"—unlike those who took a lot of convincing, these early members seemed to naturally fit. David's approach to hiring continued in the same vein: he likes to take big bets on people who are all-in.

In the years following, David and Cris completed a Star Wars-themed Myers-Briggs personality test. The results labelled Cris (the executor and the external-facing force) as Darth Vader, and David (the strategist) as the Emperor. Meanwhile, Ed's technical expertise brought these forces and strategies to life. Nubank's three co-founders are still together to this day.

Cris, a Brazilian native, had been an insider in the financial system working at Itaú Unibanco; however, she had grown frustrated that she was only "making the rich richer" and wanted to build something for all of Brazil. "We started primarily from a place of outrage," Cris says. "We couldn't stand having to pay the highest interest rates in the world, some of the highest fees in the world and have some of the worst customer experiences in the world." David had initially named Nubank "EOS," but they collectively renamed it to "Nu," which both sounded close to new and meant nude in Portuguese—in line with the transparency they wanted to create.

Ed graduated from Princeton University with a degree in computer science, but he's always been a builder, tinkering and coming up with business ideas or ways to automate things. One of his early successes was building a database to organize the mobile workforce for a newspaper delivery agency, which allowed him to make enough money to start traveling.

After graduation, Ed was unsure if a career in technology was the right path, so he took a detour and worked at BCG in New York, then a tech-focused private equity firm called Francisco Partners, which led him to London. These experiences gave Ed insight into how tech companies grow and age, providing valuable lessons on what to avoid as a startup. Chief among these lessons was for startups to avoid being riddled with legacy technology. After an MBA at INSEAD in France, he found himself as the engineering lead for a Uruguay-based data measurement company, Scantech IT, and suggested a complete overhaul of their technology stack. It was old, quickly degrading, and would not stand the test of time.

Ed was fired from that first role. He had walked into a rather complex situation where the CTO of the company was also the founder's spouse. In the battle between technology and love, Ed lost. He was summoned to the airport by the company's CEO, who was about to take a flight. "You're fired. You're creating too much noise for me at home," Ed recounts of the conversation.

Fortunately for Ed, David was a board member of Scantech IT and he appreciated what Ed had tried to do. Just as Ed was about to return to Chicago to ship software code and live out of his parents' basement, David invited him to Brazil to start a bank instead. Although Ed's CV was not typical for a CTO, he saw this as an opportunity to prove himself as an operator. He became the initial engineer, helping turn ideas into concrete prototypes, and took on the role of CTO at Nubank.

Together the three co-founders formed a formidable team. As Hugh Strange, VP of Product, says, "David's conviction was infectious, giving himself and others the sense that they could survive anything." As Nubank grew and adapted, so did David. The skills required to run a seed-stage startup and to stand at the helm of a $50 billion public company are worlds apart. "David has [borrowed] advice from smart people around him to inform his leadership philosophy."

As for the other co-founders, Cris's relentless energy enabled her to overcome any roadblock, from Mastercard approvals to regulation. "Obstacles require a focus on what is within our control: doing what's best for our customers. Success is a natural consequence," says Cris. Ed's obsessive drive to deliver led him to code much of the early infrastructure that underpinned Nubank. Hugh compares Ed to a stack rank priority program in human form, taking the number one issue from the top of the list and executing against it. When information security was the big problem, Ed would "just disappear and do that until it wasn't a problem anymore."

The three were a perfect storm to bring Nubank into the world, and collectively covered all of the challenges that Roelof had put to David.

Nu Culture

Before David even had a team or co-founders, he wrote the company culture.

Ringing in his ears was something he kept hearing: The ethos of any business is started by the first 10 to 15 employees in the first four to six months. "Either you build this culture strategically and proactively or it gets built by itself. You wouldn't just engage with your children when they are 20 years old—at that point it is too late. Similarly, if you don't [formulate your startup's] culture before it has 100 or 1,000 employees… Good luck!"

David brings up the US Declaration of Independence: "You still see Americans going back and reading the document; 200 years later it still reflects what the culture of the country is about." Similarly, Nubank's culture document has barely changed in its 10 years of existence. Company culture is "the cement" with which you build "the skyscraper."

Nubank carefully distilled its values and has kept these consistent throughout its 10-year history:

1 We are hungry to challenge the status quo,

> **2** We build strong and diverse teams,
>
> **3** We think and act like owners,
>
> **4** We are smart, efficient, and above all...
>
> **5** We want our customers to love us fanatically.

This playbook still guides David's daily decisions. In one instance during Nubank's scale-up phase, the team thought they had achieved stronger product-market fit—profitability had spiked among several customer cohorts. To understand this, the product team dug deeper and found that an engineering error had prevented loan repayment reminders from being sent. As a result, customers missed repayments, incurring additional interest fees. Some saw a profitable opportunity, but David prioritized transparency. He instructed the engineer to notify customers and refund any overpayments. *We want our customers to love us fanatically.*

Leaders at Nubank nurtured a culture of shared ownership across the engineering and product teams. As Vice President of Product, Hugh Strange empowered his team to own the metrics of the problems they were solving, "to give them autonomy, so they can work efficiently and [leaders will] not get in their way." For Hugh, success hinges on trust. With strong product and engineering partnerships, you can let the teams work their magic.

Small House

Nubank came together in a "casinha" (small house in Portuguese) in the South Zone of São Paulo. At this stage, the company comprised the founders, core engineers, and a couple of designers. Hugh Strange joined as Nubank's first product manager in time for the public launch:

"Building a generational bank inside a small residential home had its quirks. As the team grew, the kitchen became a makeshift office with laptops on top of the stove. It was mayhem in the best possible way." In fact, the toilets at the back of the house flushed thunderously. Nubankers would have to mute a call while someone flushed the toilet because it sounded like you were in the bathroom.

At the time, Ed was living upstairs in the house along with a few other key engineers. Cris bought bedsheets for one engineer as his were ratty and old. Inside the casinha, the personal and professional lives of Nubankers blurred, but when people talk about the casinha period, it is with great affection. That family-like camaraderie created something out of nothing. Cris shares: "We joked that the first employee screening took place as soon as the candidates arrived at the casinha. Some turned around and walked away. Those who remained really believed in what we were building." In the later days, the casinha would become mythical among Nubank employees, with Nubankers delineating the era they were at Nubank by which office they were in. Nubank has even recreated the casinha in one of their large Brazilian offices today.

Nubank is not the first company to run a startup from a house in its early days. Facebook got off the ground in a summer house around the corner from Stanford University, as did DoorDash. Instacart ran their company out of a house in San Francisco, as did Twitch until it got so crowded that their landlord evicted them. Physical space is a key tenet of culture and from the beginning signals to employees that working for a startup is not a normal experience.

This was the calm before the storm. In 2014, Nubank was hit by the first of many regulatory challenges. If Nubank did not launch in the next three months, before the new regulations came into force, they would have to apply for a banking license. The team urgently needed to partner with Visa or Mastercard to launch their cards. Visa didn't reply, so they went with Mastercard.

Today, there are many barriers to entry to launch a credit card in Brazil, including regulatory, but back in 2014, all you needed was to meet the requirements of Visa or Mastercard.

Credit cards involve several parties working together, including the credit card holder (buyer) and merchant (seller), the issuer (the buyer's bank), the acquirer (the merchant's bank), and the payment network (such as Visa or Mastercard, who process transactions between the buyer and merchant's banks).

When a purchase is made, the merchant's payment system sends the transaction details via the payment network to the issuer—in this case, Nubank. The issuer verifies the card's validity and available credit, approving or declining the transaction. Each month, the issuer sends a statement to the cardholder detailing the charges. The cardholder must then pay at least the minimum amount due to avoid penalties and interest.

Once the Nubank app was functioning, onboarding the first customers was slow. Hugh arranged to meet influential people, gave them a card, and then manually inducted them via a rudimentary back-office system. "It was a customer at a time. But that's how it got built."

The initial weeks of Nubank's launch in 2014 were anticlimactic; not much happened. But at some point in October, Cris and the brand team's press release got picked up by a niche local technology magazine, *Ol Yal Digital* (Portuguese for "the digital look"). All of a sudden, Nubank's signups started to grow exponentially.

Early adopting customers were so impressed by the step change in digital banking services that they invited their friends. Nubank's extraordinary referral engine works to this day. After observing many other fintechs balloon to 50,000 users and plateau, Hugh's reflection on Nubank's success was that they continued to ensure that spark of magic for every customer on the platform, for years. The spectrum of possible magic moments was vast: "It could be the seamless acquisition flow or the customer service, or just that [a neobank] existed." Nubank captured purple magic in a bottle, and its users were happy to share it around.

Tech Stack

While David and Cris secured licenses and the Mastercard partnership, Ed had the monumental task of building a bank from scratch with a three-month timeline. Today, this can be done with the help of third parties who plug together like a jigsaw to create a bank.

So how did Ed do it? Limited by the lack of third-party providers in 2014 Brazil, Ed would have to forge his own path. When Ed talked to Tata Consulting Services about outsourcing the build, he was told it would take 18 months and cost $2 million—Nubank's entire seed round. The fraud module alone would cost one million dollars.

"At Nubank, we wanted to be the system of record [for banking infrastructure], to own our destiny, especially in the markets where we operate," says Ed. There was no other answer but to build in-house.

To Ed, third parties are a recipe for fragility. If someone will sell you something, they will sell it to everyone else. "If a third party is your system of record, and they can't reconcile your debits and credits, how do you explain that to your customers?"

In the US, Simple Bank had given Ed inspiration and conviction in the idea for Nubank. They had wonderful UX. But Ed also watched them run out of ideas to innovate, as they were a UX layer on top of an old bank. Strategically, Simple Bank didn't go deep enough into the banking stack to be fundamental and sustainable. Simple Bank ended up being acquired for less than the VC funding that they raised.

Bringing a bank to life in three months came at a high cost. As Ed puts it, "Everything people do to be balanced, healthy, and to make things sustainable for themselves—I did the opposite." Ed justified this grind as his opportunity in the driver's seat, one which he couldn't bear to squander. David and Cris were hiring and negotiating contracts, but Nubank would collapse without the engineers to deliver the product.

David laid down the gauntlet to the engineers—if Nubank could launch in February, David promised the engineers more equity. The team cut corners but shipped the product hastily. That was all that mattered. The team launched marginally later than planned, in March, but recognizing their effort David delivered on the equity. The engineers, to this day, treasure the extra stocks they were granted, not least for its financial returns but also as David's gesture of appreciation.

After this, Ed made a deliberate point to draw a line under the experience. Now that a minimum viable product (MVP) was shipped, Ed saw the next step in Nubank's journey as mass-scaling. Therefore, the tech stack was built with scale in mind. Ed avoided monolithic design, as found in the tech architectures of legacy banks that are built as one huge block. He strove to do the right things around security and modularization. He set the team up in a healthier way so that when units of developers were added, productivity was not compromised. For Ed, "The scalability is [rooted in] a healthy, functioning team, as opposed to headcount." Knowing how "technical debt" ridden and what hostile work environments big tech companies can be, Ed wanted to prevent these causes of brain drain at Nubank.

Pausing growth at the MVP milestone was Ed's proudest moment at the fintech unicorn. "Pumping the brakes, creating some space, establishing that [building Nubank] wasn't sprint [after] sprint. It had been a sprint to getting a product, then a long game." He "was terrified of the cultural impact of a premature scale-up," and the resulting enormous headcount that would be "necessary to apologize for [and rebuild] the parts of the product that weren't ready [if rolled] out to millions of customers."

Quality customer technology was built at pace with Nubank's growth and became its identity and differentiator. This was never the core competence of banks, who were vendor integrators. Nubank's tech stack was built from the ground up.

Data is like gold to Ed: "Your ability to use your business data is your ability to understand your customers. From creditworthiness of customers to determining if they are being defrauded." One haunting month's end, the data in Nubank's system did not stack up. This is the number one rule of banking: The left-hand side must equal the right-hand side. Ed reflects, "I think we tried too hard to reinvent some of the wheels. We could have [asked] experienced folks from the industry, what is the domain model [for various features]?" instead of building everything as custom tech. Despite scaling flawlessly for millions, Nubank's system stumbled for a tiny fraction of users. Of their five million customers, around 100 customers' figures did not add up. The memory gives Ed chills.

Customer-centricity

Every year, Nubank gives its customer service agents a day off, and the rest of the company takes support calls. This began as a way to show appreciation for customer service agents but the day has since morphed into something deeper, to ensure that product teams are aligned with what customers feel on the ground. The atmosphere is lighthearted, with many foreigners (Gringos) at Nubank speaking down telephones with their heavily accented Portuguese.

One year, following the annual customer service call day, the Nubank team became concerned. Were they automating enough processes or just plugging the gaps with customer service agents?

To find out, Ed and Hugh, as CTO and Head of Product, embedded themselves in the customer service teams. "We had programmers next to people taking calls. I'm not sure it was the best for productivity, but it was amazing for improving feedback between what was happening on the frontlines and the people developing the products." Where many product, engineering, and customer service teams are adversarial, Nubank found a way to marry their interests together through shared culture and Hugh and Ed's close friendship.

Over the following six months, Engineering and Product automated low-hanging fruit in the customer operations journey, from handling chargebacks digitally to building operational dashboards for agents and connecting end data sources. "If your customer service doesn't have the right information up to the second, they don't have enough autonomy to do the right thing," Ed shares.

Customer attention was not Nubank's currency. They wanted to get users off their app. In the early days, Ed thought "Any customer service contact is a bug," but he evolved to see magic in customer service as he spent longer with their teams. When a customer called about a defrauded card, Nubank would first ask if they were ok, then reassure and refund the customer, rather than asking for a police report and interrogating on the details. Later, they would go back to verify the information.

Ed stresses that "each time you speak to the bank, they should remember what you said last time," as opposed to the "left-hand, right-hand split brain" that we often see in non-communicating departments. Pinpointing a phone's GPS location during a credit card transaction wasn't rocket science, but nobody had seen transactions on a map before. When an early customer's payment for a toasted sandwich went through twice, Nubank bought him a toaster by way of apology. Eventually, the Central Bank of Brazil recognized Nubank as offering the best customer experience in the nation.

Even when faced with challenges to their core business, Nubank has embraced change. In 2019, the Central Bank unveiled Pix, a free and instant transfer system. The bank's chief hailed it as a system that "eliminates the need to have a credit card." Pix has quickly become Brazil's favorite way to pay, with transactions now exceeding those of credit cards. Nubank leaned in, registering far more Pix accounts than any Brazilian incumbent bank and launching Pix no Crédito (Pix on Credit), allowing customers to make Pix transfers using their credit card limit.

No one has a net promoter score (NPS) like Nubank, especially in financial services. Customer satisfaction is their North Star metric. Much of the money other players put into marketing, Nubank invests straight back into customer service—word of mouth markets itself.

Talent

When building a world-class team, David applied the same approach to finding his early employees as he had done with his co-founders: "We were going to have to work *hard* for a very long period, and I wanted to find people that understood that quickly... I was buying culture fit and mission, and selling vision and purpose. Hiring is hard. Really hard. What have I learned? First, the pedigree is much less important." When David reflects on his hiring mistakes, the common denominator was hiring for prestige; David cautions against "relying on a CV too much as a measure of talent.' Instead, David wished he had searched for motivation earlier.

That said, closer to the IPO, Nubank brought on a series of seasoned executives. David had built a strong relationship with Nigel Morris, Founder of Capital One and QED, the fintech investment firm. David saw Capital One as a major inspiration and began to poach their key talent to strengthen the roster at Nubank. Indeed, Nigel and David first met years earlier at the private equity firm General Atlantic. Nubank was modeled on Capital One from the very beginning.

Nigel recalls David approaching him:

David: "I think we can build a Capital One in Brazil. Will you help me?"
Nigel: "No, I don't think so, David, I'm just not sure if I have the time to do that."
David persisted.
Nigel: "I'll tell you what, I'll come back and help you understand the credit card business as I understand it."

When David later returned, having established immense early traction, Nigel remembers him asking, "Will you invest now? Will you invest in me?"

Nigel did: "Of course, the rest is history."

For Nubank's Head of Product, Hugh Strange, the recruitment of former Capital One staffers was a testing moment—he initially felt intimidated by the new hires. "I think anybody that had been [at Nubank] for a while would be lying if they didn't say [they were intimidated], because you're giving up some of your scope. [However] it turned out to be fantastic." Help was arriving. People who had lived through hyper-specific parts of what Nubank was experiencing brought their playbooks. As part of this, Nubank reorganized the company, giving Hugh two extra years of life at Nubank with new challenges.

Many scaling companies misstep, Hugh observes. They are either "blindly loyal" to all current employees, unaware of the talent "out in the market that can help the company grow," or they do the opposite, installing an "entirely new slate" of leaders, which "demotivates the people who were already there." Nubank found a middle ground, where they kept the old guard motivated to bring in a new kind of energy.

Ringing the Bell

"First they ignore you, then they laugh at you, then they fight you, and then you win."

Widely attributed to Indian activist Mahatma Gandhi, the quote hangs in Nubank's São Paulo office—a reminder that Nubank has lived through each of these stages. For a long time, the competition ignored Nubank and vice versa. Building Nubank was a relentless struggle of moving quickly to survive. Nubank had always been the underdog. So, there was a level of cognitive dissonance among early employees when they rang the bell on the NYSE.

Nubank started talking about 100 million customers back when they had two million customers and talking about two million customers when they had zero. So, part of the IPO process involved reflecting on what could be their next audacious goal.

As an engineer, Ed did not like the big bangs and that's exactly what an IPO felt like to him: "Oh, I hated that. No control, it doesn't scale gradually, you just have to roll it out and hope for the best." However, the IPO was a chance for Nubank to reward the customers and employees who had traveled with them on the journey.

Nubank dual listed their stock in both the United States and Brazil, to enable all of their customers to buy the stock if they wanted, as a reward for coming on the journey with them. This was the largest number of retail investors ever participating in a Brazilian IPO, allowing 800,000 Nubank customers to become shareholders. It was the first-ever program in Brazil to allow customers to participate for free in a company's equity offering.

Staying Together for a Decade

Despite all the ups and downs, all three co-founders still play an integral role in Nubank. As Ed puts it, "We try to have very candid communication. It helps that none of us [have] big egos. [We] make decisions [based on what's] best for the company, not for our careers, and not for our egos."

A test of this dynamic was Ed's transition from CTO to individual contributor, after eight years and scaling the tech organization to 8,000 engineers. David and Ed always knew this moment would come. But they couldn't agree on the right time for Ed to transition and who the right person would be to replace him. Ed feared that prematurely swapping out may compromise the tech. David worried Nubank would miss opportunities to move at their maximum velocity without more experience.

For Ed, once Nubank reached several thousand engineers, "that's when it got weird. That role changes so drastically as you scale up. By that point, it was very specialized [and] far from building the code and things that gave me energy."

In the classic CTO-CEO dynamic, Ed appealed for conservatism and not "scaling faster than we can digest," whilst David pushed for parallelization. To Ed, "that tension was healthy for the company but hard for us." In the fog of war and information asymmetry, it can be hard to trust intentions and that the other person understands the implications of what they are asking for.

Mercifully, this challenge was not political, but rather a debate over what was best for the customer. But "you can get spun up," which is good for driving innovation forward, "but those same [emotions] make it hard to negotiate [with] a level head. It's sort of like a funhouse set of mirrors," that distort clear thinking.

"When I think back to finally stepping away from the CTO position, I wish I'd done it sooner and made David's life easier." At the time, Ed felt "I know what I'm doing. The results have been good." Ed recommends being open, as he "missed opportunities to teach and build trust." He continues, "So much happened at Nubank and [there's] so much love for each other in the process. But that makes it harder, not easier, right? Because the stakes are beyond yourself. You feel you're defending a larger thing than even your team. [Nubank] was for the customers."

David's role as CEO also evolved as the neobank grew.

"I'll always be a founder. But I don't think that means I always need to be the CEO. Those two roles are very different. In fact, at times, they are the opposite." Crucial to being a CEO is managing. David prefers the vision and innovation, admitting, "I've redefined the CEO responsibilities in a way that fits my interest, and that fits the company." Seeing the two roles as distinct will help him let go one day: "I'll be fine giving up the CEO title and will continue to be a founder forever."

The challenges Nubank tackles aren't isolated to Brazil or Latin America. They're global issues we all face. As David highlights, "There is a huge opportunity to reinvent banking globally. This is the single biggest industry in the world, [with] a $10 trillion market capitalization. Even today, after 10 years of fintech, incumbent banks have something like a 99 percent market share in every single vertical, in every single country. So we're in the early days of reinventing banking. The next decade is about expanding globally."

Nubank is truly a testament to bringing a vision into the world. By focusing on an immense market, hiring people who were truly passionate about solving the problem, and relentlessly focusing on the customer, Nubank achieved the impossible. They faced so many near-death moments along the way but their customers and team willed it into existence. Nubank stands today as a purple giant in the Latin American tech ecosystem. It's time to watch Nubank go global and hit the one billion customer mark.

TIPS FROM THE TRENCHES

1 Be an outsider. perspectives enable first-principle thinking. David, not native to Brazil, could envision a new banking paradigm for the nation. But he could not do it alone. David bet on talent aligned to the mission over pedigree.

2 Go after big markets with big ambitions. Nubank's mindset was long-term from inception, aiming for 100 million customers before they had cleared two million. The first rule for founders who want to change the status quo is to tackle big markets.

3 Focus on NPS. Nubank unequivocally focused on its customers and made NPS their North Star metric. Nubank invested in a memorable customer experience and relied on word-of-mouth referrals to grow, as an alternative approach to marketing. Owning their own tech stack was a critical enabler in achieving that customer experience.

05
SVB vs. the Newcomers
Bank Blowups and Unlikely Beneficiaries

It started as a Tweet, then a Thread, then a Twitter storm. But I first saw the queues. Driving through Silicon Valley, a noose of people tightened around the block, drawing my gaze from the road. At the red light, I flicked between news channels, seeking an explanation—a voice echoed, "This is an extinction-level event [that] will set innovation back by 10 years." The voice was Garry Tan, the CEO of Y Combinator, the renowned accelerator responsible for spawning Airbnb, Reddit, Stripe, Dropbox, Coinbase, and DoorDash. He warned, "One-third of Y Combinator startups will not be able to make payroll in the next 30 days... This is a national security issue." Rounding the corner, I drove past the queue's source: Silicon Valley Bank (SVB). People with outstretched arms implored the security guard to let them in. I was witnessing a run on the bank.

But unlike in the 2008 financial crisis, this time it was entrepreneurs and venture capitalists swarming local bank branches to withdraw their deposits. And thousands more were online, transferring funds to alternate, more sturdy, institutions. Many were portfolio companies instructed by their investors, fearing SVB would freeze deposits and lead to bankruptcy filings. When everyone is withdrawing their cash, you're incentivized to do the same, *just in case*. Alarm spiraled on social media, extending queues. SVB's CEO went live to the national press, instructing customers: "Don't panic. Stay calm. Don't panic." This only stoked the hysteria. $42 billion was withdrawn on 9 March alone—almost a quarter of the bank's total deposits.

Friday 10 March 2023: The bank collapsed in a spectacular fashion.

With SVB unable to meet the additional withdrawal requests, the California Department of Financial Protection and Innovation took possession of the bank and appointed the Federal Deposit Insurance Corporation as a receiver.

Not knowing what was on the other side of the weekend, many startups took emergency fundraising action. Parker Conrad, founder of the leading payroll and workforce management tool Rippling, raised $500 million to ensure it could cover payroll for customers who needed it on Monday. Others were not so lucky.

Chipper Cash, the African peer-to-peer payments unicorn, had been hit for the second time in six months. SVB had led their Series C round, and cryptocurrency exchange FTX spearheaded Chipper Cash's Series C extension. Most of Chipper Cash's assets were stored across the two platforms. FTX collapsed in November 2022, followed by SVB in March 2023. Chipper Cash's valuation is expected to be marked down significantly in its next equity round.

Concerns about contagion mounted—11 percent of US banks had worse unrealized losses than SVB. Over the weekend, the Federal Reserve stepped in to prevent any wider impact. The US government announced it would protect all SVB deposits, even those over the $250,000 FDIC insurance limit. Many SVB customers held venture funding rounds of millions at the bank. Therefore, 94 percent of SVB deposits were uninsured. These losses would have obliterated the US startup ecosystem. In the UK, HSBC acquired SVB's subsidiary for £1. SVB's US banking division was sold to First Republic Bank.

Two months later, First Republic Bank collapsed and landed in the hands of J.P. Morgan.

Since incorporating in 1983, SVB has survived the dotcom crash and the 2008 financial crisis. So why—in seemingly stable economic conditions—did SVB fall?

Anatomy of a Banking Collapse

For decades, one institution had become the de facto bank of choice for venture capitalists, startups, and innovators—the aptly named Silicon Valley Bank.

SVB carved a niche by providing innovative financial products that others wouldn't. They banked startups, traditionally considered undesirable clients for their high failure rates. SVB built up a network of investors with whom startup clients could connect, offered venture debt (debt financing to venture-funded startups), and even made direct equity investments into their customers. SVB's strategy was to make low margins on upfront banking services, to become the innovation ecosystem's chosen financial partner. In theory, this would generate greater long-term profits: These companies would grow and need more complex financial services.

Two Bank of America executives devised the idea for SVB over a poker game in 1983. The executives felt startups and venture capital funds were underserved by existing financial institutions. SVB would solve that. Headquartered in the heart of the tech ecosystem—Santa Clara in California's Silicon Valley—it took the bank 36 years to reach the $100 billion deposit milestone. And one additional year to add $100 billion more. Fueled by a boom in venture capital investing, by 2022 SVB had become the 16th largest bank in the United States. SVB's startup clients have matured into multinational companies including Airbnb, Block Inc. (formerly Square), Pinterest, and Roblox.

Then in 2023, SVB was sunk by what are widely considered the lowest-risk assets on earth: US Treasuries.

SVB, like all banks, employed a portion of consumer deposits to get a return. With a surge of $100 billion of new deposits in

2020 alone, SVB sought a safe and profitable way to invest these deposits. The Covid-19 pandemic was roaring; central banks worldwide, including the Federal Reserve, had set interest rates at near-zero to stimulate economic growth. In this environment of low inflation and low interest rates, SVB chose to invest in "safe," long-term US government bonds, known as Treasuries.

US Treasuries are essentially an "IOU" issued by the US government to fund spending. When you buy a Treasury, you lend money for a set period, earn regular interest payments (coupons), and your original investment is returned at maturity—in SVB's case, almost 10 years away. Long-term bonds are illiquid. SVB could not easily convert bonds to cash if all depositors demanded their funds back.

SVB's strategy began to unravel with inflation.

Coming out of the pandemic, global spending mushroomed. Russia's invasion of Ukraine forced global gas and grain prices higher. To curb inflation, central banks increased interest rates. This impacted SVB—when interest rates rise, existing bonds become less attractive, as newly issued bonds offer higher yields.

Almost 60 percent of SVB's assets were tied up in these old, low-yielding US treasuries, now worth less than what SVB had paid for them.

Although SVB planned to hold these securities until maturity, in the meantime their balance sheet held significant unrealized losses. If SVB had to sell any Treasuries—say to fund increased customer withdrawals—SVB's assets would not equate to the amount of deposits. In a bank-run scenario, a fire sale would push their Treasury valuations lower.

To mitigate against this scenario and to free up some cash, on 8 March, SVB offloaded all $21 billion of its available-for-sale Treasuries, at a $1.8 billion loss. In tandem, they announced plans to raise $2 billion in capital by selling SVB shares, which they would reinvest in higher-yielding assets to plug their balance sheet loss. Unfortunately, SVB did not communicate this plan proactively enough.

Spooked customers made a run on the bank.

The $21 billion that SVB had freed up could not cover the $42 billion withdrawn in a single day by panicking customers. The bank faced a liquidity crisis. Had SVB been able to hold the bonds to maturity (about 10 years), they would have had the assets to meet withdrawal demands. Though a poor investment strategy, it wouldn't have destabilized the bank. But they didn't have a decade—they had two days. With their assets tied up in long-term bonds, SVB simply couldn't meet the sudden surge in withdrawal requests.

The largest banking collapse in US history—Washington Mutual, with $308 billion in assets—sank incrementally over an eight-month period, culminating in the 2008 financial crisis. SVB, narrowly smaller with $299 billion in assets, toppled in just 48 hours.

Any bank is susceptible to a bank run, as they loan out customer deposits to make money. However, SVB's collapse could have been avoided with a diversified portfolio and ensuring enough liquidity to meet short-term withdrawals.

SVB had failed to learn from inflationary history. In the 1970s, the US economy was facing double-digit inflation. Excessive government spending and oil embargoes drove up prices. Consumer purchasing power eroded. To curb inflation, the Central Bank raised interest rates. Savings and loan associations (S&Ls) were the collateral damage. S&Ls used savers' deposits to fund long-term mortgages. But when interest rates rose sharply, S&Ls were paying more interest to savers than they were receiving from mortgages that had been issued at fixed low rates. The S&L industry, valued at $23 billion in 1977, was virtually wiped out by 1981, its net worth plummeting to negative $44 billion. Interest rate movement is a vital consideration when banks make investment forecasts.

The wider market environment had further compounded SVB's problems. For years, near-zero interest rates had made venture capital—with its promise of high returns—an attractive option for capital deployers. But rising interest rates had tempted investment away from high-risk venture capital toward savings accounts and liquid short-term government bonds. Venture funds were struggling to fundraise, so investing in fewer startups. Funds being deposited in SVB began to peter out.

2023 witnessed an unprecedented number of bank failures in the United States.

After SVB was seized by regulators, concerns over the health of other mid-sized banks proliferated. Over the prior year, the average US bank's assets had lost around 10 percent of their value. Like dominos, within 48 hours of SVB, Signature Bank failed. First Republic, which acquired SVB's assets, succumbed months later. Five institutions collapsed with almost $550 billion in combined assets—the largest total of any year in US history.

Victors of the SVB Fallout

In the SVB fallout, clients scattered. The major financial institutions—Bank of America, Chase, and Citi—saw an explosion in new deposits, as did digital challengers.

SVB's private banking had a stark competitor: SoFi. What began as a niche student loan provider had expanded its offering as its clients aged, to include mortgages, investment products, and personal loans. SoFi was closing in on traditional consumer banks, listing publicly in 2021, with a market capitalization of $6.8 billion.

The collapse of SVB also created a clearing in the business banking sphere, allowing other digital business banks to thrive. These challengers had been quietly putting down roots, offering companies a lightning-fast onboarding process—able to bank in just 10 minutes. Many challengers held their deposits with regulated banks that "rent out" their banking license for others to use, in return for a revenue share or fee (although this model has recently come under increasing scrutiny from regulators).

Of these so-called "shadow banks," Jeeves is now valued at $2 billion, and Mercury at $1.6 billion. As the run on SVB unfolded, Mercury rushed to increase their FDIC-insured deposits overnight. Challengers partnered with various banks to stack

FDIC-insured deposit coverage and protect client deposits for up to millions.

However, these newcomers were not immune from interest rate threats.

Mercury in Retrograde

Just over a year old, Mercury had already secured $30 million in startup capital.

But in 2020, the digital-first banking provider for startups lost 60 percent of its revenue with one announcement. States across the US imposed "stay-at-home" orders as the Covid-19 pandemic surged. A recession loomed. To stimulate the locked-down economy, the Federal Reserve slashed interest rates to near zero, a strategy not taken since the 2008 global financial crisis—and before then, not in the Central Bank's 232-year history. The announcement blindsided Mercury.

At the time, 60 percent of Mercury's revenue came from interest on client deposits. With rates cut to zero, this income vanished.

How did the startup survive its upended business model?

Mercury's resilience was rooted in its founder's childhood. Founder and CEO Immad Akhund, the son of Pakistani immigrants, grew up mostly in London. Seeing his parents adjust as minimum wage workers in the UK, having been relatively middle class in Pakistan, Immad promised himself he would be his own boss. In his words, though his parents were "jolly" and optimistic, they "gave up so much to move me to London... So I owe it to them to do the best I can." His childhood paper round and a job at a grocery store instilled in Immad a strong work ethic—and an urge to escape tedious work.

Twice an immigrant, first to the UK and then to the US, Immad leverages his cross-cultural experiences to identify problems ripe for tech solutions. Witnessing differences in banking structures, customer experiences, and product expectations across countries sparked questions. Immad wondered, "Why aren't payments instantaneous in the US? Why do I get charged fees for things here and not elsewhere? Why is this mobile app unusable? To be an entrepreneur you have to imagine a new world, and that's much easier if you come from a different world. If you've only seen one world, it's hard to imagine something else."

Immad's vision translated into a series of startup successes. In 2008, he co-founded HeyZap, a Y Combinator-backed social network for mobile gamers. HeyZap pivoted to selling developer tools for mobile game monetization and, in 2016, was acquired for $45 million. Immad joined Y Combinator as a part-time partner. Soon, he wanted to start a new venture.

Of five potential ideas, a B2B neobank serving startups was his favorite. When HeyZap had gone through Y Combinator, Immad observed other fintech founders did not boast years of banking experience. If they could do it, he probably could too. To validate his idea for a B2B neobank, Immad sought the opinions of over 100 lawyers, fintech entrepreneurs, and venture capitalists. Each conversation gave him a little more conviction that this idea was feasible.

Basking in the afterglow of his previous exit, Immad had investors' attention. He was emboldened to "swing big" and make a difference. While Mercury's impact may not be as direct as saving lives, it supported the backbone of the US economy: Small businesses. Accounting for 99.9 percent of all companies in the US, small businesses drive economic growth, job creation, and innovation.

Immad assembled the best people from his previous startup. With his co-founders, he then sought out a name. "Mercury" evoked the ancient Roman deity of commerce and tempered their futuristic aims with history—as Immad puts it, "a bank never wants to be too new." But the most crucial lesson remained: "The only way your startup can really die is if you run out of money or give up. That's suicide." Y Combinator famously ends each batch with a talk from Partner Dalton Coldwell on not giving up, or as he puts it, "committing suicide." Most other problems are solvable.

So Immad preemptively raised money before Mercury needed it. Of their $6 million seed round, they spent only $3.5 million. Within months, they secured another $20 million, maintaining Mercury's well-stocked war chest. A favorable fundraising environment allowed them to continue this strategy, as did their founder's ability to convince investors. Paul Graham, founder of Y Combinator, has described Immad as one of the best fundraisers he has ever seen.

Mercury's financial reserves proved vital.

To swiftly gain the regulatory compliance required to operate, Mercury would partner with other banks. Months went into their first integration with BBVA, but the partnership fell through. The setback was crushing; Mercury would have to restart their banking partner search and agreements from scratch. Without licensing, they could not ship products. Healthy cash reserves provided Mercury with a life-saving six months of runway.

Then, 11 months into building Mercury, the pandemic and resulting interest rate cut upended the revenue model. By now a fourth-time founder, Immad was unphased. Mercury's journey had been mostly up and to the right. $30 million from a roster of prestigious venture capital funds meant Mercury was well capitalized when the crisis hit. Staying calm, Mercury pivoted its revenue stream to card interchange fees: The small percentage merchants pay on customer card transactions. This new revenue model rode the tailwinds of the pandemic e-commerce boom. With traditional bank branches closed, Mercury experienced an influx of startups flocking to digital banking platforms. They proved adept at turning adversity into opportunity.

Three years later, SVB collapsed.

Following SVB's failure, Immad noted an "initial bump of about $2 billion in deposits," as an estimated 20 percent of SVB customers migrated to Mercury, increasing the neobank's customer base by two-thirds. Mercury now banks over 100,000 startups across the United States.

Despite Mercury's clear triumph over the established SVB, Immad encourages founders not to dwell on competitors: "No one has high morale when thinking about competitors. You're worried about them and it doesn't get your creative juices going as a product team." It often leads to copying features rather than innovating. Instead, Immad stresses the importance of talking to customers. "Build what they want; you'll build the correct thing way further ahead of other people... and leapfrog the competition." All founders need is a clear "vision" of what they want to build. By relentlessly talking to customers, the company will stand apart.

Between the pandemic and SVB's collapse, Mercury became a unicorn.

Immad bore the scars from three previous startups. These learnings refined his strategies at Mercury and disrupted business banking. Yet, the question lingers: How had Immad conquered two entirely different industries? There are many roots of Mercury's success, but as we spoke, five came up:

1 Create flywheels
Twitter played a pivotal role in SVB's demise but was vital in acquiring Mercury's earliest customers. Immad had 60 angel investors, including the founders of Twitch (acquired by Amazon for just under $1 billion), Eventbrite (went public at $1.8 billion), famous actors, and sporting icons. Immad asked each to tweet about Mercury. Playing on the psychology of trusted recommendations—especially for business banking—the endorsements drove a steady flywheel of customers.

2 Streamline growth through API integrations
Mercury streamlines financial management for startups by seamlessly connecting with third-party tools. APIs allow for easy data exchange (Application Programming Interfaces allow two software to communicate, sending data and requests, just as a telephone network enables two people in different places to speak). At Mercury, these simplify accounting and revenue recognition with established services like Pilot (accounting) and Stripe (online payment processing). By partnering with Stripe Atlas (company registration), Mercury enables new companies to open a business account instantly, while they incorporate.

The fintech's "Treasury" solution offers high-yield deposits by seamlessly investing balances via Morgan Stanley and Vanguard. Mercury even expanded to offer venture debt.

3 Prevent internal conflict

With minimal office politics, Mercury teams have a blinkered focus on serving customers. Immad's philosophy is each role has "defined lanes and if it's not in my lane, I will not create a conflict over it." Immad will voice his opinion, but each leader has the final say on their domain. "We all have low egos... Being humble is part of [Mercury's] code."

4 Question assumptions

Immad encourages all employees to be first-principle thinkers, shedding assumptions and instead basing decisions on core truths: "Ask why does it have to be like this?" Curiosity is core to Mercury's approach, whether it's pattern matching—scanning data to identify sequences—to improve engineering, or customer support. Immad even runs a podcast named "Curiosity." As Immad puts it, "Why is Mercury better than a bank? Because we asked these questions." Immad views the CEO role as a constant learning process. "Every six months it's a completely different job. You have to know completely different things."

5 Don't get stuck on the milestones

When Mercury became a unicorn, it didn't change Immad's drive, routine... anything really. Immad explains, "[For] 15 years I was trying to hit this goal post and become a unicorn. You think everything changes once you hit [it] but nothing changes. I wake up and have to do the same thing."

With this framework for growth, Mercury was on an upward trajectory—even without SVB collapsing. But it was not the only fintech profiting from the fallout.

Jeeves

Nine months after launching publicly, Jeeves became a unicorn.

Initially focused on corporate credit cards, Jeeves emerged from secrecy—known as "stealth mode" in startups—the year after completing Y Combinator's 2020 summer cohort. Dileep Thazhmon, Jeeves' founder, pivoted the fintech to become an all-in-one expense management platform spanning countries and currencies. In doing so, Jeeves secured over $300 million in funding (in less than a year). Chinese tech giant Tencent was among the investors propelling Jeeves' valuation to over $2 billion.

Just like Mercury's founder, Dileep was an immigrant and had not worked in finance. As an outsider, he could view banking through an objective lens. By adulthood, Dileep had lived on four different continents—in Nigeria, Germany, and Qatar, before settling in Florida. Dileep then studied at Stanford, alongside David Vélez, founder of Nubank. Jeeves embodies Dileep's multicultural upbringing. Raised on multiple continents simultaneously, the fintech now operates in over 25 countries.

How had Jeeves achieved this astronomical growth—reaching a valuation of over $1 billion—in less than one year?

Dileep's motivation played a vital role.

Acutely aware of his privileged upbringing, Dileep had questioned early on, "What am I doing with it?" To Dileep, entrepreneurship was magnetic. Startup building was "that intersection between something that gives you intrinsic motivation [what you enjoy], extrinsic motivation [potential remuneration], something you're good at, and something that you can learn from." Even with the risk of failure, that "learning curve that you come up against" was rewarding to Dileep.

Dileep believes that if you fall in love with the process, the outcome will follow, not just in entrepreneurship but in any endeavor. "My personality: Whether it's a small problem or a big problem, [I'm] gonna be working about the same velocity. It's all-consuming for me." Though these days, not without balance, Dileep attests. "Today, I'm a much better co-founder than two years ago, just because I've done things like go to the gym." Work-life balance encourages you to enjoy the founding process more, fueling endurance.

Jeeves was not Dileep's first venture. His first startup, co-founded with his brother, was in marketing automation. Although a different domain, he honed the skill set of company building, a process Dileep likened to "building a muscle." That first venture, Jeeng Ltd, had to pivot, let people go and bring them back, but ultimately was acquired for $100 million.

Growing another startup was familiar territory. But building a bank, with its regulatory hurdles, would ensure Dileep's learning did not plateau. For Dileep, "There are problems I'm not excited about, even though [they have] a good market opportunity. [That] I can't bring myself to spend five, six, or seven years of my life to go all in [and solve]. Fintech definitely has more challenges than a lot of industries because it's regulated. Especially if you're doing it internationally because each country is a little bit different." The challenge of fintech both excited Dileep and made him nervous.

He needn't have worried—Jeeves was disruptive. Here's how you can be too:

1 Solve a pressing pain point

For multinational corporations, Jeeves solved a salient pain point: Managing expenses across currencies and borders. Traditionally, companies had to set up separate banking systems in each country—a slow, expensive, and bureaucratic method. Bookkeepers had to track payments between countries and convert currencies to report assets.

Previously, moving funds between countries could take seven days; Jeeves can do it in 24 hours.

Jeeves' advantage? A modular infrastructure stack. This "plug-and-play" approach lets them launch in new markets faster than building from scratch, reducing the partnerships required per country. When entering a new country, Jeeves simply switches out the bank issuing cards. Customers connect to Jeeves' user-friendly interface, which acts as an "abstraction layer" to the complex banking systems powering customer cards and accounts. This distinct fintech architecture is particularly valuable in regions like Latin America, where traditional banking solutions are inefficient and outdated.

With each country Jeeves expands to, the platform is a more comprehensive solution for managing global finances.

2 Be wary of the strings attached to money

To bring this product to life, Dileep secured $380 million in funding. Though he cautions against celebrating fundraises:

"As a second-time founder, you realize that raising funds is not *necessarily* something to celebrate. You're basically getting a mortgage. It should be something that helps you [grow] better, faster, stronger. [But it can] cause a lack of discipline. It's money that comes with strings attached and you have to deliver a lot on the other side. So the pressure goes up significantly. [Consider] what's the most efficient amount of capital you need to raise to get to the next stage of your journey?

"And [choose] the right partners. A lot of times, people only look at the capital. They don't look at the partners coming on board with that capital. They'll be tied to your company and might have different incentives to you."

At Dileep's previous company, they raised a substantial Series A of $12 million. Within two years, Dileep was forced to make half the team redundant when the product failed to gain traction. This experience taught him to own up to mistakes and communicate honestly with employees when things don't go as planned. Raising money was vital to Jeeves' success, but it was not without sacrifices.

3 Reframe downturns as opportunities

At his previous startup, Dileep weathered the 2008 global financial crisis. Surviving a market slump, to Dileep, is thriving. And in his experience, when the market inevitably recovers, companies emerge with better unit economics and less competition.

So as the startup ecosystem faced a downturn in 2022 that saw client deposits wither and contributed to SVB's eventual collapse, Dileep saw an opportunity for Jeeves to become stronger and "go on defense." The near-recession would clear out their competitors and force Jeeves to build discipline around outgoings. When the economy buoyed, they would go on "offense."

But the economy did not buoy. SVB and other US banks went under due to heightened interest rates. Finding the silver lining, Jeeves was able to attract experienced executives from well-established companies, such as a Chief Compliance Officer from card-issuing platform Marqeta and a Chief Product Officer who had built the PayPal app and ran Xoom, both peer-to-peer payment platforms. The downturn enabled Jeeves to gather a world-class team.

Jeeves, an SVB portfolio company, went on the offense during the weekend of SVB's collapse, launching Jeeves Pay, a credit solution that let global companies pay US vendors without a US bank account and offered accelerated onboarding.

4 Hiring is most important at the start

Hiring starts with the founding team. Dileep suggests founders should be able to perform any business function at a 60-70 percent ability level in a company's early stages. Dileep "spent 20–30 percent of [his] time on finance before hiring a capable CFO." This time has since reduced to 5 percent. As a company scales and hires, the founder's attention shifts to new areas. That initial team should address all aspects of the business.

As founders delegate control, employees will inevitably make decisions that turn out to be incorrect. Unexpectedly, Dileep sees this as beneficial: "Even if you think [a decision is] wrong… Sometimes there is value in letting someone make that call and learning from it being right or wrong." As a founder, "You have to give [employees] the space to fail. Failing is good learning." Handing over some of the reins to employees is vital for retention.

As startups bloat, more balance is needed between A* talent and hiring at scale. Dileep says, "If you're a 240-person company, every single person can't be at that [elite] level because it'll take you [too] long to find that talent and it's hard to keep it. So I look at it more as a balance." But even if you hire all the right people, product-market fit can manifest in peculiar ways; the unexpected is always lurking.

Indeed, startups are chaos.

This was underlined when Jeeves had their first DoS (denial of service) attack, where 83,000 logins were attempted, trying to crack the system. Some might have panicked. Dileep hailed the attack as a sign of growth—they had become big enough to be a target. To Dileep, "Chaos is an opportunity." The cyber-attack was a chance to overhaul their security systems.

Embracing the unexpected. Harnessing the opportunities that arise from chaos. *That* enabled Jeeves to become a unicorn so quickly.

Yet, just as Mercury's founder admitted, Jeeves reaching a billion-dollar valuation changed little for Dileep. "As a second-time founder, it definitely didn't hit the same way. People on the outside think it's better than it is." Perhaps haunted by previous experiences of having to make redundancies and the responsibility that comes with investors, Dileep admits, "Then people on the inside, like me, think it's worse than it is. The truth is probably somewhere in between."

Although Dileep's celebration was muted, Jeeves has started to conquer global digital banking, just as its founder had set out to. Meanwhile, other US banking unicorns infiltrated the industry in a more *accidental* manner…

SoFi: "We'll Give You a Billion Dollars"

"They were like, we'll give you a billion dollars. (We didn't want a billion. We didn't want to dilute ourselves further.) And I remember them saying, if you don't take it, we're going to fund your direct competitor with a billion dollars. So we took a billion and honestly, that level of funding both for the balance sheet and for operating capital was huge," recounts Ian Brady, Co-founder, SoFi.

By 2015, having achieved product-market fit, SoFi's team began to consider an IPO and pitched growth-stage venture fund SoftBank for a $250 million investment. SoftBank wanted to invest four times that, leaving SoFi no choice but to accept. This—at first, unwanted—capital proved invaluable. SoFi kept innovating its product, funded new teams and laid the foundations for that hoped-for public listing.

But unlike Jeeves' rapid rise, SoFi's route into the banking industry was more accidental. SoFi started as a student loan provider. As their graduates aged and competition multiplied, they sprawled into offering banking products—auto loans, mortgages, and investment products—before eventually metamorphosing into a licensed digital bank. One that was insulated from SVB's collapse.

As the largest banks in the United States toppled like dominos, this fledgling fintech's audacious strategy allowed it to emerge unscathed—but how?

From the outset, SoFi solved a glaring injustice with a well-defined business plan. The inception of SoFi (Social Finance, Inc.) had been an exercise in structured research, innovation, timing, and adaptation. Mike Cagney, Dan Macklin, James Finnigan, and Ian Brady met at Stanford Graduate School of Business. All had previous expertise in finance and shared a desire to pursue entrepreneurship. Looking for a market to apply these skills to, they landed on student loan financing.

The segment was immense. In 2011, university fee loans represented just under $1 trillion of US consumer loans and this was growing. For some recipients, repayment was a decades-long process. Yet many borrowers with high-interest student loans were coming out of prestigious business schools and into high-paying jobs. They were what SoFi called "HENRYs"—high earners, not rich yet. The common profile of a HENRY was a 28- to 31-year-old, early career professional with a median salary of $125,000 and an above-average FICO credit score of 740.

Although HENRYs needed student loans, they had a reasonable job earning history and strong future potential. SoFi's underwriting model accounted for these factors to refinance their existing student loans at lower rates (approximately 5.99 percent for recent graduates and 6.49 percent for current students, down from a standard 7 to 8 percent). HENRYs would save money and their loan repayment experience with SoFi would be more favorable.

The co-founders' confidence in the concept for SoFi was rooted in solid mathematics; they believed they could access capital at a significantly lower cost than the standard loan rates, and student borrowers were low-risk loan profiles. In addition, a recent US policy change required all accredited loan providers to be listed equally by universities when offered to students—up until that point universities could prioritize "preferred" lenders. The legislation created an opportunity for disruption in the provision of loans across all universities.

To transform student loan financing, the SoFi team needed initial investment, not least because their product was money. Back then, fintech was a nascent space. Venture capitalists were not receptive to the unusual idea of a company raising institutional capital to turn around and use those same equity dollars from its balance sheet to fund loans. The team received "over 100" rejections.

The SoFi team failed to fundraise.

But they did find some traction with Stanford alumni. Several investors who had declined on behalf of their venture fund were interested in angel seeding the company in a personal capacity. Through a series of $50,000 cheques, the SoFi co-founders cobbled together a $4 million Series A round—by today's standards a pre-seed or seed round—at an $8 million post-money valuation ($4 million pre-money). Ian notes this was incredibly dilutive, but they didn't have an alternative funding path. These angels funded SoFi's pilot student loan scheme for students at Stanford GSB.

Doing so, the team gleaned a key insight that would shape their go-to-market strategy for future funding rounds: Alumni were willing to fund lower-interest-rate loans for students from their alma maters, partly fueled by loyalty and partly by the data—these borrowers were relatively low-risk investments compared to alternatives in the wider market.

As alumni funded loans, other benefits became clear. It precipitated a word-of-mouth marketing funnel. Prospective students would hear about SoFi via alumni, leading to more loan applicants. In turn, students had an even greater propensity to pay back the loan to save face with their alumni community. SoFi's pilot program then yielded data that demonstrated their student loans were almost risk-free, by targeting specific segments; this data prompted more alumni to participate in loan funding. SoFi's initial funding strategy was a success. They had validated the Social Finance thesis.

Soon SoFi was able to offer student loans to MBA students at better rates than the federal government could provide.

This called for a marketing effort. SoFi built demand via paid advertising channels and organic leads by visiting business school campuses and meeting students. They leveraged the credibility and networks of alumni to grow their customer base. It took a lot of hustling, but eventually Brady got SoFi listed as a recommended lender by the financial aid offices of Stanford and later other prestigious universities. They had identified inexpensive ways to acquire customers at the start of a growing personal finance journey. SoFi's loan program was on an exponential trajectory.

SoFi started off with a small pilot at Stanford University in late 2011, funding 100 students, each with an average loan of $20,000. Six months later, SoFi had expanded to 79 schools and processed $110 million in loans. They were on a run rate of around $25 million per month.

But two specters overshadowed SoFi's success.

Their growth had a limited lifespan. Offering low-interest rate student loans to HENRYs from prestigious universities was a finite segment. And the student loan market was being flooded. The new legislation presented student loan providers equally, leaving only one differentiating metric when choosing a loan provider: Interest rates. Others were now also offering competitive rates.

SoFi did have one novel differentiator—networking events with alumni. To reinforce their position, they dashed to ensure their existing client base was retained. SoFi grew with the HENRYs to offer follow-on banking services. Their theory? Soon after student loans were paid off, their customers would likely start looking at auto loans, mortgages, and home equity loans—SoFi could go there next. The fintech had already earned client trust.

By 2015, SoFi had become one of the largest lenders in the United States, providing $6 billion in loans. That same year, SoftBank invested (or pressganged SoFi into accepting) $1 billion.

As SoFi grew, they began offering additional products. In launching "SoFi at Work"—an employee benefit that assisted in refinancing and repaying loans—the fintech reached more customers for their existing core product offering. SoFi separately introduced stock and crypto trading, launching SoFi Invest and partnering with trading platforms like Coinbase, and SoFi business accounts.

However, customer trust did falter.

In 2018, the Federal Trade Commission charged SoFi with making false claims about the savings customers could achieve on their student loans. They agreed to back up any statistics with evidence and set about restoring that trust among their customers.

Not long after this they struck a public branding deal to have naming rights over the NFL's Los Angeles Rams stadium—the SoFi Stadium.

To bolster its position as one of the first significant fintech companies, SoFi sought to vertically integrate. In 2020, they unlocked strategic abilities by acquiring Galileo Financial Technologies. SoFi —alongside Robinhood and other major fintechs—were already using Galileo as their payment processor and for associated services. The acquisition strengthened SoFi's infrastructure. The technical capability leap enabled an expansion of offerings and accelerated SoFi's path to a banking charter.

A decade after its founding, SoFi went public through a SPAC (special purpose acquisition company) and now trades on the Nasdaq stock exchange.

By 2022, SoFi had built a membership-based licensed bank. What started as a student loan provider had ballooned to encompass checking and saving accounts, trading opportunities, and financial planning.

A year later, when SVB failed, SoFi was an established and trusted alternative for consumer banking, capable of pouncing on the giant's private banking clients. Although smaller, SoFi had managed to shield its business in the fallout.

At first glance, both banks had exposure to "risky" liabilities—SVB's clientele were startups, which have a high propensity to fail, and SoFi provided debt. But where SVB had weaknesses, SoFi was weather-tight. Perhaps having navigated the uncertainties of startup scaling more recently, SoFi had a closer grip on its business model than traditional banks.

SoFi's investment risk was spread; SVB was highly exposed to illiquid long-term government bonds that were vulnerable to increasing interest rates. Debt securities made up less than 2 percent of SoFi's portfolio, so it was insulated from the rise.

SoFi's customers were diversified; SVB was entirely reliant on the venture landscape that was suffering leading up to the bank's failure, whereas SoFi clients were distributed among high earners and businesses across many industries.

SoFi adapted when economic conditions changed; SVB's deposits were declining but they made no move to serve a broader market than the innovation sector. Years prior, faced with student loan competition, SoFi had expanded to a full suite of financial services for their customer segment. Then to continue growth, they sidestepped to serve all financially secure customers.

Today, SoFi's principal business remains loan generation. Revenue stems from net interest (that its consumers pay) and securitization (fees earned from packaging loans and selling them to investors). Yet in expanding, SoFi has become a challenger to traditional banks. In 2023, the year of SVB's collapse, SoFi announced $1.76 billion in revenue and the following year started recording a profit. The neobank was closing in on the giant, as were the other incumbents.

Venture Debt

Venture debt is a vital and integrated part of the capitalization strategy of venture-backed companies. Popularized in recent years by SVB, Western Technology Investment (WTI) has been in the game since 1980. In that time, WTI has helped more than 1,400 companies across major innovation sectors finance their growth, while minimizing dilution.

The collapse of SVB, a major player in venture debt, highlighted WTI's advantage by revealing flaws in how banks typically structure loans. Borrowing venture debt from a bank often comes with a hidden cost in the term sheet: A requirement to use their banking services. Startups who had borrowed from SVB had their money locked up in an insolvent bank. By contrast, as a non-federally regulated entity, WTI doesn't incentivize or require its founders to bank with anyone.

Maurice Werdegar, Chairman of WTI, views venture debt as empowering entrepreneurs "to own more of their companies and have more control over the timing of their financings" rather than relying on VCs. "[Venture debt has] also helped the venture syndicate because the time to liquidity has lengthened so dramatically that people were looking for filler." This additional capital complements venture rounds, plugging gaps between a startup raising new funding rounds, achieving milestones, and ultimately reaching liquidity.

Maurice continues, "If you look at venture 25 years ago, there was an assumption that you would invest and exit in 10 years. That is a fallacious concept today." The model of VCs deploying capital over 10 years, expecting their first investments to have paid out, emerged when the liquidity cycle was shorter. Back then, venture debt was modelled differently too. Maurice recalls, "25 years ago, venture debt was asset-based financing and so you needed to be buying equipment."

Market turmoil creates opportunities in venture debt, as promising companies often face liquidity issues. When worldwide Covid-19 lockdowns were enforced and the stock market plummeted, WTI leaned in. Maurice recalls that for "six or nine months, we felt like we were the only people in the market, [which was] frozen. So we had a good run of [financing] great companies over that period." But it was not WTI's first success.

In 2004, Maurice had the chance to lead an investment into Facebook, on behalf of WTI. "[They] needed venture debt because there was no cloud at the time. They were burning through servers. Our money financed the purchase of equipment to run their network. The original deal was for $300,000 but was shut down." A week later, the President of Facebook, Sean Parker, called, saying they had pulled out of the venture debt deal, but he was reopening the equity round to three friends. Maurice had worked closely with Sean at his previous company Plaxo and spoke with an air of familiarity: "I remember saying, *screw you, man*." Sean responded, "*You're a friend*. And so it turned out I was one of the three people [who joined the equity round led by Peter Thiel]." The others were PayPal mafia member Reid Hoffman and Zynga founder Mark Pincus.

As demonstrated by WTI's portfolio, Maurice Werdegar debunks a common myth about venture debt: "This is not financing for companies that can't raise money. This is a very strategic layer of capital for founders who want more tools in the toolkit, have different pockets of capital, and create a balance. Even in the best companies, if you're building ARR [annual recurring revenue] for one or two more quarters, it will increase your valuation. Supplemental capital is an important tool for that game."

SVB's collapse drove more startups to WTI, one of the longest-standing venture debt firms, which has lent over $7 billion to fuel startups' growth.

The Future of the Newcomers

2023 was a seismic year. It marked the most assets to collapse in US banking history, with five established banks upended—at the epicenter was SVB.

Following a government bailout, SVB was able to stabilize its operations and regain its footing as a commanding force in the banking sector. Under new leadership and a restructured business model, SVB has leveraged its deep roots in the innovation sector to continue catering to the particular financial needs of startups and venture capitalists.

Before the dust could settle, a new legion of fintechs emerged.

The meteoric rise of SoFi, Mercury, and Jeeves (in less than one year) sheds light on a new banking era. SVB seeks to re-establish itself as the go-to institution for the entrepreneurial community. But it must wrestle with digital-first newcomers, not least those mentioned, but also Ramp (corporate credit cards), Brex (the AI-powered spend platform), and Navan (business travel and expense management)

The rapid pivots, groundbreaking products shipped over a single weekend, and world-class teams compiled all whilst SVB floundered, may mark the first shots in a war. One that leaves the future of finance in question—tugged between the established banks and the newcomers.

TIPS FROM THE TRENCHES

1 Don't commit startup suicide. Most startups die when their founders give up. Not much else will kill you. If you never concede defeat, most likely you will live to fight another day. As famed NFL coach Vince Lombardi said, "The Green Bay Packers never lost a football game, but on a few occasions we ran out of time."

2 Reframe negatives as opportunities. Whilst SVB's collapse threatened an industry-wide contagion, it also created a gap that newcomers could fill. Dileep, the founder of Jeeves, reminds us that the startups that manage to emerge from recessions do so streamlined, with well-defined business models. The founders of Jeeves and Mercury, though

seasoned entrepreneurs, had no grounding in finance. This "lack of experience" allowed them to reimagine banking, unencumbered by industry traditions.

3 Create flywheels wherever you can. SoFi and Mercury leveraged their angel investors' influence to create an early flywheel of customers.

06

Monzo vs. Status Quo

Crowdfunding £1 Million in 96 Seconds

Tom Blomfield and a dozen or so others shook off more than just the cold evening. Winter and London are an unpleasant combination: marked by rain, grumpy residents, and days bruising to nightfall as early as 3 pm. On these long evenings, it is customary for Brits to find refuge in pubs and bars. Just a stone's throw away from "Silicon Roundabout," East London's huddle of tech start-ups, Ask for Janice was the bar that Tom and the dozen or so ex-employees opted for. They had just been fired. Or quit—the accounts are muddied. One thing is certain: one neobank splintered into two of Europe's most successful companies. A mutiny made two fintech unicorns.

Fueled by gin and rounds of the multiplayer chess game Bughouse, the ex-employees and friends looked at one another and questioned, why not do this ourselves? In this quaint bar, they resolved to start a neobank: "Mondo" (now known as Monzo). With white-washed brick walls and plywood classroom chairs, Ask for Janice was an unlikely venue for the founding of one of Britain's generational companies, particularly a banking startup. But tech doesn't always play by the rules.

Fast forward eight years, Monzo is one of the UK's biggest banks and one of the most valuable companies in Europe. Monzo today commands a valuation of over $5 billion, processes over $100 billion in payments per year, and as of June 2024 has over 9 million customers.

Monzo's co-founder Tom has since penned a number of deal-breaker startup rules to his blog: "There's now a great deal of literature laying out the unbreakable rules for startups. Despite studying this literature, I've managed to break each of these rules, in some cases more than once. In every case, I have come to regret it." These include:

1 Choose your co-founders carefully: "Your relationship will be like a marriage, but even more intense."

2 Keep company money separate: "Be very clear who's paying and under what terms. Is the money going to be repaid? When?"

Tom reflects on his experience with the previous neobank he was part of as a lesson in carefully choosing co-founders—skill matches alone don't always guarantee success. Leaders with different approaches to company building, culture creation, and execution styles can clash.

From GoCardless to Monzo

Tom was already armed with technical experience in building fintech. Prior to Monzo, he co-founded GoCardless, with Hiroki Takeuchi and Matt Robinson, a platform for small businesses to collect recurring direct debits. They met in a hacking group at the University of Oxford. At the time, Tom was set on building a dating app but given the opportunity, Tom leapt to join them as their CTO. Initially, the co-founders shared responsibilities without a formal CEO, but later funding necessitated official roles. Just weeks before Tom's graduate job start date at McKinsey & Company, GoCardless was accepted into Y Combinator. Tom couldn't refuse.

GoCardless went on to have its own tumultuous journey. After a biking accident in 2017, co-founder Hiroki was paralyzed from the chest downwards. Five years later, as CEO, Hiroki led GoCardless to unicorn status.

Feeling that GoCardless was in a good place and with Hiroki taking the CEO role, Tom had returned to the US to join fellow Y Combinator dating startup: Grouper. The app gathered men and women from major dating apps for group activities. Tom was running growth until it folded a year or two later. It was here that he met Jonas Huckestein, a gifted developer. As Grouper wound down, Jonas convinced Tom to travel the world as a digital nomad working part-time gigs. Tom, an avid kite surfer, agreed. Just weeks before they were set to fly, Tom was presented with an opportunity to help start a neobank back in the UK. He decided to join and convinced Jonas to lead their programming. So talented was Jonas, that when they left this effort to form Mondo, he wrote one-third of the startup's back-end software single-handedly, much of which is still deployed today.

After the initial neobank attempt collapsed, in that quaint London bar, Ask for Janice, Tom and the team raised their glasses to starting again with their new venture, Mondo. They identified two priorities: Build a digital banking app and get regulatory approval to hold people's money. They knew how to do the first. The second was steeped in mystery.

Predicting the receipt of a banking license by Christmas, the team hurried along to build an MVP app, which they called "mini-bank." Regulatory approval proved more stubborn. The Bank of England had reservations about someone under 30 running a bank, so with Tom as CEO, experienced banker Paul Rippon took the role of Deputy CEO and Jonas was CTO. They were joined by Gary Dolman (CFO), Tom Foster-Carter (COO), Jason Bay (Chief Customer), and Ruth Doubleday (Chief Risk) among others. With 15 people dedicated to the task, it took two years and four months for Mondo to get its license, overcome any final queries from the UK's central bank, and open unrestricted current accounts. Whilst they were waiting for the license, the team launched to customers.

How did Mondo get their cards off the ground? Tom recalls, "We ended up making friends with a guy at GPS [a card processor]. We hung out with him for three or four hours just chatting about card schemes—he was a card nerd and just loved that we were builders and coders. He had found all these ways to get around the normal rules and get a card program launched ASAP. But then he delivered the bad news: 'It's going to take you at least six weeks to get these cards set up, to print them, and get approved.' He paused and winked. 'But as long as you don't tell anyone...' He took a stack of 20 cards out of his drawer and just pushed them across the table. 'I'll give you the API keys. These cards will work straight away.'"

GPS was Mondo's card processor and Wirecard was the sponsor bank. Munich-based Wirecard held Mondo deposits in a ring-fenced client-monies account. The German fintech has since been disgraced for defrauding billions of dollars from investors. Wirecard's COO—with links to money laundering, gambling and Russian intelligence—has vanished.

Alpha, Beta, Go

The team launched while they were waiting for the banking license. With cards and a sponsor bank, Mondo rolled out their MVP to 500 alpha testers. To work around regulations, this early version of Mondo was a pre-paid card. Customers deposited £100 upon signing up and in return Mondo sent them a fluorescent hot coral ("aka bright pink") card in the post, which often sparked a conversation when a customer pulled it out of their wallet. Four months later, they expanded their sample size to 3,000 users, the maximum TestFlight (Apple's app testing sandbox) would allow. With £1.5 million in worldwide transactions and ecstatic feedback, the team sensed they were onto something.

Until Mondo, pre-paid cards had predominantly been used for kids' accounts, such as those offered by GoHenry (founded in 2012), and for individuals who were financially excluded and unable to obtain full bank accounts. Mondo found a new use. The first 3,000 customers had to come into Mondo's office to pick up their cards because the functionality to collect postal addresses or send out cards by mail had not yet been developed. Conveniently, this process allowed for a unique opportunity where all 3,000 initial users met Tom face-to-face, many of whom continued to attend company events for the next five years. Mondo couldn't have been closer to its customers. These first 3,000 customers all received "alpha" printed on their cards.

With a successful alpha, Mondo extended the service through a beta. Mondo's beta rollout exceeded its target of a few thousand users, attracting a staggering 500,000 signups. Taking a leaf out of Gmail's book, Mondo deployed principles of exclusivity and scarcity in their early strategy. Unlike many apps that incentivize users to refer friends with monetary rewards, Mondo introduced the "Golden Ticket" system. After using the account for about two weeks, users would receive a single golden ticket, a one-time-use invitation that allowed a friend to skip the queue and get a Mondo account immediately. This approach created a sense of exclusivity and urgency, leading to approximately 40 percent of Mondo's signups in 2017 coming from Golden Tickets, without any cost to the company.

Stuck on the waiting list myself, at number 70,246, over a few weeks I inched closer, but at a painful speed. Then I snagged a golden ticket from a friend, much like you might step into a night-club line with a friend who arrived earlier and queue jump. Again, those beta users received a card with "beta" printed on it.

Mondo embraced the spirit of "doing things that don't scale" when it came to getting the cards to customers. Mondo collected addresses through the app and manually posted cards directly from their office. During busy sign-up periods, the entire team halted their regular tasks to stuff pre-paid cards into envelopes, ensuring they caught the last post of the day. The process also provided an early indication of "product-market fit," as customers were signing up faster than Mondo could ship out cards.

Mondo created a viral loop: the eye-catching coral card piqued interest, driving app downloads and waitlist growth. The frustration of a long queue, combined with the promise of real-time spending insights (a novelty in 2015 UK banking), heightened users' desire for the product. The process heightened their delight at finally getting that coral card and they'd tell all their friends. At the time, most had to wait for month-end bank statements and parse through strings of numbers to understand what they might be spending on. Students managing loans and young professionals juggling living costs yearned for the real-time visibility of money running low, making them perfect early adopters.

Banky McBankface

Just as their brand had gained so much traction, in 2016, Mondo was sued for trademark infringement by a fintech with a similar name and considerably more funding. Mondo recast this predicament as an opportunity and asked their users what the neobank should be called. They received 12,500 submissions in 48 hours.

Unequivocally, the users came back with "Banky McBankface." That same year, a public vote to name Britain's new $287 million polar research ship had resulted in a just as unexpected winner: "Boaty McBoatface." According to Tom, to whittle down the submissions, Mondo had three criteria:

1 The name should start with the letter M (we love our logo!).

2 The name should represent us and work across different languages and cultures.

3 It can't be Banky McBankface.

The team shortlisted Mido, Milo, Moolah, Moola, Money, Mundo, Moneta, Midas, Mango, Mint, and simply, M. As they were deliberating between Mido and Milo, co-founder Jason Bates shared on Slack that "Monzo" was available and trademark-free, something vital after the recent mess.

Six customers had proposed the name that was ultimately chosen. Among them were Matt from Bristol, who had studied a rock called "Monzonite," and another customer, Ashley, who recalled "Monzo" was slang for money as a child in Scotland.

They ran with it.

In the meantime, Tom's previous co-founder took the opportunity to play a prank on Tom. It was rumored that Monzo was the frontrunner for the rebranded name, so they purchased the web domain getmonzo.co.uk. On the home page, prospective Monzo customers would find the message "Congrats on the rebrand. Lots of love" and promptly find themselves redirected to sign up the rival neobank they had initially helped to start.

Coral Cards: Product-Led Growth

With a viral loop to attract users, Monzo shifted its focus to product-led growth, aiming to build a platform that increased in value as more users joined. Between the five-minute onboarding, data visibility, and coral card, Monzo had a product people loved. Without a banking license, the team lacked access to the necessary payment infrastructure; so they concentrated on perfecting the details they could control. One notable feature was the inclusion of accurate merchant logos on transactions, replacing the usual cryptic company names found on bank statements. Jonas, one of the co-founders, introduced the idea of adding emojis to push notifications, such as a plane emoji for airline tickets or a coffee cup for café purchases.

Monzo introduced features designed to enhance the user experience as more friends joined the platform, coining the phrase "Monzo with Friends." Tom shares, "Our drive was to make Monzo work better if you invited your friends to use it." Starting with peer-to-peer payments based on your mobile phone contact list, Monzo introduced several innovative features including split the bill, request money, and shared tabs. The effect was a Venmo-like experience inside a bank account, never before seen in the UK.

Users could request money from friends without Monzo accounts via their personal Monzo.me link, which allowed payments using other bank cards or Apple/Google Pay, with Monzo covering the transaction fees. This feature included an upsell for Monzo, as clicking the link with the Monzo app installed would deep-link directly into your Monzo account with all payment information pre-populated.

Along the way, in 2016, Monzo began transparently publishing its product roadmap online and taking input from the community on what features should come next, gaining customer goodwill.

At the beginning of 2017, only 5 percent of Monzo users had 10 or more friends on the platform. By the end of the year, this number had surged to over 40 percent. Data revealed that users who joined with 3 or more friends on Monzo had a 70 percent chance of being a weekly active user (WAU) by day 90, compared to a 50 percent chance for those without friends on the platform.

This network effect, along with product-led innovations, propelled Monzo to reach 1 million customers by September 2018, all through organic marketing. Today, the majority of Monzo's users are in the UK, mostly in their mid-30s, and have a rich set of features to select from including Monzo Pots (interest-earning savings), Monzo Premium and Plus accounts (offering additional perks for a monthly fee), Joint Accounts, and more.

Fundraising

Passion Capital's pre-beta £2 million investment was crucial to Monzo's early headway. Founding partner Eileen Burbidge had taken a bet with backing Tom and Monzo. Eileen was previously an investor in GoCardless, having hosted the company in Passion Capital's London co-working space for several months after the company finished Y Combinator.

Once Monzo secured a banking license, Thrive Capital in New York led the neobank's Series A. In tandem with their first few fundraises, Monzo asked their early users to participate, by launching a crowdfunding campaign on Crowdcube (a leading UK crowdfunding platform).

- **Raise 1: £1 million in 96 seconds**
  In 2016, just a year after launching, Monzo made headlines by raising £1 million in a mere 96 seconds. This round was led by Passion Capital, and bolstered by the crowdfunding campaign,

marking an impressive start to their fundraising efforts. Monzo had not even opened up its beta waitlist yet.

Monzo effectively utilized "scarcity" and "exclusivity" strategies in their crowdfunding campaigns. Anticipating high demand, they set up a pre-registration system, allowing existing customers to invest before the general public. To maximize participation, individual investments were capped at £1,000. In addition to owning shares in the company, supporters received an "investor" label printed on their debit cards, a perk still honored today. Investors were also given the privilege to skip the main queue and gain access to a Monzo card if they didn't already have one.

The fundraising campaign had attempted to launch earlier that week, yet the crowdfunding site collapsed under the onslaught of traffic. By Thursday, the campaign relaunched and sold out in record-breaking time. Monzo ultimately raised £1 million from 1,861 investors out of the 6,500 who had pre-registered. This was a significant milestone, especially considering that at that time, Monzo only had 3,000 cardholders who had collectively spent £1 million using their cards.

Monzo followed up with two additional crowdfunding raises over the next few years.

- **Raise 2: A brilliant ballot raises £2.4 million**
  To address the disappointment of those who missed out in the previous round, Monzo introduced a ballot system designed to give everyone an equal chance to invest. This innovative approach resulted in raising £2.4 million, showcasing Monzo's commitment to fairness and community engagement.

- **Raise 3: £20 million in two days**
  Celebrating its new unicorn status, Monzo achieved another record-breaking raise by securing £20 million from 36,006 people in its community via their app. This impressive feat accomplished in just two days underscored the popularity and growing influence of the challenger bank.

Experimentation

Although product-led growth was Monzo's most effective scaling tactic, they experimented with other organic growth tactics.

To evaluate the paid social media advertising skills of a potential hire, Monzo tasked the candidate with setting up and running four small Facebook campaigns. The first three campaigns focused on highlighting product benefits, such as "No FX fees," "Turn off your overdraft," and "Instant notifications." While these campaigns performed adequately, the fourth campaign, "Help us build a bank you'd be proud to call your own," outperformed the others by nearly 300 percent.

Monzo also organized events at some of London's top companies—including Wise (formerly TransferWise), McKinsey, and the BBC—offering 50 to 100 Monzo cards and a 20-minute presentation during lunch breaks. Attendees could skip the waiting list and get a card immediately, making these talks highly attractive. While this strategy was not effective for user sign-ups, it proved to be an excellent recruiting tool, generating a significant influx of job applications shortly after each event.

Additionally, Monzo ran hackathons that allowed early adopters to explore and utilize the app's API. These events generated user-driven ideas, such as rounding up spare change, which were later incorporated into the product. This collaborative approach fostered innovation.

Yet there was no room for experimentation with Monzo's second priority: Gaining regulatory approval proved more fiddly. By Tom's accord, getting a banking license was one of the single greatest hurdles in Monzo's journey. Many sleepless nights were spent putting together packaging, going back to the regulator for clarifications, and repeating. The Bank of England is strict and meticulous. Directors of banks are personally liable for fraud and losing customers' money, which can result in years of jail time. As such a young CEO of a bank, they put Tom through the wringer. Monzo hired lawyers and consultants to run mock interviews with Tom, but they all thought Monzo was wasting its time. Tom recalls,

"It was like an immune system fighting against a foreign body. The reception I got in the US was dramatically different."

First, they love you...

In the UK, Monzo stuck out like a sore thumb. The front page of Monzo's first pitch deck said "We're building a powerful financial control centre for a billion people around the world." This was not the sort of ambition that the UK tech ecosystem was used to. "Digital banks" weren't yet a popular idea. At first, the UK media latched onto this in the most positive way.

Monzo's journey to becoming a well-known name in the fintech industry was significantly bolstered by early media attention. Eileen Burbidge, Monzo's first investor and partner at Passion Capital, played a pivotal role in this. She was given one of the earliest prototype cards and was so impressed by the payment push notifications that she tweeted about it. This tweet caught the attention of TechCrunch, leading to an article and even eliciting a response from the founder of another leading European neobank, N26, who remarked that the feature was nothing special.

At that time, the UK press was becoming increasingly interested in startups. David Fincher's film *The Social Network* also signaled a cultural tipping point for startup enthusiasm. Monzo's bold and ambitious project to build a new bank from scratch resonated with the British press, who often favor underdog stories.

The flipside to becoming a household name, however, was the tide of public opinion. Monzo was using world-class machine learning to identify fraud and real crime was stopped as a result. Monzo's safety measures were so effective that one Friday afternoon the office was forced to evacuate; a ring of money launderers they had shut down had threatened Monzo with an acid attack.

An unfortunate side effect of Monzo's fraud prevention was that innocent accounts were occasionally frozen for days whilst suspicious activity was investigated. This led to a BBC-commissioned documentary criticizing Monzo for wrongly freezing customers' accounts. After the program aired, a giant block of ice was placed outside Monzo's office. Whether this was a PR game by the traditional banks, financial criminals getting their own back or simply a British rejection of innovation, it was the start of a difficult time for Monzo. With every product release—often purposely launched before it was fully baked so users could help shape it—the press accused Monzo of losing its edge.

False news about Monzo also buoyed in the British press. In 2019, the media latched onto a rumor that Monzo might be IPOing soon and announced it to the world. In reality, Monzo had shared with their crowdfunded investors that they would be waiting a long time to get their money back, likely five to seven years or more for a public listing on the stock market. But in a copywriting error, Tom had written on the new CFO's job description that Monzo could IPO in the next three years. The media caught wind and it was national news.

Monzo's culture

Monzo's first office was a scrappy cordoned-off section of a larger office near Old Street. Every morning at 10 am a few dozen people stood in a circle, shared what they were working on that day and ended by high-fiving each other. Everyone was covered in Monzo merchandise. Most days ended with beers and very heated matches of Worms on the PS4.

The neobank's first and core tenet was transparency, something that existing banks lacked and Monzo brought to the next level. Monzo let their users invest in their early funding rounds; empowered users to name them; shared Monzo's product roadmap on Trello, an online project management tool, for anyone to see; and even ran internal meetings publicly on their online forum, including weekly progress check-ins.

Nurturing a culture of internal mobility, Monzo encouraged employees to upskill in new domains. Tristan Thomas is an apt example, starting his Monzo career off as a customer service agent who then took on community management, veered into marketing, and ended up as the Vice President of Marketing for a unicorn by the end of his tenure.

Monzo hired Tristan as a community manager when he was in his early twenties. With a degree in Economics, a year of experience at a startup in Egypt where he learned Arabic, and self-taught web development skills, Tristan was hands-on and impact-focused. Tristan was a perfect fit because he represented Monzo's customer base—young, city-orientated, and socially conscious. Without experience in employing marketing agencies or building teams, Tristan naturally took on tasks like writing Twitter posts himself, embodying the scrappy, hands-on approach that Monzo needed in its early stages. After two attempts to hire a Chief Marketing Officer, that didn't work out, Tom realized he had the answer in front of him—Tristan.

Tristan was not alone. Other community managers and customer service agents could collect "badges" in other departments by getting involved in their work.

As Monzo scaled, they continued making thoughtful gestures to keep this culture alive. Free meals are common in the US startup landscape but were rare in the UK at the time. Monzo provided free lunches every Wednesday to bring employees together and held beer tastings during weekly knowledge-sharing sessions. In one initiative, over two weeks, the team anonymously complimented each other; these were curated and sent to each member, creating space for gratitude.

Tom explains that Monzo matched this transparency and empowerment with "violent execution." Every employee had the autonomy to make decisions, so long as the outcomes were not irreversible. This generated immense productivity and pride in the company.

Navigating Monzo's culture, however, was not smooth sailing. Their mission was "to create the best bank in the world." As Monzo's workforce mushroomed, some employees envisioned a bank that was a total departure from what went before. A bank so radical that it wouldn't charge users or even aim for profit. Those employees thought that their salaries came from Monzo's investors, as opposed to being paid out of Monzo's future revenue. During this period, Monzo refined its mission to "making money work for everyone." That included making sustainable revenue for Monzo's shareholders.

From the beginning, Monzo was a mix of new-age tech talent and seasoned bankers. "We tried to blend the two, not entirely successfully," Tom shares, combining the "slow and risk-averse" with the "scrappy" techies.

Regardless, the initial Monzo culture was "very fuzzy, warm, people-loving, left-leaning." Tom divulges, "We saw the ways that banks typically made money as evil. For some people that extended so far as to think that if banks made any money, that was evil. This was problematic because people wanted to work on features that helped customers and made their lives better. Not many wanted to work on features that made money or even lending." Tom eventually steered the ship to emphasize, "We can both build a great consumer product that people love and make money in ways that are fair and transparent." Capital One veteran TS Anil would take over as Monzo's CEO after Tom and double down on Monzo's lending capabilities.

Growing Pains

Growing at 5 percent week-on-week, compounding to 1,000 percent over a year, brought issues for Monzo. Luckily, people loved the product and the matching customer service. When helping them resolve issues, agents sent emojis to users, who matched this energy in their responses: "I love Monzo. Can I marry the app?"

But in the push for rapid user growth, costs ballooned. Each pre-paid card customer was costing Monzo £65 per year, an unsustainable figure. The reason? Back then, Monzo was mostly constructed from third-party APIs. Monzo had built a beautiful front-end mobile banking app; however, features including login authentication and real-time spending notifications were performed by expensive external providers. As middlemen, these third parties each took their cut.

As Monzo transitioned from a pre-paid debit card to a licensed bank they made a conscious effort to reduce outgoings. They ground down their cost-per-user to around £20 by making smart architectural decisions and building in-house. Harnessing their transparent culture, they asked their users to help. Tom wrote to users: "Monzo's biggest cost at this point? Stripe top-ups (for migrated users), so it would be amazing if you could all fund your account with a bank transfer."

Monzo's agility stemmed from their microservices architecture. Unlike traditional banks with monolithic systems—imagine a giant, unchangeable block—Monzo built their platform with independent, modular components. This allowed Monzo to update or replace specific functions with ease and explains why traditional banks struggle to ditch paper statements—as the functionality is buried within their outdated system.

In the 1990s, when traditional high-street banks first went digital, they used what are now legacy programming languages such as COBOL and FORTRAN. Traditional banks never updated their systems, so many still run your customer data on antiquated software. Why does this matter? There are so few programmers left who are versed in these legacy languages, that banks are forced to pay millions of dollars to specialized programmers to fix issues when bugs crop up. By contrast, neobanks like Monzo have been built mobile-first, using modern software languages and techniques. An equivalent software comparison would be a Netflix stream versus a movie stored on five separate floppy disks.

Underlying advances in technology enabled Monzo to build a digital bank from scratch in a matter of weeks, instead of years. Although Monzo built many banking services in-house, many key aspects of your mobile banking service today are made possible by a host of different niche startups. For example, onboarding via scanning your passport and taking a selfie, investing in stocks and shares, and creating snazzy neon cards. There are hundreds, if not thousands, of these off-the-shelf functionalities for neobanks to choose from. Perhaps *you* could even build a bank...

Passing the Baton

Today, none of Monzo's co-founders remain. Tom stepped down as CEO during the Covid-19 pandemic, citing physical and mental stress: "I felt a deep, deep anxiety bordering on depression. I wouldn't use the words rock bottom, but it wasn't a happy time." Monzo's CTO Jonas followed in Tom's footsteps. As did deputy CEO, Paul Rippon, to spend more time alpaca farming in the UK with his wife. During this period, board member Eileen Burbidge stepped into an interim position to support with Tom's transition.

Just six months prior, TS Anil joined as CEO of Monzo's United States operations. Following the exits, he assumed the role of group CEO and steadied the Monzo ship. Under his leadership, Monzo has introduced a blinkered focus on credit through personal loans. With Monzo Flex, "You can flex any Monzo transaction and pay it back later, you can even do this retrospectively." Monzo initially had never intended to be a credit-led bank, but that may be what is needed to bring Monzo to the public markets in the coming years.

After building two Y Combinator-backed unicorns (Monzo and GoCardless), Tom Blomfield is now a partner at the accelerator. "It's the same now" as it was back when Tom went through the program, teaching founders to be "insanely focused and scrappy." Tom's main takeaways were "launch the product early to users, talk to them, and iterate... Does anyone care about what you're building?" Tom explains that as a founder "you've got this idea of how the world works, but that's just a starting point. You need to confirm that normal people, actual customers, agree with your worldview. It's as simple as that." This goes against the grain of traditional entrepreneurship approaches: "Writing a really long business plan, doing loads of marketing research, raising $20 million, building in secret for three years, launching it, and hoping that customers will come." In Tom's words, "That is a bad approach."

Enter Revolut

Whilst Monzo was distracted with its sights set on dominating UK banking, a new player emerged, driven by a far simpler motive: Frustration. Nikolay Storonsky, a former trader, was "pissed off" (his words) with the outrageous fees banks charged for international transfers. Having spent an inordinate amount of time transferring money internationally, he was determined to build a better solution. As a former trader, he wanted to offer the interbank foreign exchange rate (FX) to everyday consumers.

Revolut burst onto the scene in 2015, shipping their FX app within twelve months. Their initial product was "a little buggy and childish," by founder Nikolay's admission. But Revolut tackled a major pain point: Unfair foreign exchange fees. Back then, the company had such a small headcount that they would all fit in a small, furniture-less meeting room, some standing or sitting on the floor, for the daily catch-up.

As time went on, Nikolay saw a wider opportunity. Banks did a lot of things wrong. And so Revolut spread its wings into commission-free trading, credit, and a full suite of financial products. Revolut wanted to be better and cheaper. At everything, for everyone.

Despite Revolut joining the ranks of Britain's digital challenger banks, Monzo's founder Tom Blomfield never viewed Revolut as a competitor. Tom had set his sights beyond other neobanks, to a bigger target: Disrupting the entire traditional banking system. First in the UK and then the global incumbents, by building a wonderful customer experience. That didn't stop Nikolay from claiming Revolut was number one, qualitatively and quantitatively, at most public appearances. Including onstage at TechCrunch Berlin 2017, when speaking alongside Tom and German neobank N26's CEO, Valentin Stalf.

Until recently, one thing you couldn't do in the UK with Revolut, however, was get a loan. Nikolay publicly criticized Britain's red tape, high taxes, and the Bank of England's "extreme bureaucracy."

Even as his company was being audited by the UK regulator. Having leveraged hundreds of thousands of UK-based customers as bargaining power, at the time of writing, Revolut has just resolved a multi-year battle with the Bank of England, the UK regulator, to get a (restricted) banking license.

Cut-throat Culture

Where Monzo embraced transparency, Revolut thrives on a culture of ruthless efficiency. Some call it cut-throat—employees survive or leave.

Revolut has been known to hire two people for the same role and have them compete to deliver the best outcomes. When interviewing, instead of asking applicants for their experience, Revolut has asked candidates to do the job for a week. This approach streamlined Revolut's hiring decisions and they got "free work" out of the interview process. One anonymous applicant divulges, "The surprise came when I received the [interview] task: to get the company as many clients as possible, with each one depositing €10 into the app"—at least 200 clients in a week to have a chance at progressing to the next interview phase. Those who couldn't execute were executed. A former Revolut country manager recalls, "When I joined [Revolut] there were seven country managers. Only one was left a year later. Two were fired within seven weeks of joining."

At this neobank, no one can hide behind job titles. There are no product managers at Revolut; only product owners, who have extreme ownership over given services, or countries in the case of general managers. It is a meritocracy. This is exemplified in Alan Chang's rise from a graduate business analyst to Revolut's Chief Revenue Officer. But also a case of survival of the fittest: Alan was revered and feared in equal measure at Revolut. As was Revolut's founder, Nikolay, who once allegedly threatened on Slack, "Those who don't rectify and hit results will not get their bonus and will be terminated immediately."

One Neobank to Rule Them All

As Monzo approaches 10 million customers in the UK, the neobank is experimenting with US expansion. Revolut? They are live in over 35 countries.

From its inception, Revolut has been a multicurrency and multicountry neobank. Instead of seeking individual country licenses, Revolut hacked the Eurozone. Seeking a banking license in more lenient Lithuania allowed them to scale across the European Union and the UK, despite Brexit. By contrast to Monzo, which first set its sights on dominating British banking, Revolut's core technology was designed to serve multiple countries from the start.

Revolut's technology, team, and funding are a potent combination. Revolut, armed with more resources than Monzo, has global ambitions. Having launched in Latin America, Revolut has set its sights on challenging established players on the other side of the globe. Revolut's next competitor? Nubank.

TIPS FROM THE TRENCHES

1 Product-led growth. Instead of relying on traditional marketing channels or distribution partners, Monzo grew its user base organically. Launching product features, such as "Monzo with Friends," enhanced network effects and drove virality.

2 Choose your co-founders carefully. Ensure your vision, culture, and execution styles are aligned before embarking on a venture together.

3 Open communication is vital for building a strong company culture. Monzo even used it as a marketing tool, broadcasting internal meetings and their growth plans for all to see.

07
The Everyman vs. Wall Street
One Million Percent Returns on Robinhood

u/JeffAmazon was in a work meeting when he realized he was making 10 years of his salary, every 30 minutes that went by. Peering under the table at his phone, his palms slick with sweat, a single stock in his portfolio was rocketing. GameStop. Where did this miraculous tip-off to purchase this stock come from? For many, memes on Reddit.

The next day, he requested to work part-time in his sales operations role at Google, which involved running SQL queries for various sales teams and spinning up reports for sales agents on the ground. A few days later, he decided to quit and trade stocks full-time. As u/JeffAmazon puts it, "I kind of lost my mind. There were just too many numbers on the screen."

Known as Alvan Chow outside of Reddit, his username u/JeffAmazon was inspired by former US President Donald Trump's infamous blunder when he referred to the CEO of Apple, Tim Cook, as "Tim Apple."

Alvan is a quiet fellow who grew up in Southern California. His twin brother "Alan Chickin Chow" is the number one YouTube Shorts influencer in the United States, with 50 million subscribers. After studying for a degree in business at the University of Texas,

Alvan spent a stint at Oracle in the Bay Area and then joined Google's Sales Operations team.

Alvan shares that he is a student of the great US investors: Warren Buffett, Charlie Munger, and Michael Burry. GameStop first snagged Alvan's attention when he saw Michael Burry, the famous short seller, expressing his interest in the stock. GameStop Corporation is the world's largest video game and electronics retailer. Listed on the New York Stock Exchange as GME, the brick-and-mortar retailer struggled to compete with the rise of e-commerce. For months, Wall Street hedge funds—which pool money from high-net-worth individuals and institutions to invest in assets for high returns—had shorted the stock.

"Short selling" is a bet against a stock's performance. The logistics: Borrow shares to sell at the market rate (high price), expecting to repurchase them (cheaply) and return them, pocketing the difference as profit.

When Alvan discovered that the underdog stock GameStop was up 12 percent in a single day, he investigated. The stock price spike had been caused by famed Canadian internet entrepreneur, Ryan Cohen, disclosing that he had purchased a 10 percent stake in GameStop. Cohen believed the company still had life in it and was undervalued. Alvan bought some shares.

Like many pandemic-induced stock enthusiasts, Alvan would wake up at 6 am to fit in three hours of trading before work. To decompress in the evenings, he read Reddit, which he saw as "the perfect combo of memes and [stock market] content." Alvan tells me that nobody read ideas on Reddit expecting to make money: "It was just a cesspool." But binding the memes and outlandish notions, there was camaraderie.

The largest of these Reddit subforums, r/WallStreetBets, was notorious for stock tips that would lose money. Alvan became an early and memorable figure in r/WallStreetBets, where GameStop caught the internet's imagination.

In months, GameStop soared from a few dollars per share to hundreds, fueled by online characters like Alvan and famed YouTuber RoaringKitty. Alvan explains that at first, "Between

September 2020 and December 2020, there were probably a couple of hundred [people] online talking about [GameStop]." These were everyday folk.

Then, in the dark forums of Reddit during the home quarantine of Covid-19, a frenzy ensued. Millions piled into GameStop. Demand intensified when serial entrepreneur Elon Musk tweeted "Gamestonk!!" to 187 million followers and a link to r/WallStreetBets. The frenzy generated the epic stock returns that saw Alvan quit Google: "My ego, despite my best efforts to keep it down, inflated to infinity. And then I started to make a bunch of risky decisions and risky trades."

At the epicenter of these transactions was Robinhood, a stock-broking platform with zero trading fees, which also offered margin trading (where consumers can borrow money to purchase stocks). Robinhood was seeing unprecedented trading activity. Against the odds, the platform's infrastructure processed quintuple the normal amount of transactions without a hitch.

GameStop's stock price was skyrocketing. Some of the US's largest hedge funds, having shorted GameStop, would be forced to buy back borrowed shares (to "cover their shorts"). This scramble to repurchase would propel the price even higher, known as a "short squeeze."

Meanwhile, Alvan explains, the everyman "was just trying to make a trade—we didn't care who was on the other side."

Then without warning, Robinhood halted the purchase of GameStop shares.

Alvan sat in front of his computer. His pupils were dilated, his knees weak, his arms heavy. Alvan had started to lose touch with reality. Maybe he already had for some time. He had put every ounce of his savings into this stock. His thesis: He'd be set for life. GameStop was going to squeeze. Wasn't it?

At one point, he had hit a 1,000,000 percent return.

But Robinhood's suspension of purchasing GameStop would decimate the stock price, with lots for sale and no one able to buy. The opposite of a squeeze. Was this how Alvan would lose it all?

Robinhood

It was 3 am, and Vladimir Tenev's phone was buzzing insistently. The co-founder of Robinhood pried his eyes open and answered. The line crackled. Due to the unprecedented volatility and volume of trades occurring, the National Securities Clearing Corporation (based on the East Coast in Washington DC, where it was 6 am) was demanding an additional $3 billion safety deposit from Robinhood—within 24 hours.

As a margin trading platform, where users can buy shares with borrowed money, Robinhood was required in periods of heightened volatility and volume to increase their safety deposit with the NSCC. The deposit protects the public in case margin traders (Robinhood's customers) lose money and cannot repay their debts to the platform, mitigating the risk of trading-platform insolvency. The more volatile the market, the bigger the deposit Robinhood needs to place with the NSCC.

Robinhood faced bankruptcy and as you can imagine, it's *very* hard to raise $3 billion in 24 hours. The only way out was if the market stabilized, then Robinhood's deposit obligation would reduce back to an amount they could forecast and maintain.

GameStop predominantly fueled the market mania, with Robinhood, the go-to platform for commission-free trades, at the heart of the retail investor (everyday people) surge. In the face of the regulator's daunting ultimatum, Vlad considered a risky move: Restricting trades of GameStop. Doing so risked alienating and infuriating the customers that had grown Robinhood into a multibillion-dollar company. But what was the alternative? Caught between a financial abyss and a potential user revolt, Vlad was in a precarious position, though at first he did not realize it.

Robinhood had restricted the trading of MoviePass in 2018, without too much backlash. But when Vlad decided to suspend the trading of GME, the reaction was like nothing he had seen before. The result was market panic and a crash in valuation for the "meme" stock.

At least that's how events played out, according to Vlad. WallStreetBets users are more suspicious. Robinhood's revenue model is based on selling data to hedge funds (such as Citadel), who aggregate the data, sell it, or use it to take positions against retail traders. By freezing GME purchases, Robinhood caused the stock price to plummet, reducing hedge funds' losses and decimating many retail investors' gains. Were they bowing to pressure placed by their main source of revenue?

Robinhood had been set up with the intention of democratizing investment. The platform's name was borrowed from the folklore hero who stole from the rich to give to the poor. Its previous name, CashCat, had less noble origins, with a product called Cash Stats that allowed you to track stock news, much like r/WallStreetBets.

So how did the tables turn, so the everyman Robinhood was trying to uplift lost out? We must dive into the platform's founding story to understand.

Early Days

When Vlad Tenev was five, his family relocated from Bulgaria to the United States. Vlad lived through Bulgaria's currency fluctuations, which instilled in him the importance of currency stability—in its absence, copper cookware was a store of value. Vlad explains, "We had this closet in our household with copper pots and pans, where the wealth would be stored."

Years later, Vlad's path crossed with Baiju Bhatt at Stanford University. Their friendship was sparked over a mutual fascination with math. Upon graduating, Baiju journeyed to New York to work as a quantitative analyst in a pioneering algorithmic trading firm. Meanwhile, with an undergraduate degree in math, Vlad found the job market challenging. At the time, companies had no appetite for math graduates. Leaving Stanford, Vlad foresaw no great prospects. In part, that's why he went to grad school.

Whilst Vlad pursued his PhD in theoretical mathematics at UCLA, the 2008 financial crisis was a real-time lesson for Baiju;

traditional market frameworks were inept at handling severe volatility.

Convinced of opportunities in digital alternatives, Baiju persuaded Vlad to leave his PhD. Vlad didn't want to be a researcher and his advisor offered the safety net he needed: Vlad could return to his PhD if the business didn't work out.

Together, Vlad and Baiju created an algorithmic trading startup from a humble shed in San Francisco, later relocating to New York to fine-tune their product. The initial trading model flopped, but they struck gold by discovering an unintended market—institutional investors craved the technology infrastructure they had developed. It mimicked the advanced trading capabilities of elite proprietary trading firms (who trade with their own capital) and made these capabilities accessible to all institutional investors (who trade with clients' capital).

Many institutions were wrestling with outdated systems, built upon remnants of original 1980s technology. Top hedge funds were willing to pay big sums for a product like Vlad and Baiju's, to get an edge over their rivals.

Maths Meets the Market

2011: The Occupy Wall Street movement surged through New York's veins. Activists voiced their frustration over the escalating economic disparity in the United States. Following the 2008 crash, this disparity was exacerbated by the financial industry's grip on politics and markets. This climate gave rise to an idea. Vlad recognized that empowering ordinary individuals to invest in the financial markets was crucial for diminishing wealth inequality.

The prevailing barriers—complex, costly investment processes and the exclusivity of advanced financial instruments to wealthy or institutional investors—needed dismantling. Ultimately, providing a consumer app was closer to Vlad and Baiju's mission.

Their vision was clear: Create a platform that democratizes investment, making it feasible for the common person to engage with the market. Robinhood was born, a company that focused on encouraging new and overlooked investors into the market, with an enticing user interface and a product engine geared toward engagement.

One of Robinhood's many innovations was making fractional stocks available on the market. Berkshire Hathaway for example, which costs several hundred thousand dollars per stock, became available in $1 increments. Warren Buffett and Charlie Munger disliked this innovation, comparing Robinhood to a casino as everyday stock traders swarmed the annual Berkshire Hathaway shareholders meeting. Another pioneering aspect of Robinhood was zero-commission trading, back when consumers were expecting to pay between $5 and $10 in fees per trade.

Transitioning from a complex professional trading platform to a user-friendly consumer app was a monumental leap. Vlad and Baiju, understanding the complexity of serving two divergent audiences, stood at a crossroads: Advance with the successful yet exclusive quant firms (who use quantitative analysis and mathematical modeling to make investment decisions) or innovate for greater inclusivity? When Vlad and Baiju debated which path to go down, they wondered if they could serve both audiences.

So Vlad began working on the high-frequency trading software from 4 am to 4 pm. He would sleep for four hours and from 8 pm to 4 am would work on the platform we now know as Robinhood. Early pitch decks were convoluted, struggling to explain Robinhood's dual product. Eventually, they shut down their high-frequency trading (HFT) arm. There weren't enough hours in the day to pursue both opportunities.

Vlad and Baiju gathered their world-class CalTech infrastructure developers into a small conference room to explain their new direction. Vlad and Baiju wanted to make an app for retail trading, to ship as soon as they got regulatory approval, which should take three to six months.

The developers were skeptical; iOS (Apple's operating system) was not their specialism. Initial investors also pushed back on Vlad and Baiju, doubting that a team of mathematicians could build a world-class consumer product. Vlad and the team took that criticism personally, mastering those skills investors had questioned.

Choosing the path less traveled, they launched Robinhood. By allowing the average person to trade without commission fees, the platform was a gateway for casual investors. Robinhood planned to make money through Payment for Order Flow (PFOF), meaning they route your trade to a market maker who can execute it. The market maker benefits from combining wholesale orders, and in return, they pay Robinhood a small commission. Making money through PFOF enabled Robinhood to charge zero fees to users.

From Robinhood's announcement that they were launching a commission-free trading app, to securing SEC approval, took a year. During this time, Robinhood's waiting list ballooned to a million eager subscribers.

Scott Sandell, Chairman and Chief Investment Officer of renowned venture firm NEA, joined Robinhood's board. Not long after, he recalls, "Somebody mentioned that we had surpassed eTrade [in profitability]." eTrade was a competing trading platform worth $20 billion, with Robinhood comparatively worth a mere $250 million. Yet eTrade had close to 3,500 employees, while Robinhood hovered around 100. Scott attests, "I thought to myself, wow, this company's cost structure is an enormous advantage, [it] is about 1/35th of eTrade. And from that moment forward, I knew how disruptive the company could be." Robinhood was doing what discount stock brokerage, Charles Schwab, had done over the phone for the generation before. With technology as an enabler and a far lower cost base, Robinhood could lean into one of NEA's key theses: "The most powerful model in the world is free."

In May 2017, just two years and two months after launching their app, Robinhood reached unicorn status (valued at over a billion dollars) and served two million users. The platform was a hub to explore, acquire, and trade stocks. Despite its rapid growth, the company preserved its commitment to quick product launches with new offerings like cash management services and cryptocurrency trading.

However, the launch celebrations were short-lived. In late 2018, a critical software update from a senior engineer inadvertently disrupted the equity ordering mechanism. Chaos ensued. Sales were processed as purchases and vice versa. That morning, Vlad stepped into an office spiraling into disorder. With every passing minute, a deluge of transactions were being mishandled. Clients were losing substantial sums of money. The immediate challenge was identifying the affected transactions and the extent of the issue.

The dilemma was stark. Halting the platform would prevent any trading, thereby averting further erroneous transactions, but

it would also block legitimate market participation, potentially causing additional customer losses. The time required to isolate the fault and restore service was uncertain, raising concerns about prolonged inactivity, customer dissatisfaction, and negative media attention.

Vlad decided to keep running, trying to contain the damage. It was all hands on deck. He was up for about 36 hours. Everyone slept in the office. Once the fault was fixed, the team had to untangle the immense bookkeeping mess. Following the outage, Robinhood committed to compensating customers with valid claims, maintaining its radical customer focus.

After the fallout, Vlad recalls a heated debate. Should they fire the engineer responsible? Vlad wanted to for a long time but his head of engineering was clear: When you fire someone for making a mistake, people will hide mistakes. And then you'll find out about them when it's too late and they're *big* problems This was far from the last problem Robinhood would encounter on its meteoric rise.

Not least because its competitors' services were augmented with robots…

Nutmeg

While Robinhood was democratizing access to the stock market with its commission-free trading platform, other fintech pioneers like Wealthfront and Nutmeg advocated a more hands-off approach to investing. These fintechs focused on the benefits of automated, diversified investment management. AI-managed stock trading simplified the investment process and "robo-advisory" allowed users to achieve their financial goals with minimal effort and expertise.

Nick Hungerford founded Nutmeg in 2011 to challenge the exclusivity and opacity of the traditional investment world. As a former stockbroker, Nick was disillusioned with the barriers that kept everyday people from accessing professional investment management. Nutmeg was his solution: An online discretionary investment management platform. Instead of users making their own trades, Nutmeg manages investments on behalf of its customers, tailored to their individual goals and risk tolerance. This innovative approach rendered professional investment management accessible and straightforward for everyone.

Establishing Nutmeg was tough. Initially, Nick experimented with the idea of a "dating website for money managers," but this concept proved too challenging to implement. Undeterred, he pivoted to an online discretionary managed portfolio model. Getting Nutmeg off the ground required immense perseverance; Nick lived on the sofas of his classmates and faced numerous rejections from investors. Despite these hardships, his dedication paid off. Nutmeg's intuitive, user-friendly platform struck a chord with consumers, allowing the company to grow its user base significantly.

Nick faced a staggering 45 rejections from investors before finally securing funding from venture capitalist Tim Draper on his 46th pitch. Nick recalls, "I drew a line in the sand, and said that if I haven't got a 'yes' by December I would go and get a job." This turning point was crucial, leading to further investments, including $60 million from Goldman Sachs in a subsequent funding round.

Despite his success, Nick chose to step down as CEO in 2016 to prioritize his family, a decision influenced by his move to Singapore and his wife's career. Nutmeg's eventual sale to J.P. Morgan for approximately $1 billion in 2021 marked the culmination of Nick's vision and hard work.

Nutmeg's story is a testament to Nick's relentless pursuit of excellence and his belief in making high-quality investment management available to everyone. Nick was so dedicated to Nutmeg that he recalled his friends used to tease him, "We love you but you gotta start talking about something else. You're getting boring."

In his final years, Nick's focus shifted towards giving back. Diagnosed with terminal cancer, he and his wife founded Elizabeth's Smile, a charity supporting children who lose parents to illness. In the process of preparing for the end of his life, Nick created a series of videos detailing the Nutmeg story and his perspectives on the world for his daughter to enjoy one day. Nick's wife, Nancy Hungerford, shares that he had an unparalleled "will to win. He sees the very best in people, the version of you that you want to be." Nick approached building Elizabeth's Smile with the same conviction as he had with Nutmeg.

Nick's legacy extends further; as a Venture Partner at Portage, he had the chance to invest in other fintech startups. His openness about the highs and lows of entrepreneurship, combined with his enduring commitment to his family and community, continues to inspire many in the fintech and startup ecosystems.

I was fortunate enough to sit down with Nick a few months ahead of his passing. As fellow Brits, fintech entrepreneurs, and Stanford graduates we hit it off quickly. Nick had a great sense of humor but also championed doing anything to your utmost ability. My conversation with Nick, in part, influenced me to bring this book to life.

"A gift of a dying man. Don't waste your time. Don't hide from the ups and downs. Do things to 110 percent."

Wealthfront

What do most of these unicorn fintechs have in common? Product-market fit (PMF). Founder of rival automated investor Wealthfront and General Partner at Benchmark, Andy Rachleff, coined the term. "It means you have proven your value hypothesis. In less technical words, you have found a market that is desperate for your product. Needing your product is not good enough. Initial prospects must be desperate."

Not only do you need to find product-market fit, but "to generate outsized returns you have to be right and non-consensus."

How do you know you have product-market fit?

To Andy, "Word of mouth (by far the most important issue) and retention (which is necessary, but not sufficient [alone])" are the best indicators. "You know a market is desperate if customers want to reach across the table to get it from you—now! In other words, they are willing to pay for your product with little proof or they [already] tried to build the solution themselves." In the earliest of stages, Andy continues, "to optimally apply this methodology you must create an organization that is built to learn rather than built to execute."

Then once you have found product-market fit in one market, Andy likens expansion in adjacent markets to bowling pins. "For each new bowling pin [or product] you must start with early adopters who will buy an MVP and then build a whole product [before starting] an entirely new adoption lifecycle. The whole product from one pin may share some elements of another pin's whole product, but it always has some unique elements of its own. Adjacent markets make themselves known through requests." As that first pin gains traction, customer requests will reveal related markets and pain points to solve.

Following this recipe, at Wealthfront, Andy and his team initially created a product tailored for a niche yet enthusiastic audience: Young technology professionals. This group prioritized an exceptional user experience over traditional metrics like assets under management. Wealthfront first targeted engineers at Facebook, followed by those at LinkedIn, and gradually reached other prominent tech companies through word of mouth. By securing a strong foothold within this specific segment, Wealthfront was able to develop a comprehensive product. Leveraging their loyal user base, Wealthfront subsequently expanded into adjacent markets.

Andy concludes, "You can follow my proposed process exactly and still fail. That's because an outcome is a function of the quality of decision you make, the extent to which you took advantage of the data available to you, and luck."

Andy argues that execution and metrics such as customer satisfaction (NPS) are irrelevant compared to the signs of product-market fit.

Beyond the pursuit of profit, financial markets also hold the potential to drive positive social change...

Stock Trading for Good

Stock trading is not always underpinned by hypercapitalistic tendencies.

Stanford Professor Saumitra Jha's research explores how financial markets can nurture social cohesion and reduce political polarization. Saumitra demonstrates that financial literacy and participation can help individuals:

1 Make better financial decisions

2 Share common economic metrics

3 Focus on the common good

These benefits can rebuild trust, reduce global conflict, and create coalitions for socially beneficial reforms. Historically, medieval Muslim traders in Indian ports enjoyed centuries of peace due to complementary business relationships. In Japan, rapid 19th-century modernization saw ex-samurai receive public bonds, aligning their interests with broader societal goals, averting conflict, and promoting economic growth.

In one notable experiment, Saumitra examined the effects of financial market participation on political behavior. Participants who were given financial assets and incentivized to trade them were between 4 percent and 6 percent more likely to vote for pro-peace parties. These effects persisted for at least a year and were more pronounced among inexperienced investors, who began to resemble experienced investors in their political attitudes and voting behaviors.

Financial innovations can align diverse groups' incentives, foster peace, and support comprehensive reforms. Indeed, Robinhood's role in widening financial participation was guided by principles.

Principles Beneath the Decisions

When facing a moral dilemma—such as whether to halt stock trading to prevent erroneous transactions, which would affect market prices—how do you make a decision? Across the vignettes of this chapter, we've glimpsed Vlad Tenev's guiding principles as he steers Robinhood, reflected in the company's values:

1 Safety first: Robinhood is a safety-first company
2 Participation is power: At Robinhood, the rich don't get a better deal
3 Radical customer focus: We exist to make our customers happy
4 First-principles thinking: We make bold bets and challenge the status quo

Stanford runs a course on building entrepreneurial skills for students to take on their venture-building journeys. Vlad has joined each year, offering his perspective as an active founder, with the Robinhood story continuously evolving. The class is co-taught by

Jack Fuchs, former investor and operator-turned-lecturer, and Scott Sandell, Chairman and CIO of the venture firm NEA and aforementioned previous board member of Robinhood.

I had the chance to join first-hand and hear Vlad share his principled entrepreneurial decision-making framework.

"Safety first" guided Robinhood to halt trading during a technical error in 2018. "First-principles thinking" guided Robinhood to return to an in-office culture, after initially announcing the company would be fully remote. "Participation is power" guided Robinhood to innovate in the first place to make stock trading commission-free.

Ultimately, lecturer Jack Fuchs explains, "Having a solid set of principles [to resolve] conflict will help you and your organization make better decisions." Yet Jack warns against "principles that have words like *always*, *never*, *first*, or *at all costs* because these overshadow every other principle." When Robinhood halted the trading of GameStop (to prevent the need to raise an additional $3 billion NSCC deposit), they were taking a "safety first" approach to preserve the platform's life.

Game Stopped

Within a month of GameStop's ascension and plummet, the US Government's Securities and Exchange Commission (SEC) put together a hearing on the incident to unpack what had happened and why so many consumer investors lost money.

The hearing, titled *Game Stopped*, summoned an eclectic collection of speakers. YouTube star and r/WallStreetBets advocate Roaring Kitty represented retail investors. The CEOs of Citadel and Melvin Capital attended as the key hedge funds involved. Robinhood CEO, Vlad Tenev, dispelled suggestions that freezing the purchase of GameStop (GME) on his app was to appease hedge funds—a key source of revenue for Robinhood—at the cost of consumer investors. In Congress, Vlad confirmed, "We don't answer to hedge funds."

The hearing concluded in a 44-page report highlighting the need to "reflect" on "the forces causing brokers to restrict trading," "payment for order flow," "trading in dark pools," and "short selling." The report acknowledged that whilst GME as a meme stock had "tested the capacity and resiliency of our securities markets," it had also democratically unlocked "broad participation." Roaring Kitty testified, "I like the stock. I'm as bullish as I've ever been and I remain invested in [GameStop]."

Robinhood emerged from the GameStop controversy, but not without scars. At the time of writing, Robinhood's assets have only just returned to the levels seen in 2021 ($98 billion) but are on the rise as it continues its mission to democratize access to the stock market, going from strength to strength in 2024. Most recently it expanded its service offerings with a Robinhood Gold Credit Card (after acquiring credit card startup X1 for $95 million in 2023) and the purchase of cryptocurrency exchange Bitstamp for around $200 million in cash. According to Vlad, Robinhood's next chapter seeks to "build a world for our customers [in which] all of their assets are custodied at Robinhood and every financial transaction goes through Robinhood."

As for Alvan Chow—u/JeffAmazon, who stoked much of the discussion around GameStop on the Reddit subforum r/WallStreetBets—his life was transformed by the stock, which has been immortalized in the Netflix documentary *Eat the Rich: The GameStop Saga*. Alvan missed cashing out at the absolute peak of GameStop's meteoric rise. But having bought early, unlike many retail investors, he made a tidy sum—approximately 100,000 percent return on investment. GME empowered him to escape the daily grind at Google. To this day, Alvan remains a professional trader and after a two-year hiatus Roaring Kitty (real name Keith Gill) has begun tweeting about GameStop once again. By some estimates, Keith increased his net worth from $50,000 to over $250 million through stock appreciation and option calls. Alongside other meme stocks, GameStop allowed retail investors to dream big and, for a fleeting moment, shook the very foundations of the US financial system.

TIPS FROM THE TRENCHES

1 Target a cost innovation. By cutting trading fees, Robinhood improved the whole trading market, forcing other platforms to follow suit. Robinhood's business model and technical efficiency enables it to price below the market rates and handle immense volume.

2 Ultimately, you can't always be a nice CEO—you have to make difficult choices in a crisis. Not everyone will like your decisions but a clear guiding set of principles will aid your decision-making and provide a framework to navigate the grey areas.

3 Pivot when you have to, with conviction. Robinhood's mathematical and precise approach to app design showed they were a force to be reckoned with, despite not having more conventional design skills on the team.

This chapter is dedicated to Nick Hungerford for his work at Nutmeg democratizing access to money management and for founding Elizabeth's Smile, a charity supporting bereaved children.

08

Crypto vs. the Global Financial System

Missing Billions and $700 Million Pizza

Chris Larsen sensed he was about to be fired.

The chair of Prosper's board had summoned him for an unexpected meeting. Chris was exhausted and his lending startup was deteriorating. As he made the journey down from San Francisco to Palo Alto, Chris thought back to his previous Sequoia- and Benchmark-backed business. There, he'd successfully navigated the dotcom crash to IPO one of the break-out companies of the last decade: The online mortgage lender, E-Loan.

Now his board chair had suggested lunch at the Rosewood Hotel on Sandhill Road. But Chris had lost his appetite. And though expected, when it came, the news was difficult to swallow. Reflecting, Chris admits, "I know it was right, but it's hard to get over something like that."

Chris would never lose control of one of his startups again.

A good thing too, considering his next company, Ripple Labs—responsible for creating the XRP cryptocurrency—would go on to be valued at over $10 billion.

Crypto

After Prosper, Chris found himself back in the wild. It was 2012. Web 3.0 (a new era of internet that emphasizes user autonomy over data) was just gaining traction and it became clear to Chris that blockchain (the distributed ledger technology that enables this user autonomy) could restructure our financial hierarchies. A few lines of code were capable of replacing national and supranational money systems.

Towards the end of World War II, the Bretton Woods Conference established the US dollar as the world's primary reserve currency, underpinning international trade. This dominance remained unchallenged for nearly 50 years—until crypto. The rise of blockchain-powered currencies and China's economy now pose the first significant threats to the US dollar's hegemony.

General Partner and leader of a16z crypto, Chris Dixon, provides a powerful framework to think about the different eras of the internet in his book *Read Write Own*:

- **Web 1.0, The "Read" era (circa 1990–2005):** Early internet protocol networks democratized information. Users could consume or "read" but had limited ability to contribute content.

- **Web 2.0, The "Write" era (roughly 2006-2020):** Corporate networks democratized publishing. Users could create and share content through social media and other platforms. However, these platforms have now been monopolized by big tech players who monetize user data for their own financial gain.

- **Web 3.0, The "Own" era (present-day):** Blockchain networks enable users, not just corporations, to own and control parts of the digital services they use. This new era offers unmapped possibilities:

  a Decentralization and ownership: Users can own and control their data and digital assets, contrasting the current model of large corporations controlling user data and content.

b Economic empowerment: Blockchain networks can redistribute economic benefits to users and creators rather than concentrating them in the hands of a few corporations.

c Transparency and trust: By embedding rules and governance in code, blockchains can ensure transparency and prevent the abuse of power in digital interactions.

d Innovation and creativity: This open and permissionless nature can lead to a new wave of creativity and entrepreneurship.

Bitcoin, the first cryptocurrency, began circulating in 2009. As is often the case with novelty, some loved it and others hated it. There was much speculation over Bitcoin's founder; the cryptocurrency's whitepaper attributed the innovation to the pseudonym Satoshi Nakamoto, whose true identity remains a mystery to this day. Since its formation, Bitcoin's value has appreciated exponentially. To illustrate this, one of the earliest recorded purchases with Bitcoin—$30 on two Papa John's pizzas—is now equivalent to just shy of $700 million.

Unlike centrally governed currencies, Bitcoin is decentralized and mostly unregulated. As a result, Bitcoin's early days found its most prolific use on the dark web to trade drugs and move money without the watchful eye of authorities. Although some scorn this, it is also the case that many modern digital payment services found their initial customers in the gambling, pornography, and gaming sectors. Today, as we are just now contemplating the impacts of Web 2.0 and social media on our society, Web 3.0 offers the potential for a new internet that is co-owned by its users, not just a centralized set of powers.

Bitcoin's proponents have not always helped quell anxieties surrounding decentralization nor aided the currency's reputation. A sub-faction of fans, known as "Bitcoin Maximalists," strongly believe that Bitcoin should be the only cryptocurrency. Some extreme adherents of this view have been known to engage in aggressive actions, such as hacking critics and supporters of rival tokens.

Ethereum, now the second largest cryptocurrency and block-chain platform, was theorized much later, in 2014 by Vitalik Buterin, a teenage programmer and mathematician in Canada. First hearing of Bitcoin from his father, Vitalik had big dreams. But he never imagined that just a few years later he would have amassed one of the greatest networks of computing power in the world. Ethereum, like Bitcoin, uses blockchain as its underlying architecture. However, Vitalik's co-founders were divided over whether Ethereum should be a non-profit, leading to the ousting of Charles Hoskinson. The for-profit advocate took revenge by founding Cardano, a rival blockchain supporting smart contracts and decentralized apps—nicknamed by the media a potential "Ethereum killer." Regardless, Ethereum remains the first-mover in enabling other programs and protocols to build on top of it, effectively creating programmable money.

A third major cryptocurrency is XRP, co-founded by our protagonist, Chris Larsen, in 2012. According to the *Wall Street Journal*, Ripple was "the third-largest cryptocurrency by market value" over a seven-year period starting in 2013. Yet in this fast-moving industry, that is always changing.

These alternatives to Bitcoin are known as "altcoins." XRP is one of the only altcoins to have penetrated commerce as a usable currency; rather than a speculative store of value, XRP targets businesses. Created by Ripple Labs, XRP can be used for e-commerce, peer-to-peer payments, and international transfers. Unlike traditional currency conversions, XRP settles payments in seconds and boasts minimal fees. Bitcoin often takes an hour and traditional bank transfers a full working week.

Unlike Bitcoin, which has no central control, XRP is supported by a team of developers at Ripple Labs, though Chris Larsen is quick to highlight, "There's a distinct difference between the distributed ledger and the company. We don't control the ledger. We don't control the currency. We own a lot of it, but we can't reverse that transaction. That's as decentralized as anything out there. And that was a project before the company existed." The differences continue: Where Bitcoin can be continuously "mined," bringing new coins into circulation, the total supply of 100 billion XRP was released at its inception.

Just how did Chris, recently fired from his job, create the third most valuable cryptocurrency in the world?

The Ripple Effect

Ripple Labs was rooted in Chris' earlier ventures.

Chris Larsen's entrepreneurial journey began with E-Loan, an online mortgage lender he co-founded with Janina Pawlowski in 1997. Frustrated by the high fees and lack of transparency in their previous mortgage broking roles, they envisioned a more efficient system. They initially funded their venture with $450,000 from friends and family and later secured venture capital.

However, by 1998, E-Loan faced financial difficulties and nearly sold to Intuit for $130 million. But Yahoo interrupted the deal, offering a $25 million investment, which Chris and Janina accepted. Within a year, E-loan controlled as much as 25 percent of the online mortgage market and was the first company to provide consumers with FICO credit scores for free online. In 1999, E-Loan went public and settled at a valuation of $1 billion.

Then the dotcom bubble burst. E-Loan, like many other dotcom darlings, struggled long after the recession. In 2005, Puerto Rico-based Banco Popular took E-Loan private for $300 million in cash, despite the company having processed $20 billion in mortgages.

By this point, Chris had left the company and was onto his next venture—Prosper Marketplaces.

Prosper was launched as the first peer-to-peer lending platform in the United States. The marketplace connected borrowers with individual and institutional investors, cutting out traditional banks as middlemen. Throughout Chris's leadership, Prosper would process over $20 billion in loans. But that didn't stop the board from asking him to step down.

By 2012, Chris had distributed $40 billion of private credit and built two digital fintech unicorns. Now released from his CEO duties, Chris began to explore his next steps.

The idea of a global, non-government digital currency had been circulating for some time. In 1998, Peter Thiel co-founded the peer-to-peer payments platform that would become PayPal. That same year, Beenz, a universal online currency, gained popularity, as did Flooz, which was earned through online purchases and redeemed at participating merchants. Although more akin to a coupon system than a true currency, Flooz pierced mainstream thought with its commercials featuring actress and comedian Whoopi Goldberg.

The concept resurfaced with social networks and gaming, in which digital currencies became ingrained. In many popular online games, such as Farmville on Facebook, users bought digital coins to fund in-game features.

Web 3.0 unleashed the first true realization of non-sovereign currencies.

Blockchain technology is the backbone of cryptocurrencies, acting as a public ledger that records all transactions in chronological blocks. Data stored in each block references the data before it, establishing provenance. Unlike traditional databases controlled by a single entity—such as governments controlling currencies or banks overseeing payments and charging a premium—transactions are transparent to members of the blockchain network and stored across interconnected nodes. This makes it nearly impossible to tamper with data, given each node has a record of what has happened previously, preventing fraud. As well as being secure, blockchain gives ownership of data to users, rather than to a central body (which is efficient but can be corrupted by errors or bad actors).

Vital in fintech is that blockchain makes money programmable. It allows code to be written directly on top of crypto tokens, to automate actions such as investment triggers based on market conditions. The creation of Bitcoin ushered in a new era of digital currencies and with it conferences, enthusiasts, developers, and investors.

During this advent of Bitcoin, Chris was introduced to three programmers—Jed McCaleb, David Schwartz, and Arthur Britto—who were trying to build a better Bitcoin that was faster and consumed less energy. Their project would eventually become the cryptocurrency XRP, and together the four founders would establish Ripple Labs, a company leveraging XRP for business applications.

But within a year, the co-founders' collaboration spiraled into conflict.

Chris reflects, "A co-founder—if it's the right co-founder—is probably the one person [with whom] you can share stress. To everybody else, you must be 100 percent certain, no matter what challenge. If you get three co-founders it's like 3D chess. It's just too complicated."

Ripple Labs' controlling founders, Chris and Jed, had the largest equity and equal voting shares. Unable to agree on a direction forward for Ripple, nor who should be part of it, their degrading relationship almost sank the crypto platform. The stalemate was resolved by a vote: Ripple's shareholders backed Chris. Although ousted, Jed would still become a billionaire and build rival open-source blockchain Stellar, which facilitates fast and inexpensive cross-border payments. Jed has been slowly selling off his XRP ever since.

Chris did not feel threatened by the rival.

In fact, Chris is a fan of competition. "It's good to have a competitor you're gunning for, whether it's SWIFT [global financial messaging infrastructure for banks] or some other fintech company. That's a good motivator." E-Loan vied with Home Loan for market share. Prosper's primary competitor was the P2P loan platform Lending Club, whose CEO was Chris's arch-nemesis. These rivalries spurred the startups to innovate. At Ripple, Chris set his sights on a larger opponent: The existing banking system and financial infrastructure.

The next hurdle for Ripple was finding product-market fit. But Chris emphasizes it cannot be rushed. "In the early days, you're trying to get clarity around the mission, core values, and strategy, be okay with not having product-market fit as a company for a couple of years. That's how these things typically play out."

Chris likens going to market with a currency to building open-source software. Both rely on network effects: Currencies need users to have worth and open-source requires a community to build value. To find the best applications for their cryptocurrency at Ripple, Chris and the team were "wandering in the desert, letting a bunch of smart people experiment." Ripple tried various services, from wallets to custody and charity. Eventually, they started to find product-market fit in cross-border enterprise payments.

Chris acknowledges his expertise lies in the earlier stages: "I'm very comfortable with conflict and uncertainty. Once you get product-market fit, that's about measurement, accountability, and KPIs. I get pretty bored with that." Once Ripple Labs found product-market fit in 2017, Chris recruited Brad Garlinghouse as CEO and graduated to become Ripple's chairman. In Chris's words, "I'm just not good at that part of it. I'm good at the early part." Chris sees his role as helping Ripple's CEO: "Brad is in charge. The key is never to give anybody the impression that they can go around Brad [through me]."

With Brad at the helm, Ripple and its cryptocurrency, XRP, gained momentum. Its valuation climbed steadily following the announcement that just over half of XRP tokens would be placed in an escrow account, for gradual and controlled release to the public. By the end of 2017, XRP's market capitalization had peaked, briefly surpassing Ethereum to become the second-largest cryptocurrency after Bitcoin.

Then on 11 November 2022, the cryptocurrency exchange FTX collapsed.

The crypto industry shrank in value by 70 percent within two weeks. FTX's CEO, Sam Bankman-Fried, was extradited to the United States to face criminal charges over misused customer funds. He is now serving 25 years in federal prison for fraud.

FTX's crash had been set in motion by a report revealing that Alameda Research, a trading firm also owned by Sam Bankman-Fried, had unlimited credit and the ability to maintain negative balances at FTX. Alameda had been illegally "borrowing" from FTX customer funds to cover their investment losses. The result: An $8 billion hole in FTX's balance sheet.

Within days, Binance, a rival crypto marketplace and one of the largest shareholders of FTX's cryptocurrency FTT, publicly announced the sale of their entire FTT holding. The cryptocurrency's price plummeted and triggered a surge of withdrawal requests from FTX customers. FTX didn't have the funds to cover customer withdrawals and was forced to file for bankruptcy.

Although Ripple Labs lost only 1 percent of its liquid assets in FTX, XRP suffered in the resulting crypto winter, with increased regulatory scrutiny and shaken investor confidence. But Ripple was resilient.

Having been in the ring for many of the great booms and busts of the last few decades, Chris shares the upside of weathering "bear markets," meaning a prolonged period of falling stock prices and deflating investor confidence. "In the dotcom bust, I thought we did our best work. If you have a good culture and enough financial horsepower to survive, the short-termers leave and the committed people stay." Whilst fundraising becomes difficult and "more expensive," Chris highlights that "talent gets cheaper, a lot of things get cheaper. I thought great work came out of the dotcom crash." His optimism continues: "I saw a lot of great new [business] models coming out of the crash. Don't let a crisis go to waste."

Nor a period of market buoyancy. "Raise money when you can," Chris stresses, as "when you need it, you might not be able to get it…" Chris reflects on FTX and other crashes: "Now they feel like another cycle. It's just one of those things that will pass."

Chris is bullish about crypto's long-term prospects. "The world needs this different kind of currency. It's very useful. [I predict] every human will have a part of [crypto] in their basket."

Facebook thought so too.

Libra: Diem's Demise

In a dim office at Facebook (now Meta), Libra co-creators David Marcus, Christian Catalini, Morgan Beller, James Everingham, Kevin Weil, and Christina Smedley began hatching a plan to grow a new global digital currency out of the social media giant.

It was early 2018. Ripple's XRP was vying with Ethereum to be the second-largest cryptocurrency and Facebook had fallen foul of the public and political eye, embroiled in scandal. Cambridge Analytica, the political consulting firm, had illicitly harvested Facebook user data to provide voting profiles of 87 million Americans and target them with personalized social advertising. Some alleged this swayed the US election result.

Against this backdrop of public disgrace, David Marcus, the former president of PayPal, started covertly hiring for Facebook's blockchain currency operation. Named Libra—in reference to the ancient Roman weight measurement of a pound (lb) from which the British Pound (£) originates—the cryptocurrency would have connotations of stability.

Tapping into Facebook's 2.4 billion users, Libra could be the new gold standard for global currency exchange.

David Marcus's journey into payments and blockchain began at age 23. Faced with financial pressures, he dropped out of college and left his job at a bank to start his first company, an alternative telecom provider in Switzerland. After selling this startup in 2000, he founded another venture that pivoted to focus on mobile payments and eventually sold to PayPal. Six months later, David found himself as PayPal's president overseeing the acquisition of Braintree.

Years later, scaling Facebook Messenger, David was still frustrated with the state of payments. The internet lacked an open, interoperable protocol for money. A universal payment protocol would provide stable currency to all and enable instant, frictionless movement of money around the world. David saw Facebook's vast user base as an ideal launchpad for developing such a system and began tackling the problem. David reflects that humans "typically care about health and their loved ones. And then right after that comes money. For some people, it's before their loved ones. It's how people put food on the table. There's a tremendous amount of injustice in how money moves and the quality of money people have access to. So I feel quite passionate about it."

David had been crypto-curious for a while. In 2010 he encountered Bitcoin but found the technology "too geeky" even for him at that point, until his dear friend Wences Casares—an Argentinian entrepreneur widely known as "Patient Zero" for his role in promoting Bitcoin to prominence in Silicon Valley—convinced David to look a little closer.

In 2013, while running PayPal, David became aware of the importance of cryptocurrency. The Argentinian government approached PayPal requesting their support in preventing Argentinians from moving balances abroad. "I remember seeing the price of Bitcoin appreciate the same day... [Argentinian] people wanted financial freedom, which they deserve." It made him realize the power of blockchain technology for alternative global digital payments.

Meanwhile, Morgan Beller, after a stint at Medium, had landed on the corporate development team at Facebook. Realizing the significance of cryptocurrency and the potential Facebook held as a launchpad, she created a pitch deck on why and when Facebook should consider it. Morgan sent it to various key figures at Facebook. Despite not needing to respond, many lent their time and encouragement. Among them was David Marcus.

Another was Sam Lessin, who in his earlier days at Facebook (after investing in Venmo) had explored airdropping XRP (where Sam was a seed investor) to all Facebook users.

Morgan and David knew they needed a technical expert to power their crypto project. They met with several internal employees and chose Ben Maurer, a long-time Facebook staff member. Although initially a crypto skeptic, Ben had expertise in building one of the best decentralized tech stacks in the world, at Facebook.

Whilst Morgan and David focused on high-level strategy, Ben immersed himself in technical research, studying the manifestos of

Bitcoin and Ethereum. Morgan can still "picture to this day, the piles and piles and piles of whitepapers," as Ben read up. In the crypto industry, it has become commonplace to publish a manifesto before or alongside a product launch, explaining a project's purpose, structure, technology, and economic incentives.

They gradually built their team, adding Kevin Weil (now CPO of OpenAI) as Vice President of Product. David brought in many former colleagues from PayPal and Messenger, showcasing his ability to inspire trust and loyalty among his peers. This included James Everingham to lead Engineering, Christina Smedley to lead brand and marketing, and Christian Catalini to lead the economic design of the project. Christina and Christian would later co-found Lightspark with David.

Libra's early days were an intellectual maze. There were infinite design choices. How to launch the currency? What should the technical architecture be? Should it be built from scratch or on top of existing digital currencies like Ethereum or Bitcoin? How should the currency be governed? Which partners should be involved? Where should the governing entity reside? What should Libra's relationship with Facebook be?

It took 18 months of discussions to settle upon decisions.

Morgan shares, "There were many, many, many times that we went through full-blown explorations of just adopting Ethereum or Bitcoin." Although the team recognized the potential of these cryptocurrencies, Facebook faced significant technical and regulatory risks in working with them. Only recently have Ethereum and Bitcoin received regulatory blessing as ETFs (exchange-traded funds) in the United States.

In June 2019, Facebook published a whitepaper.

It announced Libra's mission: "To enable a simple global currency and financial infrastructure that empowers billions of people." Libra wished to solve inequality. The whitepaper continued, "For many people around the world, even basic financial services are still out of reach: Almost half of the adults in the world don't have an active bank account. Those numbers are worse in developing countries and even worse for women. The cost of that exclusion is high—approximately 70 percent of small businesses in developing countries lack access to credit and $25 billion is lost by migrants every year through remittance fees."

These sentiments still resonate with Morgan: "If you close your eyes and picture the future, the world is going to be more digital than physical." The US dollar, though increasingly digitized through card transactions, is still linked to tangible cash. Morgan explains, "Being the world reserve currency is pretty awesome for America and I would argue pretty awesome for a lot of the Western world, as well." Facebook's Libra could reinforce the US dollar's importance, as the global economy migrates online.

To do so, Libra settled on a stablecoin—a digital currency pegged to a fixed value. Launched on the Libra blockchain, the cryptocurrency would be backed up by a basket of fiat currencies, notably the US dollar, and "other assets."

Unlike Bitcoin, the whitepaper outlined that Libra would have a governing association "consisting of geographically distributed and diverse businesses, nonprofit and multilateral organizations, and academic institutions." The blockchain itself would be open-sourced, following a similar format to XRP with a publicly available and modifiable ledger, overseen by the parent company. The Libra Association's 28 founding members included Visa, Mastercard, Coinbase, PayPal, Uber, and Lyft. Each invested $10 million to join the consortium, and Libra expected 100 founding members by 2020 to meet its $1 billion funding goal. The reported waiting list comprised over 1,500 entities.

Libra promised that users could seamlessly transfer money—instantly and at a low cost. Transactions could be made across borders and platforms, on Facebook's apps and beyond. Alongside the Libra currency was Calibra, a digital wallet designed to store your Libra coins.

Facebook's announcement of its cryptocurrency detonated a series of privacy and regulatory concerns. US lawmakers called for a halt to the project until Congress and regulators had assessed it. Concerns were primarily over Facebook's track record on data privacy and the potential for Libra to be used for money laundering and financing illicit activities. Beyond the United States, Central Banks across the world scrutinized the project. The Bank of England and Bundesbank, among others, issued statements that they would carefully examine Libra and apply tough regulatory standards. The G7 nations set up a forum examining the risks of digital currencies to the financial system.

A month after Libra's whitepaper's publication, co-creator David Marcus was summoned to Congress. David reflects it was an "honor to testify in front of the Senate and the House. I'm an immigrant, I'm proud to be an American. It was a privilege to address the Senate and defend my project." Yet "many [were] asking questions without wanting to hear my answers... they had already decided."

David's testimony did little to alleviate the concerns of lawmakers and regulators. Intense scrutiny and regulatory challenges ensued. Although David Marcus was previously president at PayPal, his former company led the mutiny. By October, PayPal withdrew from the Libra Association, closely followed by Visa, Mastercard, Booking Holdings, eBay, Stripe, and several other key partners.

As Morgan and David would discover, operating within a mothership had its hurdles. One government official involved in the process explained: "[Libra] spent years trying to reverse engineer their project to fix all its faults, but they could never fix being linked to Facebook. It was their original sin."

To distance the cryptocurrency from Facebook, Libra was rebranded as Diem. Facebook proposed a scaled-back and amended vision "to build a trusted and innovative financial network that empowers people and businesses around the world." However, the project was bruised by the high-profile founding member departures.

In 2020, there was a glimmer of renewed traction.

The digital currency resurfaced, announcing backing from high-profile founding members including e-commerce site Shopify and the Singaporean state investor, Temasek.

But it was not enough.

By 2022, rumors emerged that Diem was contemplating an asset sale to compensate investors. Shortly after this, Diem announced it was winding down the project, after failing to gain regulatory approval.

Morgan reflects on the Diem team's hard work which didn't come to fruition. One lesson "was making such a big splash. We had our pregnancy announcement before our product, [which] put a target on our back for every regulator in every country." Especially at a time when "the public wasn't necessarily amped about Facebook."

Why didn't Libra work? The age-old saying in startups—"ask for forgiveness, not permission"—did not apply to Facebook. To Morgan, "One of the core pillars of the crypto market is incentives, and given that we had to ask for permission, not forgiveness, there were zero regulators in the world who were incentivized for Libra to work." Libra conversed with regulators entering an unending loop.

Morgan references the children's picture book, *If You Give a Mouse a Cookie*: "[like] the book, if you give the [regulators] a cookie, they'll ask for milk, and then if you give them milk, they'll ask for a straw... So that's what our development process became. We kept going back to regulators with an updated version. And then they would say, *OK, you're good to go, except for this.*" Regulators aim to protect consumers and were cautious about crypto. But Libra was the collateral damage.

Facebook's scale was matched with scrutiny. For such an ambitious financial project, launching on the coattails of the Cambridge Analytica scandal, Morgan recalls the Diem team had to "ask for permission." And the world declined.

Lightspark

After Libra, David "realized that private companies issuing a new unit of account [currency] with that kind of distribution is problematic." In fact, he gleaned a hard-earned insight from trying every alternative possible: "Bitcoin is the only form of neutral internet money there will ever be."

Bitcoin was the only network capable of supporting an open, interoperable, and efficient payment protocol for the internet. But David recognized that Bitcoin was too slow and expensive for everyday transactions. Bitcoin's main blockchain can only process a limited number of transactions per second, as each transaction must update every node on the network. As adoption increases Bitcoin becomes congested, slowing the network and increasing processing costs.

David identified the Lightning Network as the solution to these scalability, liquidity, and cost issues—a second layer on top of Bitcoin which enables fast, low-cost transactions through off-chain payment channels for two users to transact. Fueled by his "deep sense of unfinished business," David sought to make Lightning better known, more accessible and user-friendly for mainstream adoption. Their goal was to create an enterprise-grade entry point into Lightning for exchanges and wallets. Clients would plug in, manage their own liquidity and nodes, and send and receive payments reliably without worrying about the underlying complexities of the Lightning Network. A conversion from Bitcoin into cash on Lightning "happens in, say, a second. So the only volatility risk that you have is that second. You can price that in."

As David learnt with Libra, there's not a huge consumer appetite to give up autonomy. By contrast, "Governments care a lot about controlling their own currencies and not delegating power to private institutions." Governments desire strong domestic payment systems "that use the country's national currency."

With cryptocurrencies, David asserts, "There's a lot of speculation and a bunch of technology that's been built. [But] consumer impact at mass market scale, it hasn't happened with Bitcoin [or] arguably the entire industry. Bitcoin is faring better in terms of its neutral, digital store of value, [yet] compared to all the other internet-era technologies, we're not at mass market scale."

Achieving this scale and impact is David's purpose. "It's such a wonderful moment in life when you know exactly what you want to do for the rest of it. You have absolute clarity that you're going to achieve it or die trying." Where David was previously "the grand preacher of something new and trying to get people to believe in it, to trust you," now "it's liberating to build on top of Bitcoin, where you have millions of people who [already] believe in it."

Looking back, David is still motivated by solving problems: "Anomalies that are artificially maintained for unfair reasons against consumers and businesses." For Lightspark, "It's a much more complex problem, because when you're trying to build an internet for money, you have to think about it with your horizon at 100 years. Can you think of something that will replace the internet in 100 years? No. The internet, TCP/IP (the protocol behind the internet), and movement of data on the network will still be here. We'll have AGI (artificial general intelligence) and all these things, but the underlying network tissue that will connect all of these AI agents and instances and data is still going to be TCP/IP. So what does that mean for money in 100 years? David compares "the fragments of Bitcoin on top of Lightspark" to the "TCP/IP packets on the internet, but for money." (TCP/IP packets are like a digital envelope used to send information across the internet.) This would "not necessarily be [the currency that] consumers or businesses use for everyday purchases or for payments, but rather a neutral settlement TCP/IP packet for money between us," creating a system where money can move instantly to where it's needed, anywhere in the world, at any time. "I think it will unlock a lot of value for billions of people around the world and potentially lift global GDP by a few points, if money can go where it needs to be, in real time, at all times. What's not exciting about getting the once in a lifetime chance to work on something like this?"

A former board member of the cryptocurrency exchange Coinbase, David joined Nubank's board in 2023. In 2024, Lightspark and Nubank partnered to bring the Lightning Network to Nu's 100 million customers.

Cryptocurrency, however, was not the only store of value in blockchain technology clouded by volatility, speculation, and cries for regulation.

Bored Apes, Cool Cats, and Their Invisible Friends

The most expensive artwork ever sold by a living artist is an NFT (Non-Fungible Token)—and not even a one-of-a-kind.

PAK, the artist, sold digital tokens of his piece *The Merge* over three days. Unlike limited editions, these artworks were released in a so-called "open edition," meaning unlimited pieces for sale. Each token's price started at $575 and every six hours went up by $25. The digital collectibles brought in a total of $91.8 million.

This came just months after a record sale price for a single NFT. *Everydays: The First 5000 Days* by the artist Beeple sold at the famous auction house Christie's for $69 million.

Celebrities jumped on the bandwagon, replacing their Twitter display pictures with "blue chip" NFTs by Bored Ape Yacht Club (BAYC), a collection of 10,000 algorithm-generated cartoon apes, and Invisible Friends, a series of digital characters that promote inclusivity by being invisible but for their clothing and accessories. Jimmy Fallon, Justin Bieber, Madonna, and Neymar Jr have all dabbled. CryptoPunks, pixelated collectible characters, have sold for over $20 million. Astronomical figures considering that early adopters could mint a CryptoPunk for free, and a Bored Ape for just a few hundred dollars. Now, in the fallout from the last crypto winter, many NFTs are worth close to nothing.

NFTs can be digital art, music, tickets, and more.

Before we look at what kind of value NFTs can offer their owners, it's worth understanding the tech behind the tokens. Cryptocurrencies are "fungible," meaning all coins hold uniform worth and can be used for transactions as more liquid assets and reliable stores of value. Contrastingly, NFTs are unique digital assets and therefore "non-fungible," achieving wildly different valuations. Speculation over some NFTs' perceived rarity and their rise as status indicators have driven record sale prices.

Smart contracts underpin NFTs. They enable anyone to validate provenance and ownership. NFTs can be linked to real-world assets or be purely digital. There are limitless applications of NFTs for gated communities, digital IDs, and collector's items.

NFTs' ability to prove ownership unlocks value in multiple ways. Some examples include:

1 Community access: NFTs can provide a "key" to access exclusive experiences.

2 Empowering creators: Artists, podcasters, or musicians can interact with their fans directly, instead of through third parties, and benefit financially.

3 Investment: The accumulating value of a scarce asset.

The first major NFT project that struck the world was CryptoKitties. A savvy engineer devised a fun way to help people understand Ethereum: Cats breeding on the blockchain. Comparing token IDs to DNA, users gleaned that NFTs were uniquely identifiable. CryptoKitties ground Ethereum to a halt through their popularity. In December 2017, so many kittens were minted in such a short period that pending transactions on the Ethereum blockchain increased six-fold.

Since then, billions of dollars have poured into NFTs.

The space has seen rapid innovation. CryptoPunks innovated by creating a fixed supply of 10,000 pixelated punks and a market-place for trading its collection. BAYC pioneered collector IP rights. Doodles created a "Doodle bank treasury" for NFT holders to vote on which projects the collective fund should be allocated to. Cool Cats made NFTs family-friendly.

Many well-known brands and figures have ventured into the space. Dolce & Gabbana has launched a digital token fashion line. Gary Vaynerchuk, the early Twitter investor and media mogul, has a personalized collection of NFTs that grant access to VeeCon, his annual conference with festival elements. The art is drawn by Gary himself and naive in style (think doodles), yet at their height they sold for around $70,000. Gary's brother has created a private sports community where your NFT doubles as a ticket to real-life matches.

NFTs can, and will, unlock real-life utility. But what are the externalities?

On the upside, the value of many NFTs extends beyond the digital asset. BAYC is not only an NFT collection; it is an elusive community with access to members-only events. Its members have been rewarded amply with derivative NFTs, including mutant apes, ApeCoin, and now a virtual "land" in the metaverse.

Following the success of BAYC, its parent organization Yuga Labs raised venture capital and acquired CryptoPunks. Yuga Labs has also created a cryptocurrency, ApeCoin, which they airdropped (sent) to all NFT holders. Bored Ape owners received $100,000 in ApeCoin for each NFT purchased. The coin has mostly been able to hold its value. With a market capitalization of around $500 million, this is truly money created from nothing.

On the downside, NFTs have been a breeding ground for fraud. A fake Banksy NFT titled *Great Redistribution of Climate Change Disaster* was briefly available for auction through a link on Banksy's official website. A collector named Pranksy bid around $336,000 in cryptocurrency for the NFT on OpenSea. The bid was immediately accepted, sparking questions of legitimacy, since auctions typically run for a set duration. Banksy's team confirmed it was a scam, but in an unexpected twist, the scammer returned the collector's money minus fees.

Piggybacking the popularity of the Netflix show *Squid Game*, scammers created a cryptocurrency token called SQUID. Within 11 days, the token's value skyrocketed by an astonishing 310,000 percent, reaching a peak price of over $2,800 per token. However, investors couldn't sell their tokens due to anti-dump mechanisms in the smart contract. In a rug pull, the scammers sold off their holdings, profiting an estimated $3.38 million, whilst thousands of investors were left with worthless tokens.

Scammers have exploited consumer naivety over the new asset class, taking advantage of Discord, a communication platform popular with crypto enthusiasts which allows users to create to-ken-gated channels. Clickbait lures users onto malicious links and behavioral hacks in private messages encourage the uptake of fraudulent offers.

These channels can also give rise to trolls. As NFTs and crypto languish relatively unregulated, they are accompanied by a hyper-capitalistic undertone: Those with the most can access the best opportunities. NFTs have been criticized for exacerbating eco-nomic disparities, although stock trading, property ownership, and the purchase of any asset class could be similarly blamed.

The grey area of NFTs, with some stakeholders benefitting and others losing out, has been intellectual property (IP).

For instance, Nike took legal action against StockX, an online resale platform, over their "Vault NFTs" series which featured patented sneaker designs and their infamous tick logo. Nike argued that the NFTs profited from their brand without permis-sion. StockX countered that the Vault NFTs merely served as digital ownership records for customers of resold Nike sneakers. The law-suit remains ongoing.

Finally, there's the downright strange.

In December 2021, a Cryptopunk NFT sold for $532 million; however, it turned out the buyer and seller were the same person. Twitter co-founder Jack Dorsey's first tweet was sold for $2.9 mil-lion as an NFT and subsequently plummeted 99 percent in value, which some bystanders speculate was for tax benefit.

Until recently, the exclusive platform for trading NFTs and these ensuing externalities was OpenSea.

Navigating OpenSea

In January 2022, OpenSea's latest investment round valued the NFT marketplace at $13.3 billion. It had reached defensibility with over 90 percent market share.

How did OpenSea build such a dominant platform? In part, it was first-mover advantage.

As a child, OpenSea's co-founder Devin Finzer loved the intersection of creativity and logic. "I was always looking for things that were fun, visual, interesting." Puzzles, math, and music were his strengths.

With the dawn of social networks, Devin recalls being "excited about Pinterest," for it was "a more visual consumer app." Then Web 3.0 came along, full of technological potential, but lacking aesthetics. There was space to build something radically different.

In late 2017, Devin Finzer founded OpenSea with Alex Atallah and launched its beta version two months later, backed by Y Combinator. Devin's toughest and most exhilarating moments accompanied the NFT craze of 2021; it was "an order of magnitude, 100,000x what we had seen before. We had never seen that number of users, that volume, it all happened quickly." OpenSea's team mushroomed to accommodate the unprecedented growth.

By August 2021, trading volume exceeded $3 billion.

A surge in interest from collectors, high-profile sales, and the entry of major brands into the NFT market collided at once, attracting billions of dollars. The result: Gas fees.

Most NFTs on OpenSea (the largest NFT marketplace) are stored on the Ethereum blockchain—a decentralized network of computers (nodes) that work together to validate and record transactions. Whenever you want to perform an action on the Ethereum blockchain, like transferring an NFT or sending Ethereum (ETH) from one wallet to another, you must pay a transaction fee called "gas." Paid in ETH, gas goes to the "miners" who provide the computing power to process your transaction and add it to the blockchain.

The amount of gas you pay depends on the complexity of your transaction and how congested the Ethereum network is at that moment. When there are many pending transactions, the network gets congested, as each node has to process every transaction to maintain consensus. Transactions willing to pay premium gas fees get prioritized. This can create a bidding war, driving gas fees up to thousands of dollars for a single transaction.

A key example of this was when Yuga Labs (who was behind the success of NFT series Bored Apes) launched "The Otherside," a multiplayer online role-playing game in the metaverse, where players can own virtual land and use their NFTs as in-game characters. As one of the largest mints in history, they raised $150 million in sales. However, demand was so high that $100 million in ETH was burned in gas fees.

Crypto was experiencing widespread uptake. OpenSea's breakneck scaling encountered some teething problems.

A fateful moment came in September 2021, when OpenSea failed to display accurate floor prices for NFT collections. The crucial metric represents the lowest price at which an NFT from a particular collection is listed for sale. A declining floor price may indicate waning interest. Clients were misled about the values of NFTs when purchasing on OpenSea and the issue persisted for over 12 hours before the platform resolved it—inciting fury among customers.

Co-founder Devin reflects, "Any startup founder can tell you that along the way, you're going to make some mistakes and enter uncharted territory." At OpenSea, "demand was growing faster than the company was set up to accommodate." The limited bandwidth of the founders and employees was starting to show. "You have to let things break [and] choose things you're going to fix." Devin had to pick between repairing the platform that kept going down and customer support, which "oftentimes ... was just me and Alex [Devin's co-founder] in the Discord talking to users."

This influx of new mainstream internet users exposed security risks.

OpenSea was "designed for the crypto-curious early adopter type," but had been flooded by inexperienced clients, who all of a sudden were "downloading MetaMask [a crypto wallet] and trying to get crypto." Customer support was straining to keep up. "All sorts of things can happen in Web 3.0, where users can lose their items. If they go and use that malicious website, it can drain their NFTs." And it did. In January 2022, a hacker stole $1.7 million worth of NFTs on OpenSea. Despite this, OpenSea remained up and to the right.

Until May 2022, when $45 billion disappeared. This time the losses did not emanate from OpenSea, but the impact on Web 3.0 was severe. In truth, the money did not actually vanish, but a series of calculated and unfortunate events led to 99.99 percent of investors' money in the stablecoin Terra being wiped out in three days.

$1 million invested would become just $3.

Stablecoins are cryptocurrencies pegged to more dependable assets to dampen price volatility, which enables liquidity. Stablecoins are mostly backed by real-world currencies. Terra, on the other hand, was backed by an algorithm.

Terra (UST) and LUNA were intertwined cryptocurrencies, named after Earth and its moon. UST aimed to be a stablecoin valued at $1, balanced by LUNA, a freely traded cryptocurrency. The algorithm allowed users to swap 1 UST for $1 worth of LUNA, and vice versa, regardless of market fluctuations.

If Terra's price fell below $1, traders could "burn" (remove) Terra tokens from circulation by exchanging them for newly minted LUNA tokens—like removing weight from a seesaw, it would restore the price. When Terra's price rose above $1, more Terra tokens would be minted and given to LUNA holders, increasing Terra's supply, which lowered its price, again like a seesaw. Market participants were incentivized to trade through arbitrage.

However, this mechanism failed catastrophically in May 2022.

There was a mass sale of UST and the price dropped well below $1. To increase UST's value, the algorithm burned lots of UST and minted new LUNA tokens. At this scale, LUNA was in oversupply and its price plummeted. LUNA was no longer valuable enough to restore UST's $1 peg through token burning.

Caught in a death spiral, both cryptocurrencies crashed to near zero.

In the aftermath, there were suicides across the globe and an investigation by the South Korean authorities into Terra-LUNA's infamous founder, Do Kwon, who was still trolling other Twitter users and starting Twitter wars, even as LUNA went over a cliff into oblivion.

Considered one of the top cryptocurrency projects, Terra-LUNA's collapse decimated confidence in Web 3.0. A contagion of panic triggered other crypto failures and tipped the market into the prolonged downturn known as a crypto winter.

OpenSea laid off 20 percent of its staff. Around this time, Devin's co-founder Alex stepped down as CTO. In Devin's view, "Alex's skill set is a little more on the frontier, building new things and experimenting. Alex's ambitions have always been at that zero-to-one phase. Eventually, he decided to start tinkering and do something new. It was a natural transition as the company scaled."

The crypto winter was compounded by FTX's insolvency later that year.

In this harsh landscape of autumn 2022, the fledgling crypto exchange Blur launched its beta platform and announced an airdrop—a free distribution of digital tokens to specific users—to incentivize NFT listings. While OpenSea charged 2.5 percent fees per transaction, Blur came onto the scene and charged zero. Originally developed as a tool for pro-NFT traders, Blur added analytics, sales history, and aggregated listings of NFTs across platforms. Within three months, Blur surpassed OpenSea in daily transaction volume, eroding OpenSea's 90 percent market share. To solidify their gains, Blur introduced a loyalty program to incentivize the exclusive use of their platform.

To regain lost traffic, OpenSea made a significant policy change. They would reduce royalty fees paid by buyers to 0 percent for a limited time. Previously, NFT creators had been able to set their royalty rate between 1 percent and 10 percent. The move backfired. OpenSea was condemned for abandoning its ethos by robbing creators of their royalties.

Devin reminds founders to "enjoy the ride" when startups are going well. "One learning [from OpenSea] is it's important to experience the joy and positive elements when your startup takes off. I don't think I experienced it. I tend to be pretty hard on myself."

During OpenSea's growth Devin concentrated on "all the things that were broken, [that] I needed to fix. Always look to improve yourself, but also be grateful that you have that opportunity in the first place."

Devin continues, "A lot of founders are going through challenging times. They become very disconnected from their emotions. They're just going to squash this [problem] down [and] logic the situation. During that period, I [too] was in that bucket of a rational perspective. Now, I think I've matured to the point where I try to use my emotions to guide me to make better decisions. Your emotions usually are telling you something. [As a founder] you just don't want to let them overwhelm you."

In September 2023, amid the ongoing crypto winter, OpenSea reduced its workforce by 50 percent. Meanwhile, Blur expanded its offering, launching a lending protocol for borrowing against NFTs.

Devin frames OpenSea's redundancies as powering efficiency and innovation: "[Over] almost seven years, we've built an amazing team." OpenSea's "recent restructuring" was to ensure the team "is small, tight-knit, high efficiency, high velocity, [containing] the people who are most excited about pushing this technology forward."

Despite the competition, OpenSea maintains a long-term focus. Devin acknowledges the "cooler market environment" and is investing in initiatives that will "push the space forward in the long run," rather than simply "reacting" to competitors. OpenSea adapts its strategy to competitive dynamics and the bear market. Devin continues, "When we first started the company, we had this long-term conviction that NFTs were going to be big and we planted our flag... that turned out to be a great flag to plant because then the market took off. Now we need to be a bit more strategic than before. We have to be thoughtful as we navigate the competitive dynamics and a prolonged bear market."

Battling for market share, the two NFT exchanges are now neck-and-neck. OpenSea maintains a larger overall user base, but Blur leads in trading volume.

Despite Blur gaining on OpenSea, Devin's vision for his company is not deflated: "We're still just as excited as we were back then about NFTs. In the bull market, we have to remember it was mostly collectables and profile pictures. In the bear market, it may seem doom and gloom, but there's a ton of innovation happening. The quality of projects and the scaling of blockchains is going up and up. So you have to temper your reactions to the highs and the lows."

Looking forward, Devin believes gaming is a promising market for NFTs and digital economies. In gaming, "there's already this audience who are accustomed to buying and selling digital goods online." Coupled with the innovations in AI and VR, as "the younger generation is spending more and more of their time making money inside of games," Devin predicts market opportunities. "But there's a whole host of other areas of the industry that I'm excited about as well."

In the real world, crypto enables fast, efficient money transfers beyond traditional banking. Devin marvels, "There are things we can do in crypto that are way beyond what we've already done on the rest of the internet. It's pretty damn wonderful to send money to someone with an Ethereum address. You can send a million dollars in a single transaction in 30 seconds versus having to deal with banks." However, Devin admits he still uses Venmo for everyday transactions.

NFTs have the potential to solve real-world problems. "At their worst," Devin reasons, "NFTs could just be a fad. At their best, NFTs could be a massive enabler for freelancers to get paid for their creative work, reduce fake ticket sales for popular events, and help global, remote communities connect more deeply."

He puts forward, "The technology is here to stay."

Don't Write Off Crypto

Web 3.0 also has unmapped risks. In 2024, $112 million in XRP cryptocurrency was stolen from Chris Larsen, the co-founder and executive chairman of Ripple Labs. The unauthorized access to his account was then laundered through various crypto exchanges. Though the incident was isolated and did not involve Ripple's wallets, the high-profile theft highlights the importance of robust cryptocurrency security measures. The incident is under investigation and some stolen funds have been frozen. But the remaining XRP are yet to be recovered.

Regulation looms, but its impacts are uncertain. There is an ongoing lawsuit between Ripple Labs and the US Securities and Exchange Commission (SEC) over XRP allegedly being an unregistered security. Ripple Labs has previously emerged victorious against the SEC. After that prior ruling and the SEC's overturned appeal request, Ripple's cryptocurrency XRP increased in value by 77 percent. Undeterred and true to his vow, Chris has retained authority. He sits on the board of Ripple Labs and is the controlling voting shareholder. XRP remains one of the top 10 cryptocurrencies by market capitalization in the world.

Crypto emerged as an antidote to world powers' hold on currencies, decentralizing control to servers and their network of users. Over in Asia, however, the imminent roll-out of China's state-led digital currency, e-CNY, controlled by the People's Bank of China (PBOC), overturns these ideals.

Within crypto and NFTs there will likely be more casualties, joining Libra and Terra-LUNA. Companies will continue to be shed as the still-nascent industry evolves and new frontiers are explored. Chris Dixon distinguishes between the speculative aspects of cryptocurrency ("the casino") and the practical, innovative uses of blockchain technology ("the computer").

But decentralized technology has a place. PayPal mafia member Elon Musk has warned that the US dollar is at risk of becoming obsolete: "We need to do something about our national debt or the dollar will be worth nothing." This threat, Elon claims, is driving investors toward alternative stores of value like the cryptocurrencies Bitcoin, Ethereum, and XRP.

Crypto is here to stay. Its potential reaches far beyond market hype.

TIPS FROM THE TRENCHES

1 Keep an ear to the ground for new developments in decentralized finance and novel technologies. Innovations in Web 3.0 are forecast to disrupt established financial systems.

2 Be prepared to scale explosively when opportunities arise, but remain vigilant for competitors and potential market shifts. Early market leaders in emerging technologies may face significant challenges from new entrants.

3 Remember tokens can have unending applications in real life. Blockchain relies on incentives to function and grow. Tokens (cryptocurrencies and NFTs) are often given to reward desired behaviors, such as mining or participation. These tokens may grant access, voting rights, or a share of profits.

09
Black Swans vs. the Power Law
Insuring and Betting against Crisis

O ne-quarter of Brazil, one of the most populous countries in the world, was estimated to be playing games on Vostu—until they were served a lawsuit.

Leading US-based game creator Zynga accused Vostu of intellectual property rights infringement, in other words, *imitating*. Zynga's flagship game FarmVille had been closely tailed by Vostu's Mini Fazenda (small plantation). Within two years of launching Zynga Poker, Vostu Poker surfaced, and so the claim continued. Zynga alleged that Vostu's copies were so blatant that they even contained the same software bugs.

Behind the prosecution was Zynga's founder and CEO, Mark Pincus—ironically also an investor in Vostu.

Vostu rebutted that Zynga's games copied existing concepts, and even filed a countersuit alleging the US gaming platform had imitated their games. Rather unhelpfully for Vostu's case, TechCrunch and other media outlets had lauded Vostu as the "Zynga of Brazil." Having been the largest game creator in Latin America and named one of the 100 most valuable startups in the world, Vostu lost the case and the co-founders resigned under pressure.

Today, Vostu is no longer operating.

How did this startup reach such heights, only to unravel spectacularly?

When Games Are No Longer Fun

This improbable and unpredictable "black swan" event was not the first hurdle Vostu had experienced.

Vostu was founded in 2007, the same year as Zynga, by three Harvard students: CEO Daniel Kafie, Chief Scientist Mario Schlosser, and Josh Kushner.

At the time, Mario saw social networks were gaining traction, with platforms like Friendster, MySpace, and the still-nascent Facebook. Meanwhile, Josh and Daniel had Latin American friends from Harvard's Spee Club—an elite club, whose alumni include President John F. Kennedy—and noted the absence of significant social networks in the region.

The trio settled on building a social network for LatAm and named it Vostu, from the domains available.

Upon graduation, chief scientist Mario and CEO Daniel moved to Silicon Valley and began raising money to get the startup off the ground. Mario suggested: "Anybody who wants to keep their equity has to come to Silicon Valley." Co-founder Josh, who had yet to graduate, would not. The founders had fully vested their equity upfront (Silicon Valley startups usually set vesting schedules over a number of years to plan for situations like this). Mario thought Josh should give his equity back. Josh disagreed.

Their disagreement was hollow as Vostu was making little progress.

Mario accepted a job at the famed hedge fund Bridgewater, admitting, "I didn't think [Vostu] would go anywhere frankly, but I kept the servers running." A small team of coders in Buenos Aires ran the social network: "We pivoted like 16 times." And for a couple of years, Josh (in Cambridge Massachusetts) and Mario (in Silicon Valley) lost touch.

Then Mario observed a friend engrossed in a German online role-playing game (RPG). Players could interact and trade items; Mario's friend was hooked, meticulously planning his next moves. Realizing that a game could supercharge uptake of the social network they had been trying to build in Latin America, Vostu developed a soccer simulation game. To increase users, Vostu marketed on Orkut, a popular social network in Brazil at the time. Vostu gained immense popularity and pivoted toward social games.

Channeling his global macroeconomic learnings from Bridgewater, Mario created virtual economies on Vostu, which drove in-game prices. Monitoring playtime and engagement, Vostu built simulations to predict player behavior. These insights enabled them to construct addictive features. In Vostu's agricultural game, crops had varying harvest times—some in minutes, others in hours—ensuring users returned frequently to check on their virtual farms.

In Mario's words, "It was uncanny; three months into [users] playing the game the simulation was right on the money in terms of how people were acting. We had enough experience seeing how often people play in a given day and how we could get them to come back."

Vostu quickly became a dominant social gaming provider in Brazil and other Latin American countries.

As the company found product-market fit, Mario and Josh healed their rift and resumed working together—Mario as the technologist and Josh as the strategist and capital orchestrator. Josh helped Vostu raise a venture capital round from his mentor, General Catalyst investor, Joel Cutler. Mario reflects on the early co-founder tensions: "You have to go through those things. The earlier you can get them out of the way, the better. But you cannot avoid them."

Vostu became the largest gaming presence in Latin America.

Multi-Grammy-award-winning musician Justin Bieber's team approached Vostu to develop his first-ever mobile game. In 2010, Vostu raised $30 million, led by Accel. And yet, Mario, in his role as Chief Scientist, was already looking to close an enormous new round to support the next wave of growth.

Then out of nowhere, in 2011 the team was served a lawsuit from Zynga.

Mario recollects, "For the most part, it was me fighting the lawsuit because I knew our games best. I had to tell all these lawyers, that's exactly what was copied and what was not." Alongside their legal battle in the United States, Mario had to fight dual suits in Brazil.

Eventually, Zynga and Vostu reached an impasse: "The parties are pleased to have settled their disputes and to now put these matters behind them," the companies said in a joint statement. The corporate settlement was minor—close to $50,000—but the controversy undermined Vostu's funding round. Growth stagnated with missed game deadlines and led to infighting within the company.

Zynga went on to IPO.

Meanwhile, Vostu laid off two-thirds of its workforce, with two co-founders Mario Schlosser and Daniel Kafie resigning from its leadership (although Daniel would later return as CEO before Vostu eventually dissolved).

This "black swan" moment precipitated the game developer's demise.

Out of a job and with a decimated stock value, Mario boarded a flight back to New York to figure out his next steps. Sitting down with Vostu co-founder Josh Kushner, the pair briefly considered a gamified debit card in Brazil, but "we didn't dare to go after the big banks. The lesson there was we should have gone after the big banks," Mario ruminates, as Nubank went on to do.

Josh, influenced by his mentors, particularly Warren Buffett, was drawn to the idea of disrupting the insurance industry. This resonated with Mario, who saw parallels between designing game economies and building incentive structures in healthcare: "Health insurance seemed a good analogy for what we were doing in games."

During his wife's pregnancy, Mario had experienced the inefficiency and opaque nature of US healthcare. Between friends and Google searches, he couldn't find clear answers about childbirth costs or reliable pediatricians. With his second child, Mario wrestled with the nagging uncertainty—was his wife getting high-quality care for a low price, or low quality for a high price? The idea for a new kind of health insurer stuck.

Pixels to Premiums: HiOscar.com

Games and insurance have more in common than you might expect.

Mario Schlosser and Josh Kushner learned to build virtual economies and incentive structures at Vostu. Then in 2012, Mario and Josh, joined by Kevin Nazemi, applied these learnings to a real-world problem: Health insurance.

In the United States, healthcare's intersection with fintech cannot be ignored. Twice as much of US GDP is spent on healthcare than in any other affluent nation. Yet the system is riddled with horror stories: Convoluted and indecipherable bills, unpredictable pricing, and poor patient outcomes. US healthcare lacks the essential transparency and competitive pressures needed for a marketplace to function. The dire result is no universal access, exorbitant costs (as risk pools are not spread between healthy and sick customers), and a focus on revenues over serving consumers. To illustrate the latter, the percentage of employees with deductibles greater than $1,000 has surged to over 60 percent in the past 15 years.

Oscar Health would change this.

Oscar rode the tailwinds of the Affordable Care Act (ACA), commonly referred to as Obamacare, which expanded health insurance access for 40 million citizens in 2010. The regulation required most Americans to have insurance (on the premise that spreading risk pools would lower insurance costs), provided subsidies for low- and middle-income individuals, and prevented insurers from denying coverage based on pre-existing conditions. The pool of health insurance customers grew, as did providers. So Oscar Health differentiated. The consumer-centric platform leveraged technology to simplify insurance, offer personalized policy quotes, and incentivize healthy behaviors. Selling plans on the

ACA marketplaces, Oscar's private valuation mushroomed to $2.7 billion. The company had captured a remarkable 15 percent market share within just 18 months of launching.

But in 2017, the Trump administration vowed to dismantle the ACA. The announcement shook health insurance startups across America.

Oscar was still unprofitable, having reported immense losses of $45 million in its third quarter alone. With the individual mandate penalty eliminated and subsidies cut, insurers faced uncertainty and a shrinking pool of healthy customers. Would the ACA be further undermined?

Fast forward to today: Oscar Health is trading at close to $5 billion on public markets. Trump's administration could not fully deconstruct the ACA but stoked enough uncertainty that a number of startups folded.

Oscar managed to insulate itself from the fallout.

Mario, Oscar's co-founder, initially designed highly gamified experiences with levels, points, titles, and interactive elements like coins jumping out of claims. The goal was to engage users deeply, similar to harvesting crops in Vostu's farming game. Mario believes in the power of gamification in healthcare, though "pure prioritization" has meant these features have not yet been fully implemented. Mario explains, "Oscar became so much more complicated than just building a bunch of these front-end experiences [because] we built our own claim system and payments. It has taken all this time just to get those basics right."

Oscar Health incentivizes healthy behaviors, which reduces claims, and is a testament to how gamification can be used for good. Oscar customers who meet daily exercise goals with their wearable device receive an Amazon gift card. Some can claim cash to get a flu jab. Specific actions earn discounts, sales, and double points.

By delighting its customers, Oscar has gained their trust. The majority of Oscar's quote estimates are within 10 percent or $25 of the service cost—because they utilize user data—which enables members to plan for their healthcare spending. The platform maps the best doctors for their conditions. For minor issues, Oscar streamlines care, offering virtual consultations and prescriptions. Oscar now has an all-time high NPS score of 66, indicating satisfied customers; although not at Nubank's level, it trounces the competition.

That was not always the case. Another larger competitor, Bright Health, was also "differentiating" by providing terrific customer service. Oscar Health's team felt threatened. When faced with a decision, Mario recalls, "Like those bumper stickers: '*What would Jesus do?*' We'd ask: '*What would Bright do?*'" In the end, Bright did not fare as well. After suffering losses and retracting from the ACA market, Bright Health's subsidiary in Texas was ordered into liquidation by a court in 2023. Bright's losses put it at risk of being delisted from the New York Stock Exchange. Mario reflects, "It just shows that even the right strategic thinking is not [enough to] rely on."

Differentiation allowed Oscar to outlast almost all of the other startups in the Affordable Care Act space.

Within a year of Trump's administration unwinding the ACA, Google's parent company Alphabet invested $375 million in Oscar Health. The investment accounted for a third of all digital health spending for the year—in a single round. With it, Oscar promised to expand geographic reach, hire, enhance their data and offer Medicare Advantage plans.

What strategies had allowed them to raise such substantial capital?

In part, the team. Mario and his co-founder Josh brought different but essential strengths to the table. With a "density of information," Mario excels in technical aspects and building teams; meanwhile, Josh's "simple, repetitive way" lends itself to fundraising, relationship management, and translating complex ideas into clear visions.

Mario admits to "cringing" at Josh's initial, overly simplified pitches, fearing they wouldn't be taken seriously. "[Josh] would give a bit of story, and I would explain how it works." However, Mario came to appreciate Josh's ability to gauge the audience and deliver the message concisely, citing one of Oscar Health's key early investors: "Stanley Druckenmiller, a legendary investor, is famous for listening to a venture and walking out five minutes into it [the meeting]. He doesn't have any tolerance for getting bored. [But he] only invested because I was able to explain how health-care works. So you need both."

Despite Google's colossal investment, Oscar Health's expansion unexpectedly plateaued.

Traditional health insurance giants were still gatekeeping the industry. Mario reflects that Oscar Health's team had "an incredibly arrogant view of the incumbents early on. They seemed completely backward and unsophisticated to us." These days, Mario views this through a different lens: "United Healthcare was at least an incredibly well-run company. We were focused on the wrong thing. We thought they [couldn't] build a great mobile app, and that was true. But they controlled the distribution and the hospital systems. Healthcare is all about sales and distribution." Whilst established insurers were hindered by legacy technology, their relationships with healthcare providers and sales networks remained steadfast.

This left Oscar in a predicament.

The market was starting to adopt risk-sharing, tying healthcare provider payments to the quality of care, rather than the volume of services. To keep pace, Oscar had to be agile in cultivating partnerships with providers. At the time of writing, 48 percent of Oscar Health's members are now part of such arrangements, and the company is working to increase this figure.

Aside from improving customer experience, this model has been shown to drive better clinical outcomes at lower costs. A healthier dynamic emerges between providers, insurers, and patients as value-based arrangements reward exceptional hospitals and ensure better care. By directing patients to a few providers in each city, Oscar has been able to negotiate discounts, laying the foundations for its first profitable year.

Despite the incumbent insurers' strong distribution networks, Oscar Health acted fast. Growth recovered and in 2021, Oscar listed publicly.

The global healthcare industry is worth $3 trillion. Since 2012, Oscar Health has made a sizeable dent in healthcare's largest and most notoriously complex region, the United States, disrupting the industry for the benefit of consumers.

Lessons from Oscar

Having stepped back as CEO of Oscar Health, Mario Schlosser shares three lessons out the other side.

1 Resilience

After the Zynga lawsuit and being forced out of Vostu, then raising mega fundraising rounds and facing the public markets with Oscar, Mario has battle scars. I ask him how he navigates and approaches unsuspecting crises. For Mario, resilience is "built over time; human beings get used to a surprising amount."

Still, Mario does not wish his past crisis moments on himself again. "The funny thing is, if I now picture myself getting up in the morning [with] a day ahead of me where I have to tell people bad news, I get worried. I don't want to do that, even though I already did it." Citing Google's major investment in Oscar, and the startup's subsequent stagnation, Mario shivers: "Five years later you still have that [terrible] feeling, you just will never be able to shake that kind of thing."

Mario admires PayPal mafia member, Elon Musk, for his "relentless [persistence] at putting himself back in embarrassing situations that can backfire against him. That part is admirable, that he's willing to take the pain, the heat." That's what it takes to succeed as a founder.

2 Owning your stack

If Mario were to rebuild Oscar Health from scratch, he would put more emphasis, and earlier, on owning their tech stack: "In the first two years, [Oscar] did a bound claim system. We outsourced [claims]. You have to because you have no scale whatsoever." However, the team always planned to control their infrastructure. "We made agreements with that third-party administrator to eventually buy the [claims] software from them," Mario stresses, "That was an incredibly important thing to do because it gave us the experience of coding our own software. Certainly, those things took way longer than we thought," but Oscar's team were able to run the claims in-house.

3 Naivety

Freed of CEO duties, Mario now spends time rediscovering his naivety through fun projects. Building games, he is interested in the "notion that games can keep adding to their own logic." He also experiments with AI applications. In healthcare, Mario sees promise in AI doctors: "Healthcare is so well structured, there are a set number of diseases, so you have all the contextual knowledge." Drawing on his recent experience of dislocating his shoulder—something he had done 10 years prior, outside of the United States—Mario marvels that an AI doctor would have pulled from past medical records and advised him accordingly.

These three traits have been carried forth from Oscar Health. Former employees have begun starting ventures, creating a nascent tech mafia. Oscar has even spawned competitors from its work-force. At a book launch in NYC, Mario recalls the first moment an Oscar employee resigned to build a new company. At first, Mario was taken aback, but then he realized it was a great outcome.

Oscar had hired from great brands. As an alumnus of the hedge fund Bridgewater, Mario explains, "Oscar was where most Bridgewater people went. By far and to this day." Oscar was beginning to become a brand in its own right, indeed one which many employees would launch their own venture from.

Mario embraces this possibility: "The only thing I don't get upset about is when people leave to start their own companies." Instead of departing for other insurance brands or tech companies, Mario and his co-founder Josh embolden employees to "go for it." Josh, through his venture fund Thrive Capital, "tries to support them, either invest or give advice. I try to at least invest $5,000 in all these alumni."

That network built during a startup's early days—with investors, clients, and partners—is valuable. Mario highlights,

"Something that distinguishes great, scaled leaders from [CEOs of] early-stage startups is that they know who to call."

The constellation of ventures forming around Oscar Health is a repeating pattern of so-called "tech mafias." Peter Thiel, co-founder of PayPal and the venture firm Founders Fund, was one of Oscar Health's lead investors.

But Oscar Health was not the only insurance startup in the PayPal mafia's orbit. Roelof Botha, former PayPal CFO, now Managing Partner at Sequoia, serves on the board of Ethos Life.

From Health to Life

Ethos Life was founded in 2016 by Peter Colis and Lingke Wang with the mission of making life insurance more affordable, accessible, and customer-friendly. The inspiration for the company came from a negative experience Lingke had in college when he was misled into purchasing an expensive whole-life policy that didn't meet his needs. He continued to pay for it over the years, even though it wouldn't fully cover him. Meanwhile, Peter had been contemplating insurance for much of his life. His grandfather was an insurance salesperson who started a brokerage. Peter's background gave him the foundational knowledge and confidence to tackle the intimidating world of insurance.

The founders first ventured into the life insurance industry by founding Ovid, which helped people sell whole-life insurance policies they could no longer afford. The more they researched, the more they found that the insurance industry was thoroughly broken, plagued by high-pressure sales tactics, complicated purchase experiences, medical exams, blood tests, and outdated administrative systems. Ovid was not big-picture enough to solve this. After successfully exiting the business they set their sights on a bigger prize.

Peter and Lingke considered 400 different business models before settling on Ethos. Three to four hours every day for two months, they brainstormed and evaluated ideas against competition, market size, and long-term viability. Was the problem they were solving significant enough? Was their solution truly effective?

Their diligence paid off. Despite being turned down by 39 of the 40 seed investors they pitched, the 40th investor, Sequoia Capital, saw potential in their idea. Roelof Botha, PayPal mafia member and Sequoia's Managing Partner, had trained as a life insurance actuary. The problem Ethos was solving resonated and he invested.

Ethos built an end-to-end platform with a small, elite team. This focused approach allowed them to innovate and create a more efficient and customer-friendly life insurance platform. Co-founder Peter admits, "Six of us cranked day and night in an apartment, eating microwavable dumplings and drinking too much coffee, to launch in-market as quickly as we could... We built a vertically integrated distributor to sell policies, an underwriter to price risk, and an administrator for end-to-end management of insurance, compliance, and customer processes."

Peter Colis describes a founder's journey as one of resilience: "There are going to be days when it feels like you're eating glass. But the more glass you eat, the less you taste it."

Ethos today issues more life insurance than any other player in the United States, including New York Life, Prudential, John Hancock, and MassMutual. Of the many other startups who took on the life insurance industry in the last decade, only Ethos remains at scale. Peter shares, "There's different kinds of businesses. Some businesses need to be extremely competitor focused. Some need to be very focused on client and product-market fit. We found that ours is very much the latter. The reason is that life insurance is so fragmented today—the largest carrier in the market issues 7 percent of all US life insurance premiums and it goes down from there. Even if you are the largest carrier, you're really competing with a sea of other competitors, rather than having consolidated competition."

Ethos differentiated by "becoming an underwriter and an administrator, but we stopped short of being a balance sheet provider and guaranteeing the risk ourselves." This gave Ethos the "real estate up and down the stack in which to innovate and optimize, more so than anybody else. But at the same time, we didn't have the capital drag and the regulatory drag of being a licensed life insurance carrier." By picking carefully where within the stack to innovate, Ethos was able to be more than a simple UI layer on top of existing solutions and also avoided the risk of being a balance sheet provider.

Meanwhile, another startup was similarly innovating business insurance.

Newfront(iers) and Abraham Lincoln

What do Lime Bikes, Y Combinator, and Aspen Flying Club have in common? Newfront underpins them by brokering their insurance.

Frontier technologies are necessary for innovation but come with unmapped risks for insurers. Liabilities of life sciences and deep tech can range from hazardous contamination to data theft, and even cyber terrorism. Where Oscar Health disrupted the consumer insurance industry, Newfront "de-risks human progress" for commercial ventures.

In the aftermath of crypto exchange FTX's insolvency, which left an $8 billion hole in FTX's balance sheet from misused funds, insurance companies shunned crypto. Some denied coverage to clients with FTX ties, others shied away from the entire industry. The remaining premiums became extortionate. Newfront, as a specialty tech broker, capitalized on the opportunity to gain client trust. In one case study, Newfront saved a global blockchain fintech just under a quarter of a million dollars on their annual insurance premiums.

Today, insurance covers all aspects of our world, providing the economic lubrication for trade to occur.

As Spike Lipkin, CEO and Founder of Newfront, puts it, "When you trace the development of modern society over hundreds of years, [insurance] has allowed people to take risks. The only reason you would take a risk is if there's an opportunity, right?" Today,

Newfront works with hundreds of public companies, and many innovative crypto, AI, and biotech companies, where risk has never been defined before. Spike continues, "We are thinking about what could go wrong all the time so that the entrepreneurs that we partner with can think about what could go right."

Behind the scenes, insurance has enabled everything from the healthcare system to the moon landing. Launching rockets and space exploration required massive investment and insurance safeguarded against numerous risks, from the potential failure of launch vehicles to the loss of payloads and satellites.

Insurance is not a new concept, Spike explains, gifting me a wonderful book. *Against the Gods: The Remarkable Story of Risk* by Peter L. Bernstein traces the roots of insurance back to ancient Babylonian and Chinese merchants spreading cargo across ships to avoid total loss if one sank. This risk sharing evolved into formal contracts where merchants pooled funds to recompense stakeholders of wrecked ships.

The 17th century saw a leap in probability theory by French mathematicians Blaise Pascal and Pierre de Fermat, who suggested a fair way to divide bets if a game of chance, like cards, was interrupted. Their work on expected value laid the groundwork for modern insurance. Around the same time in London, merchants and those seeking to insure their cargo gathered at Edward Lloyd's coffee shop, which has since evolved into the largest specialty insurance marketplace in the world: Lloyd's of London.

In the 18th century, Bernoulli's *Law of Large Numbers* advanced probability theory, arguing that the more times a random experiment is repeated, the more representative the results of theoretical probability. Growing global trade fueled risk management solutions.

Insurance protected shipments of cargo and now defends the shipping of innovative tech.

Founded in 2017 by Spike Lipkin and Gordon Wintrob, Newfront had ties to the PayPal mafia.

Spike, Newfront's CEO, was the first employee at Opendoor, an online real estate platform co-founded by former PayPal VP, Keith

Rabois. When Spike ventured out to found Newfront, Founders Fund, led by another PayPal mafia member, backed the company with a $9 million Series A and a $30 million Series B round. Newfront CTO, Gordon, also had tangential links to the PayPal mafia; he'd worked previously as an engineer at LinkedIn, co-founded by former PayPal COO, Reid Hoffman.

Spike's interest in insurance had been piqued at Opendoor, where he was responsible for managing property and casualty insurance. Again, in his role at Blackstone Group—one of the world's leading private equity firms, with over $1 trillion in total assets under management—Spike purchased corporate insurance.

Though proud to oversee the vital mitigation of risk, Spike was taken aback by the archaic and convoluted process. The sheer volume of paperwork, prolonged waiting periods, and the wildly varying, almost incomparable options left Spike bewildered. There was no transparent dataset to guide them on which carriers to consider, which coverages to prioritize, or how peer businesses made their insurance choices. This cumbersome process was repeated annually. And this was before any claims were handled.

Seeing the problem in insurance, Spike and Gordon set about solving it.

First, their startup needed a name. Aiming for transparency, they chose Abe Insurance, a nod to Abraham Lincoln's nickname "Honest Abe." Customers and brokers wondered if the name was an acronym. Feedback was universally negative. One broker stated they were joining in spite of its name—this was the final straw. CTO Gordon wrote a name-generation script and eventually landed on Newfront. "New" symbolized innovation, while "front" referenced insurance. With a swift decision, Newfront became the startup's new identity.

Armed with a license and a team, Newfront launched its tech-enabled brokerage platform to modernize the insurance experience for all stakeholders: Businesses, brokers, and insurers.

In an industry steeped in history, how did the upstart Newfront gain such a foothold? By serving its customers.

Data-driven Marketplace for Businesses

First-of-a-kind companies have no comparables.

Newfront helps these innovators secure initial coverage, by telling their story to the insurance markets. AI and crypto startups, for instance, face a whole new vector of risk and require specialized insurance.

Drawing parallels between risks in existing sectors—such as the money-laundering perils of remittance firms, which carriers are familiar with, and emerging technology such as crypto—Newfront uses data to illustrate clients' underlying hazards for accurate underwriting.

Some risks are particularly hard to quantify because they are compounding; early in the curve risk might appear manageable, but can exponentially escalate into a serious threat.

To serve young startups, Newfront took a counterintuitive approach: Negotiating down policy limits. This enabled fledgling companies to afford insurance, albeit with lower coverage. Insurance companies were, in turn, pleased, as startups are incentivized to manage risk in case the cost of a claim exceeds their coverage. Newfront analyses a client's cyber risk by examining the number of records held and the average loss per record. This data-driven approach allowed Newfront to slash a client's premium from a staggering $50 million (more than the startup's total funding) by proving to the insurer that lower claim limits were sufficient.

But Newfront were not just remedying insurance for consumers, they were also serving brokers.

Empowering, Rather Than Eliminating, Brokers

Insurance is a $100 billion industry, 90 percent of which is controlled by brokers matching customers with specific packages. To revolutionize insurance, Newfront would need to go after this sector.

When Newfront launched, insurtech that aimed to replace brokers was gaining traction, with numerous startups securing gargantuan investments, but Spike and Gordon could see this reasoning was flawed. From conversations with CFOs, general counsels, risk managers, and business owners, the pair concluded that skilled insurance brokers are indispensable. Newfront's model was predicated on bringing over brokers to Newfront.

The issue wasn't the brokers themselves, but the system.

Traditional brokerages relegated brokers to data collection and paperwork processing, stifling their ability to develop expertise or offer informed advice. Spike and Gordon were determined to address this.

In Newfront's early days, the average insurance broker had an NPS score of 17 (customer satisfaction, out of 100). Newfront's success hinged on technology, economics, and culture. They built a custom AMS (agency management system), which aided clients' decision-making with insights on policies and improved claims tracking. This transparency forced a new revenue model for brokers. Rather than recommending policies with inflated premiums to earn a higher commission, Newfront sought to minimize policy prices. Once they had earned consumer trust, the client would likely choose them across many packages. This culture of transparency and accountability was novel.

By transforming raw information into actionable insights, Newfront empowers customer decisions and can negotiate lower policy prices for their lower-risk clients.

Newfront has built a moat against competition from structured data.

Newfront's Philosophy

A certain mindset underpins unicorns.

Coming from real estate at Opendoor, Spike Lipkin was unbridled by the preconceptions of an insurance professional. Taking a first-principle stance, Spike could envision an alternative. This approach was rooted in philosophy.

Like Andrew Kortina, the co-founder of Venmo, Spike studied philosophy at the University of Pennsylvania. Spike wrote his college thesis on David Hume, a Scottish philosopher who championed empiricism: "Observing the world around him and forming a thesis based on observation." This philosophy parallels entrepreneurialism. Spike confesses: "So much of building a startup is just making a series of reasonable decisions based on the information available all the time. It's having a hypothesis and being willing to test it."

Accordingly, Newfront's approach is iterative: "We'll build something and immediately talk to users. We often ship something that [is not ready and] we're embarrassed about, just to get user feedback and refine, refine, refine." Spike continues, "As a founder, your job is to create a series of small, incremental steps that when done together over time, lead to something very impactful. Getting to your first million in revenue or 100 million in revenue seems hard but you break it down into 1,000 little steps."

One of the first is talent.

Attracting Top Talent

How did a small startup steal Uber's CFO?

At Opendoor, Spike had seen the painful process of insuring complex business transactions, but his true takeaway was "the keen focus on talent." Opendoor was a startup with no revenue. Spike reflects that Opendoor's CEO was targeting hires "that in my estimation, seemed to be very far out of our league. At some point, [the CEO] wanted to recruit this guy named Gotham Gupta, the acting CFO at Uber at the time."

As an outsider to Silicon Valley, Spike felt it was "wild to think we [could] just recruit one of the most experienced and sought-after people." The audacity to offer him the job stuck with Spike: "When you think about technology in Silicon Valley, you think a lot about the product." But at Opendoor, Spike learned to ask, "How do I find the best people?"

In a competitive market, recruiting top talent determines success.

Spike preaches: "If you have the right strategy and the right market, your success is entirely determined by the caliber of talent you can recruit and retain." No matter how intelligent or hard-working the founder, Spike continues, one person cannot "propel the business to take over and dominate a market. It's going to be the people you can recruit, and the people they can recruit," and so on. That's why "a lot of the early team at Opendoor have gone on to do amazing things."

Kevin Hartz helped Newfront meet and recruit exceptional talent, in return for leading their competitive Series A round.

When he was investing at Founders Fund, Kevin offered to meet with the Newfront team every week, indefinitely, if he could lead the round. Newfront agreed and has kept that promise ever since. As the founder of Xoom, Eventbrite, and later A* Capital, Kevin had an exceptional network. Whenever Newfront was hiring, Spike recalls, "Kevin Hartz would say, why don't you go meet with this person, because they're the best version I know of this role. [The team] got to see what amazing looked like and sometimes ended up recruiting those people." Seeing good talent teaches you "how to spot talent."

One such introduction was to Mike Brown from Uber.

Mike had been instrumental in building Uber's business in Asia as their second employee in the region. During his tenure, he over-saw exponential growth, managing billions of dollars in gross merchandise volume (GMV) and recruiting thousands of drivers and riders. "Immediately, we saw that Mike was the bar [of excellence they desired]." Spike invited Mike to join some of Newfront's operation meetings, so he could see how things were breaking and offer thoughts on solutions. Intrigued by the challenge, Mike ended up joining Newfront and has been with the business for five years.

Spike and CTO Gordon were amused that as founders, the hier-archy was upended. Important figures in Silicon Valley were asking to meet with Newfront. Had Spike and Gordon graduated from Stanford Business School and been hired by these important figures' companies, Spike chuckles, "I'd be 20 levels removed," reporting to someone, several tiers down from the influential figure, instead of sitting across from them.

The co-founders have stayed together for Newfront's whole journey: "Part of what's worked well for us is we have very different skills, but very similar values. I think the archetype of having co-founders with different skills is well understood, but [co-founders] need values to bring [them] together. Gordon and I were both clear, we wanted to build something impactful, for a long time."

They had their sights on market domination.

Merger

That most mergers fail did not deter Newfront, nor did the advice of its board.

According to Harvard Business School, 70 to 90 percent of mergers and acquisitions fall through. And yet, in 2021, Newfront merged with an incumbent brokerage, ABD, to expand its offerings and geographic reach. This long-standing firm was admired by many in the industry. With a strategic vision, the boutique West Coast brokerage had grown to become a national presence. Brokering insurance for Google, Facebook, and Slack, ABD observed firsthand the risks in these evolving industries.

The merger combined Newfront's tech stack with ABD's insurance talent—a compelling value proposition. Newfront was a brokerage driven by market-leading proprietary technology, while ABD had a deep bench of skilled insurance professionals and was a recognized innovator in employee benefits, insurance, and financial services.

Together, the firms would get closer to achieving their mutual mission: To transform insurance broking for providers and customers with a high-tech and high-touch platform. Under the umbrella of Newfront, they offered an alternative paradigm: Modernizing the industry through technology and data-driven solutions.

The combined entity became a unicorn, valued at $1.35 billion. This expanded footprint and market share have enabled Newfront to better compete. With a new client dashboard and specialist employees, they serve over 10,000 clients and place more than $2 billion in premiums annually.

Today, Newfront is the primary stop for building insurance offerings, partnering with companies from day one and leveraging data analytics to quantify risk. Newfront has sprawled beyond brokering insurance into employee benefits and 401(k) pensions. The brokerage is regulated in 50 states, with 50 licenses, and 100 trading partners.

20 percent of unicorns in the United States find their insurance via Newfront.

Its combination of resources, unified under one roof, creates an unparalleled competitive advantage. Coupled with recent break-throughs in AI, which Newfront is harnessing through data scientists, CEO Spike highlights this moment in time as a "once-in-a-generation opportunity" to reshape the insurance brokerage industry.

The Power Law

Where insurance bets against outlier events, venture capital relies on them.

At the turn of the century, SoftBank achieved a 2,500x return on its stake in Alibaba, whilst Naspers made a 5,500x return on investing in Tencent. In 2012, Venmo was acquired by Braintree for a mere $26 million, which was in turn snapped up by PayPal just a year later for $800 million. By 2020, Venmo alone was independently valued at a staggering $38 billion. This substantial windfall demonstrates the immense wealth-creation potential of venture investments.

In venture capital, success hinges on allocating to a winning company. Even a portfolio with many losing investments can be successful if it includes a single breakout winner. That one right investment can return the entire fund many times over.

This is the power law. It can be seen in earthquakes—rare large ones account for most global damage. In wealth, 1 percent of the world's population controls almost half of global wealth. In online traffic, Google, Netflix, Facebook, Apple, and Microsoft have more traffic than the rest of the internet combined. And in VC, one infrequent wildly successful investment drives the majority of returns for a fund. Of the startups that reach unicorn status, most value is concentrated among just a few key players.

Stanford Professor of Private Equity and Finance, Ilya A. Strebulaev, has proved this in his research. Examining all VC funds of the past 30 years, if you remove the top individual investment from each of these funds, the 95th percentile falls to the 30th percentile. Most VC funds have a standout success. For Accel it was Facebook, for NEA it was Robinhood, for Benchmark it was Uber; although tier-one firms such as these have more than one outlier over the years, sometimes several within a single fund.

"Competition means that only the fittest survive," explains Professor Strebulaev. He highlights that VCs experience a "double-edged" challenge: Competing for capital from investors (LPs) while also vying for the most promising "home-run" startups. The best venture capitalists develop a prepared mindset to spot outsized opportunities. To Ilya, this mindset means, "You believe in the vertical. You believe in this space. You study it. You meet with a lot of founders, [whom] you don't invest money in. So that when you meet *that* founder or *that* team, you [recognize] unique potential."

Over time, to ensure they had equity in home-run startups, many VCs broadened the range of stages they invested in. But in the long run, the VCs who profit have honed a skill in recognizing startups with potential. Ilya reiterates, "If you buy another lottery ticket next week, and [win] another jackpot, that's a skill."

A skill that Andreessen Horowitz, one of the largest venture capital firms in the world by assets under management (AUM), has honed. Known as a16z—due to the 16 letters between Andreessen and Horowitz.

To attract allocations in the best startups, with zero track record, a16z offered operating support to its portfolio companies across hiring, marketing, and sales. Managing Partner, Scott Kupor, explains, "We believe in finding ways to add value to companies... The idea that capital is what distinguishes one player from another is gone. I don't think it's ever coming back."

But not all firms are so conscientious. Spencer Rascoff, co-founder of real-estate marketplace unicorn Zillow, cautions about accepting venture capital: "You're choosing a partner, not just money. You want an investor that you can learn from and that will be loyal in tough times," as fundraising "ratchets up the expectations, which can be pretty dangerous."

More recently, newcomers to venture capital have sought to be that partner. Grammy award-winning electronic music duo, The Chainsmokers, have crossed into venture capital with their early-stage fund, Mantis. When international lockdowns over the Covid-19 pandemic halted their tour, Alex Pall and Drew Taggart reflected. Whilst performing for various Fortune 500 companies, The Chainsmokers had met the founders of Twitch, Dropbox, and Airbnb. These conversations sharpened the pair's curiosity about tech.

The pandemic gave Alex and Drew a valuable opportunity to hone their financial literacy and speak to experts in venture capital. With the encouragement of high-profile founders—including Michael Seibel and Justin Kan, co-founders of the popular live-streaming platform Twitch, who expressed that they would have welcomed The Chainsmokers as investors—they launched a venture fund: Mantis.

The Chainsmokers have an extensive network, which their portfolio companies can leverage to reach customers and partners. Alex attests, "Our superpower is that I can get people on the phone." Mantis offers hands-on support, from strategic advice to recruitment help. Alex prides himself on being available to answer founder questions and doing whatever it takes to help his investments succeed. The fund is committed to earning a reputation as a valuable ally in a startup's journey.

Drawing on his background in music, Alex also helps startups harness the power of narrative. To Alex, "Storytelling is the foundation of everyone's business. It's how you sell your product, hire the first customers and employees, and [pitch] the next venture investor. In some ways, it's a lost art form, but to me, it's what I enjoy working [on] with these different founders."

From caddying to working at a pet store and at Blockbuster, Alex admits "I've had so many shitty jobs. I know the value of a dollar." Putting that capital toward transformative technology gives him purpose: "I don't mind working 14 or 15 hours a day, because [venture capital] doesn't feel like work."

To use Alex's words, "At the end of the day, Drew and I don't feel very accomplished, even though from the outside that might be a crazy statement." The duo wanted to channel their energies into collaborating with innovative entrepreneurs. Doing so has prompted backlash: "When we tell people that The Chainsmokers are investors now, the reaction is, *These guys are idiots. Stay in your lane*. I love being the underdog. We've always had to prove ourselves." Far from being tourists in the space, Mantis has gone on to demonstrate its longevity.

Since its founding in 2019, Mantis has allocated to over 75 startups, at varying stages. Of the fintechs mentioned in this book, Mantis backed Jeeves, Coinbase, and X1 (which was acquired by Robinhood).

Insurance, Everywhere, All At Once

The stories of Vostu, Oscar Health, Ethos, and Newfront illustrate the unpredictable nature of entrepreneurship and the resilience required to navigate "black swan" events—and insure against them.

On the consumer front, Mario Schlosser's tumultuous journey from gaming to healthcare insurance underscores the transferability of skills like designing incentive structures and simulating economies—as well as the need for resilience in the volatile path of an entrepreneur. The rise of Oscar's own "tech mafia" highlights the ripple effect of a successful startup; as alumni venture out, they carry the founder's mindset and a valuable network, enabling them to disrupt new domains.

Indeed, Oscar Health co-founder Josh Kushner went on to found Thrive Capital at 24 years of age, which has backed many fintech unicorns including Monzo, Ramp, Robinhood, and Stripe. Josh's mentor, Joel Cutler of General Catalyst, provided the initial $5 million in seed money for the firm. Today, Thrive is valued upwards of $5 billion and has over $15 billion in assets under management.

On the business insurance front, Newfront carved out a niche by catering to innovative, high-risk businesses. Their platform aided brokers, rather than displacing them, and eventually merged with another brokerage, in keeping with the age-old proverb: "If you can't beat them, join them."

The evolution of insurance, from pooling funds against shipwrecks to enabling space exploration, underscores its vital role in facilitating human progress. Insurance underpins every fintech in this book. And as emerging technologies introduce new risks, insurers like Newfront will be instrumental in "de-risking" innovation.

"Black swan" events—like lawsuits, financial crises, political u-turns or the FTX collapse—are rare and improbable, but have severe consequences. Insurance shields innovation from risk and propels human progress.

Venture capital is another game of outliers which underpins fintech. 75 percent of startups fail. Just 1 percent become unicorns. And yet, the allure of that one breakout success continues to drive the venture capital industry's growth, innovations, and profits. In the past decade alone, VC has grown from a niche asset class to a global force influencing stock markets. Venture capital has the *power* to disrupt industries and create new ones: Robinhood's commission-free stock trading model upended the traditional brokerage industry, attracting millions of new retail investors; Nubank digitized Latin American banking, empowering the underbanked; Venmo brought peer-to-peer payments to mobiles. All of these innovations have been propelled by their investors—and the power law.

TIPS FROM THE TRENCHES

1 Be first-principled. Oscar and Newfront both took approaches that were, at the time, against the grain: Newfront aided rather than replaced brokers, whilst Oscar Health built insurance for the bottom of the economic pyramid first. Newfront continued its contrarian approach by pursuing an acquisition of a legacy insurance company despite the resisting pressures from all sides. Maintain your contrarian approach, even when chasing funding. Don't compromise your vision for short-term funding gains.

2 Build your own tech stack—if you can't, acquire it later. Many generational companies take control of their own stacks. With enough data and complexity, you cannot control each variable and deliver the customer experience you want by relying on others.

3 Be *very* ambitious. Newfront went after talent out of its league, Oscar Health took on the incumbents, and VC bets on outlier "home-run" startups.

10
Unicorns
A Blueprint for Billion-Dollar Growth

Why do some companies reach billion-dollar valuations, known as unicorns, and others fail? Why do some groups of founders and employees proliferate into controlling forces in tech—so-called mafias—and others do not?

Keith Rabois has founded, funded, or helped start 23 unicorns in 23 years and is a core member of the PayPal mafia.

"At Stanford," Keith reminisces, "only the most odd people in the class became founders. It wasn't attractive. They were people who couldn't get real jobs. After the internet exploded, becoming a founder at Stanford became cool, popular, and interesting. And then post-Facebook, it actually became trendy. So it changed the DNA of the people who became founders, shifted their natural biases."

He attests that for founders and investors, "the art" is to ascertain "the archetypes of successful founders" and replicate or back them. "What were their unique attributes? What were their superpowers? How did they present themselves? What enabled their rate of growth? And critical to these questions is, how much is consistent?"

Nine Pillars Underpinning Fintech Unicorns

These pillars represent correlations, not causes. Past performance does not necessarily indicate future success. Of course, if there were an exact formula, Keith exclaims, "The job of an investor would probably be easy." However, there's no harm in studying the actions, products, and execution of founders who have navigated the intellectual maze to unicorn status, generational company, and beyond.

Behavioral Characteristics

Pillar 1: Thrive in Chaos, Crisis, and Conflict

Unicorn founders thrive in the chaotic startup landscape.

LinkedIn co-founder and former COO of PayPal, Reid Hoffman, believes, "The first counterintuitive rule [of entrepreneurship] is to embrace chaos. You're in an uncertain environment, so you don't have perfect control over it. You learn a form of *calm triage*— similar things happen with emergency room doctors and firefighters. You're going to be very prioritized and very focused."

Amid the chaos, Jeff Epstein, former CFO of Oracle, likens his past role to a "shock absorber," ensuring the stability and safety of companies. "If things are tough, you want to be the one spreading hope and saying things are going to get better… If the company is doing badly, everyone knows, so you don't need to beat them up on it." On the other hand, "When a company's doing well, I want to try to help them do even better and be somewhat critical." Jeff's approach takes cues from "the famous saying [that] the job of a reporter is to comfort the afflicted and afflict the comfortable."

The best leaders are decisive in chaos. Jeff emphasizes, "When there are big opportunities, have you created financial flexibilities to invest in a great opportunity and invest enough? That willingness to make a decision is something that takes experience and judgment. Inexperienced people default to: We'll just do a little bit of everything… make 20 small bets and hope that something works, which is a non-decision decision."

Unicorn founders see opportunity in a crisis.

Back in 2000, in the UK, the discount travel (and fintech enabled) marketplace Lastminute.com became a household name. That March, Lastminute.com went public on the London Stock

Exchange, its valuation peaking at £768 million. It was the height of the dotcom bubble. In the United States, the NASDAQ stock exchange, heavily weighted with tech stocks, had more than doubled in value over one year.

Then the dotcom bubble burst.

Investors realized that the prices of these unprofitable internet stocks had been driven up by speculation and many had poor business models. Investors rushed to sell their holdings. Lastminute.com's share price plummeted to less than half of its issue price and the NASDAQ fell by 75 percent, wiping out around $5 trillion in market value as tech stocks crashed. Numerous over-hyped dotcom companies filed for bankruptcy. The deflating bubble sparked a recession and froze the IPO market for tech companies for several years.

Pete Flint, an early employee at LastMinute.com, recalls that what "stuck out during that time was if you are persistent and creative enough, you could solve almost any problem. Once you see that work it's incredibly empowering. Because nothing [is] impossible." Applying this to a new asset class, Pete Flint went on to co-found Trulia, a real estate listing platform, which IPOed and then merged with competitor Zillow for $2.5 billion. Both had survived the 2008 financial crisis which decimated the property market.

Indeed, the best leaders thrive in the face of conflict.

Martha Lane Fox—co-founder of Lastminute.com, who has since served on the boards of Chanel, WeTransfer, and Twitter (now X)—has some valuable advice on navigating conflict. Serving on Twitter's board during its tumultuous acquisition, Martha saw Elon Musk become a 10 percent stakeholder in Twitter, decline a board seat, and offer $44 billion to buy Twitter outright. He later backed down, sparking a legal battle between Twitter and Elon Musk, forcing the acquisition to go through. At the height of this controversy, Martha recalls someone suggesting Twitter's leadership "could all attend the Hunger Games," not realizing that "actually we all worked really well together... [it's just] no company should have to be put through that so publicly."

A vital peace preserver is the relationship between the Board Chair and CEO. Bret Taylor—now Chair of the OpenAI Board, the developer of ChatGPT—was Twitter's Chair over the takeover. In the face of media scrutiny and legal challenges, Martha recalls "he only ever presented as calm... Despite all that hideousness, he was trying to manage, He was scrabbling massively behind the scenes and doing so much work. That was an extremely impressive characteristic."

Martha emphasizes the importance of constructive debate within the board. "Debate, critiquing, and challenge are fundamental," she explains, "but conflict, actively shouting at each other, isn't helpful." To achieve this, Martha believes building trust is key. "It's about keeping people in touch outside board meetings," she continues, "understanding where people are coming from. Allowing and encouraging everyone to speak, and making collective decisions based on everyone's view, rather than just one loud voice."

Finding refuge in demanding times is also crucial for Martha. Reading, spending time with friends, and traveling were outlets throughout her career. Whether that was at work as a young founder, which she recalls was "hard, lonely, and difficult. I was young. I was missing my twenties. Even though I had an amazing business partner." Or during her recovery from a horrific, near-fatal car accident in Morocco in 2004, which left her with 26 broken bones and internal bleeding. "But I survived," she emphasizes. "I've had many moments in my life where I've gone back to those fundamentals."

Stanford Professor and neuroscience expert Baba Shiv finds that elite athletes are better at processing stress, failures, and crises than their counterparts, often presenting higher heart rate variabilities. Generational fintech founders show similar characteristics: remaining calm in chaos, being decisive in crisis, and refusing to accept failure as final. They are wartime CEOs when needed. They are adaptive and insatiable learners. They are all in.

Pillar 2: Contrarian Thinking

According to PayPal mafia member, Reid Hoffman, the best start-ups and companies are "contrarian [because] it changes the world if it's right. What's the thing that few other people see?"

Reid reflects on life after PayPal. "Everybody thought all the interesting things on the internet had [already] been done." Contrary to the prevailing attitude, he believed "the internet's really important, and everybody else is looking in the other direction." With this perspective, Reid led Greylock Partners' investment into Airbnb. "Most people thought it was creepy. No one's going to rent rooms from random strangers, [it's] too dangerous." But Reid thought, "If this does work out, it's going to be huge." Ten years later, the iconic hospitality disruptor listed on the Nasdaq.

There's no secret recipe for building up a contrarian muscle. According to Reid, you must keep "applying those lenses constantly to everything you're encountering." Even Reid Hoffman doesn't get it right every time. Blinded by his experience at PayPal, Reid passed on the opportunity to invest in the generational fintech companies Stripe and Square.

With contrarian thinking you can even reframe an economic downturn. Kevin Hartz, the co-founder of Eventbrite and Xoom (the money-transfer startup acquired by PayPal), recommends: "Lean in incredibly aggressively in those down periods... That's the dirty little secret of Google and Netflix and PayPal and Amazon. They were examples of four companies just cranking during that down period, that were miscounted."

An investor too, Kevin Hartz reflects, "In a bubble [when] things collapse, there's this massive aversion to growth. Of course, there are great fledgling companies still in the making, so as soon as everyone's running for the hills, one should step up engagement and search for great companies and trends."

To Kevin, the ultimate contrarian remains Peter Thiel, the co-founder of PayPal and Founders Fund. Kevin often asks himself: "What would Peter do?... It's always embarrassing pointing that out. But when it comes to challenging ideas, Peter is still that original thinker. [Peter questions], what if this seemingly obvious truth isn't a truth at all? He's still incredibly engaged, opinionated and curious—and always has wise words... It's a challenge to keep looking at a problem from different perspectives." Peter would ask colleagues, "If you have a 10-year plan of how to get [somewhere], why can't you do this in six months?" Could you condense a six-month plan into a week? Or a week-long plan into a day? Often our perceptions shape reality, and teams can find a way to get things done more quickly. Kevin admits that Peter is "dramatically wrong sometimes, it's the nature of a contrarian." But it's not often and Kevin likes to work with people who are usually right.

Contrarian thinking often aligns with timing. Few ask, "Why now?" Braintree's former CEO, Bill Ready, saw the *why now* of the mobile internet era. David from Nubank saw the *why now* of disrupting banking incumbents in Brazil. Contrarian thinking means actively challenging the status quo based on first principles. Why is that not possible? What if this works?

Pillar 3: Long-term Orientation, Long-term Relationships

To build a long-term company, you must build long-term relationships—from the beginning. Addressing conflict early is conducive to longevity.

Reid Hoffman encourages founders to "work with people [as if] you're planning on working with them your entire life. When you have conflicts, surface them early in productive, constructive ways. When you iterate on relationships, surface the things you like, but also the things that conflict." That way, you can create a shared mission that you both invest in. Reid advocates that two partners working together effectively achieve more than several in isolation: "One plus one is greater than five."

"You're going to want to create institutions that outlive you anyway," Reid continues. "The best way for them to outlive you is to help them get to that stage, [where it's] going without you being there." Founders cannot implement their visions alone. They need exceptional talent around them. Newfront founder Spike Lipkin emphasizes that "If you have the right strategy and the right market, your success is entirely determined by the caliber of talent you can recruit and retain." He actively pursued top talent from giants like Uber, recognizing that exceptional hires can propel a company forward. David Vélez often chose people who were all-in on the company's mission and who quickly grasped Nubank's concept, even if they lacked traditional experience. At PayPal, Reid Hoffman partly attributed the company's success to its ability to attract "very high energy, high talent, high IQ, young people."

A lot of the founder journeys chronicled in this book emphasize transparency among their teams, to build longevity. Monzo livestreamed all their meetings for anyone—even competitors—to tune into. This openness not only fostered trust among employees but also became a powerful marketing tool. Transparency and candid communication are what enabled the co-founders to get through the most difficult periods together.

The same is true for investors. Scott Kupor, Managing Partner at a16z, embraces a key tenet of the legendary venture firm: Open and honest communication. One of a16z's founding partners, Ben Horowitz, known for his direct approach, challenges Scott and the team to "sharpen the contradiction," to clarify specific points of disagreement and confront those issues. At a16z, rather than ignore the elephant in the room, the team placed it on the table and discussed the problem. Scott attests, "What I've learned, mostly from Ben, is you've just got to deal with these things. All the coping mechanisms you try to put in place just never work. The reality? As painful as a direct conversation is, the likelihood of getting to a good outcome is just so much better."

Kevin Hartz, who co-founded Eventbrite with his wife Julia, emphasizes the value of "having real partners and listening to them. Having seen a lot of messy founder divorces, it's so meaningful to win the war, not just the battle." This can sometimes mean giving tough feedback when it needs to be given, so it doesn't come back as a major issue down the line.

Sarah Smith, former Bain Capital Ventures Partner and executive at Facebook and Quora, echoes this long term orientation. Research from Bain reveals that founder-led companies are four to five times more likely to be top quartile performers in public markets. For example, an index of Fortune 500 companies with active founder involvement outperformed the rest by 3.1 times over the past 15 years.

At Quora, Sarah scaled the team from 40 to over 160 people, including hiring 17-year-old intern Alex Wang, who later founded the decacorn Scale.ai. Sarah also established Facebook's first office in Austin. To improve a CEO's chances of long-term success, Sarah offers PeopleOps office hours and a CEO 360 as part of her VC fund services, "tipping the odds in favor of the CEO." She goes on, "It's the only person in the company that doesn't get a performance review, but arguably has by far the most impact on long-term returns of that investment."

To ensure a startup survives, you need a great team to steward it. Address conflict and promote transparency to build a company that outlasts you.

Product Characteristics

Pillar 4: Focus on Customers > Competitors

Peter Thiel, PayPal co-founder, famously believes "competition is for losers." Reid Hoffman, former PayPal COO, elaborates, "Some people have mistakenly thought that they prefer competition because it validates the market. I think you [should] want incompetent competition, and no competition can be a good version of it." Reid explains that fintech as "regulated software" is a great place to start, as "other startups tend to be fewer and far between, and incumbents tend to be shackled about how they operate. Software allows you to move very fast. Fintech and payments give you that space [because of the regulation]."

The counterpoint: Competition can be a powerful motivator, whether that is the rivalry of Monzo vs. Revolut or Stripe's brilliance forcing Braintree to strive toward new heights. Indeed, incumbents push startups, too. Alex Rampell, a16z General Partner, summarizes, "The battle between every startup and incumbent comes down to whether the startup gets distribution before the incumbent gets innovation."

Co-founder of real estate platform Trulia, Pete Flint, believes that rivalry fueled his startup's success. Trulia would launch a product, only to see Zillow, a competing real estate listing platform, unveil a strikingly similar feature a month later. On occasion, Pete thought, "We must have a mole in the company. How did they do that?" But it soon became apparent that there was an optimal and natural roadmap to developing a marketplace that Zillow and Trulia were independently following and therefore overlapping. At times, Trulia improved upon features Zillow had launched. Other times it was the reverse. The two learned from each other.

Although Trulia and Zillow were competitors, together they accelerated the adoption of online real estate advertising. In Pete's words, "The biggest challenge we [both] had was getting money from real estate agents," encouraging them to switch from inefficient advertising—in newspapers or on Google—to their real estate marketplaces. "More people, with different approaches, make the market much bigger." So in some ways, Zillow and Trulia were always working in tandem.

This reframe is powerful. Venmo's true competition was cash; competitors aided consumers' migration toward digital currency. Ripple's true competition was SWIFT; other cryptocurrencies accelerated blockchain adoption.

Competition is a fine balance though, Pete cautions. "If you didn't have any competition, you're probably in a less interesting market. But clearly, if you have too much competition, it's a fool's errand."

Where rivals exist, founders have a choice: Fixate on their competitors or their customers. Eventbrite co-founder, Kevin Hartz, recalls, "I probably obsessed too much [about] competition. It can be unhealthy... Focusing on the customer is a much healthier mechanism." Indeed, Zillow's co-founder Spencer Rascoff believed,

"If we build for Harriet the homeowner, Rachel the renter, over the long term that would vanquish competitors." Pete Flint rejects the "Silicon Valley [concept] that you've got to ignore your competition." Keeping a close eye on Zillow's product shipments ensured Trulia was not blindsided. But Trulia also "carved its own path." Trulia differentiated from Zillow, adding crime maps to determine neighborhood safety and giving cost projections of owning a property.

The best differentiator from competitors is serving your consumer, as we have seen in the superior NPSs of fintechs in this book. According to venture capitalist Ali Tamaseb, over 60 percent of unicorns solve an acute problem, whilst 30 percent improve upon the existing market offerings by saving time or money. Jeeves *solved* transnational companies' problems managing finances across borders. SoFi *improved* upon the existing extortionate student loan repayments. Ripple's XRP cryptocurrency *solved* the need for pre-funded accounts when exchanging currencies. Bored Ape *improved* the quality of and market for NFTs.

Solve or alleviate a customer pain point with user-friendly interfaces, innovations, or cost efficiencies to stand apart.

Pillar 5: Democratize Data or a Service—This Can Be Afforded by Finding Cost Efficiencies

To Roelof Botha, Managing Partner at Sequoia, a common denominator of fintech breakthroughs is democratizing services. "[If] we go back to the founding of Wells Fargo, only the wealthy had bank accounts." Part of Wells Fargo's popularity lay in "democratizing access to banking services to people who otherwise were stuffing cash under mattresses." In fintech, Roelof continues, "There's a history of creating a cost breakthrough or a distribution breakthrough that enables you to provide financial products that people [previously] couldn't afford."

Indeed, many of Roelof's most successful investments democratize: YouTube makes information accessible, Square empowers small businesses to process card payments, 23andMe grants access to genetic analysis. Roelof learned this firsthand as CFO of PayPal, which democratized P2P payments for small businesses.

Democratization is enabled by finding cost savings.

Roelof explains, "A lot of new financial services breakthroughs happen because there's a cost advantage." Cost advantages can come in many forms: Technology improvements, underwriting (evaluating risk), customer acquisition, and vertical integration. Some of the most successful unicorns combine several of these.

Unlike businesses that deal with physical products (atoms), fin-tech is driven by revolutionary ideas and processes (concepts). Roelof emphasizes, "Financial services are a conceptual business, not an atom's business, so you can innovate very quickly as new technologies [emerge]. New technology enables radical cost reductions."

One of Roelof's investments benefitted from the cost advantages of developments in technology and underwriting. Square—later renamed Block, which spawned Cash App—enables offline merchants to process credit cards. Before Square, card terminals were obstructively expensive to small businesses, with high monthly fees, due to minimal underwriting data. When customers pay by card, the payment processor typically sends the money to the merchant three days before receiving the money from the card user. Therefore payment processors need data to assess the risks associated with providing credit to the merchant. In the absence of data, payment processors were charging high fees.

In our modern era, using connected data systems and the internet, Square could underwrite people at scale, reducing the need for high terminal fees. "Benefitting from the dividend of smartphones," Square could also inexpensively make hardware that processed credit cards. In doing so, Square's user base ballooned to millions of monthly merchants. Square's ability to democratize a service was underpinned by cost advantages.

Earlier in the book, we saw Robinhood democratize zero-fee stock market trading, which forced other trading platforms to follow suit. Robinhood was able to offer zero-fee trades due to its cost advantage. The virality of its service, free trading, dispelled any customer acquisition costs; Robinhood had a waiting list, whereas broker incumbents had enormous advertising budgets. The platform's tech stack reduced operating costs in comparison to its rivals.

Trulia and Zillow also made B2B real estate data publicly available, allowing consumers to make informed investments. This democratization of information supercharged word-of-mouth marketing—free customer acquisition.

Others served the underbanked: Nubank brought digital banking to Latin America. Cash App sought to serve more remote portions of the American population. Alibaba's Taobao brought e-marketplace services to China's rural communities and Alipay mapped customers' credit histories based on atypical data, such as satellite images of their harvest or mileage driven.

Roelof emphasizes, "Cost is the competitive advantage." Google's obsession with cost—vertically integrating to create their own data centers to reduce third-party fees—enabled the search engine to grow sustainably. Amazon Web Services (AWS) scaled in the same way. Capital efficiency through a lower cost base further enables startups to do more with the VC funding that they do raise, drive better unit economics, and more easily access additional capital for future scale.

While some startups democratize services by making them free, Roelof emphasizes the distinction between cost efficiency and price. "Price is not a competitive advantage. Prices we choose, that's marketing. [I'm looking for a] fundamental cost advantage," achieved by making services cheaper through efficiencies.

Democratization of services fuels virality. Fund this by finding a cost efficiency.

Pillar 6: Putting the Tech in Fintech

World-class technology stacks deliver a distinct customer experience.

Controlling their technology stack, fintechs can customize and innovate at a pace that third-party solutions cannot match.

Nubank's CTO emphasized the importance of being the system of record to ensure complete control over operations and customer interactions. Unimpeded by limitations and delays of external technology, Nubank was able to adapt swiftly to market demands and regulatory changes, setting it apart from competitors.

Possessing your tech stack can save costs in the long run. Monzo, for example, initially relied on third-party APIs, which resulted in a high cost per user. By building more technology in-house, Monzo slashed this cost from around £65 to £20 per user. Owning the tech stack, or at least the source of truth on customer data, enables companies to become a system of record. Their customers are critically dependent on them, and better still, other businesses may want to use their data to build on top of their platform.

Capital One's Nigel Morris concludes, "Velocity is only possible if you have the right tech stack."

Operational Characteristics

Pillar 7: Piggyback Platform Changes

Identify complementary fast-growing platforms.

Pete Flint, co-founder of Trulia, recalls piggybacking Google's explosive growth by providing much-needed content for the search engine and using SEO as a nascent, yet effective, marketing strategy.

PayPal similarly leveraged eBay's leading position to gain access to a large customer base and become the preferred checkout option. In turn, Kevin Hartz, an angel investor in PayPal, describes their partnership as "mutually beneficial... Most biz dev deals are terrible. Two companies want to do something, and they're usually grossly misaligned." But PayPal was an exception. "PayPal was 99 percent on eBay, so people saw it as this kind of parasite," leeching off the platform's success, "whereas we saw auctions were the first vertical, and we were going to help them diversify into more."

Serial entrepreneur and investor Kevin Hartz exemplifies the strategy of building upon existing platforms, having founded

Xoom, a cross-border money transfer service that leveraged PayPal's infrastructure (acquired by PayPal in 2015). He went on to co-found Eventbrite and A* Capital. Kevin observes that successful platforms often act as springboards for others: "Stripe's entire business is a platform for others to build payment applications upon." This reflects the growing trend where companies offer APIs and tools, empowering developers to seamlessly integrate functionalities like payments into their applications.

"If you look at tech history, when a new platform emerges, whether it's the Windows operating system or it's iOS and the iPhone, whether it's PayPal or Stripe, developers build on top of those new platforms, and that's where a tremendous amount of value accrues." Kevin has seen this happen "time after time" and laments the "misnomer of calling anything that's built using OpenAI a wrapper." So when the tech industry knocks these products "calling them *just a wrapper on top of OpenAI*, a thin wrapper that doesn't add value, it discounts what has been achieved through history." There is a pattern where "a great platform gets developed and released to the world," and great companies are built on top.

In launching ChatGPT, OpenAI's CEO Sam Altman has "unleashed the power of LLMs." Developing these foundational large language models (LLMs) that ChatGPT relies on "took a very separate expertise." Just as OpenAI was built on LLMs, Kevin argues, "We should be working with founders that are building to extend its capabilities, because there's an infinite number of ideas that can be built on top of OpenAI."

Piggybacking does not have to be restricted to emerging technologies. Tencent's WeChat Pay successfully beat Alibaba's Alipay in the Red Envelope War, jumping on the cultural tradition of sending red envelopes at New Year. In turn, many startups have built on top of Alipay and WeChat Pay.

Whilst complementary fast-growing platforms can turbocharge growth, one unicorn founder advocates another trait, above all others…

Pillar 8: Harness Network Effects

Pete Flint, co-founder of Trulia and the VC fund NFX, has based his investing thesis on network effects—where value proposition grows with user adoption. What unites the likes of Twitter, Amazon, Apple, Meta, Uber, Salesforce, and Tesla are network effects. They create the strongest form of defensibility, alongside scale, branding, and embedding—meaning software that is so integrated into operations that it's almost impossible to switch providers such as Salesforce's CRM or Visa's payment network. According to NFX, approximately 70 percent of value creation in tech can be attributed to network effects.

NFX has identified 16 types (and counting), so you can bake them into your startup's strategy. They range from direct network effects (such as a telephone, where both parties require hardware for the service to work) to two-sided marketplaces (examples being Alibaba and Venmo) to data network effects (powering recommendation engines or AI models) to user-contributed content (for example, social media) to attracting complementary products (products built on top of Braintree) and monetary network effects (like Bitcoin gaining value the more widespread it becomes).

Jeeves, the corporate cross-border finance platform, illustrates this principle well. As Jeeves expands into more countries, the more valuable its service to transnational corporations. This breakneck growth provides value for its customers and establishes a defensible moat of network effects. But it is hard to get from zero to one. Startups that rely on network effects typically require VC funding to reach a critical mass of users.

Both Zillow and Trulia faced the classic "chicken and egg" problem typical of early-stage marketplaces: Attracting enough suppliers (real estate listings) to draw in consumers, and vice versa. Trulia initially tackled this by scraping listings from broker websites and leveraging SEO to attract users. Similarly, Zillow focused on providing value through its "Zestimates," offering users property valuations before it had a comprehensive listings database. The same solutions to the "cold-start" problem can be applied across industries. Once scaled, the winner reaps most of the profits. With Zillow and Trulia, a merger created a decisive market leader that had defensibility from network effects.

According to James Currier, General Partner at NFX, "Having a network effect is *the single most predictable* attribute of the highest-value technology companies—other than perhaps having a great CEO."

Pillar 9: Blistering Velocity

Should the market require it, the best startups move at lightning speed, or Blitzscale, prioritizing speed over efficiency (as outlined in Reid Hoffman and Chris Yeh's book *Blitzscaling*). When faced with a crisis, these founders find a way through—repositioning their product offering or business model or even expanding into new verticals—and follow this path with conviction.

"In PayPal's case, [users joined for the] free credit card processing and $10 bounties. The press and eBay [which later acquired PayPal] all thought we were going to die. You've got an exponential cost curve of credit card processing because your transactions are going up and you're giving free credit card pricing. But [PayPal's critics] didn't realize once you got the network established, you could flip over to become a master merchant." With significant traffic, PayPal could negotiate better rates with credit card companies and profit from being the market leader.

Reid shares, "Part of Blitzscaling is pouring on the gas, spending capital, both financial and human, really inefficiently. Normally this seems like a bad way to take risks and [a great way to] lose money. But if the prize is big—something with network effects, [like] Airbnb, PayPal, LinkedIn, Facebook—then the prize makes it worth pouring on that gas." In those cases, "It's worth spending intensely and inefficiently to be first to market scale—the returns are still very much worth it."

Nevertheless, since fintech is often a low-margin, high-volume business, startups must have a clear line of sight for their unit economics, once they reach a critical mass of users.

Blistering velocity also applies to pivoting products. Robinhood began as high-frequency trading software before pivoting to an app for retail trading. Venmo began as a means to purchase MP3s from musicians until its founders stumbled upon a larger problem: The need for mobile peer-to-peer payments.

Startups must also be agile in pivoting revenue models, as external market conditions shift or mature.

Some are forced. The Federal Reserve's interest rate cuts during the Covid-19 lockdowns decimated digital business bank Mercury's revenue model overnight, which had relied on earning interest on client deposits. To rebuild this 60 percent decline in revenue, Mercury identified that e-commerce was flourishing during the pandemic and shifted its primary revenue stream to card interchange fees, with a small commission paid by merchants for each customer card transaction.

Again, in the wake of SVB's collapse, Mercury again took brisk action. Partnering with FDIC-insured institutions over the weekend, they ensured millions in deposit coverage for their clients, surpassing the protections offered by SVB and traditional banks.

Other revenue model shifts were not forced, but rather evolutionary progress. Zillow, after merging with Trulia, commanded enough market share to implement an auction-style pricing model—as Google does with search rankings—in which real estate brokers bid for premium positioning on their website.

If agility is responding to setbacks, just as vital is pinpointing tailwinds of growth that you can profit from.

Once product-market fit is achieved, companies rapidly add additional products, services, and geographies. As increasing competition eroded SoFi's differentiator of offering lower-interest-rate student loans, the startup was forced to diversify its revenue model, adding new services. Recognizing they had a loyal client base whose banking needs swelled as they aged, SoFi expanded into other verticals: Car repayments, mortgages, and investment products, eventually morphing into a licensed digital bank.

We saw Alibaba expand from B2B into B2C marketplaces to fend off eBay and then launch a payments service (Alipay) to serve its e-commerce platform. Witnessing this growth, Tencent's WeChat branched into payments (WeChat Pay). In an ever-changing market, startups that succeed adapt products or revenue models with blistering velocity.

These nine traits that unicorns have in common—these blueprints for billion-dollar success—have been absorbed by early teams and carried forward into new ventures, transforming how money operates across the globe.

Fintech Super Founders

How do the case studies of *Fintech Wars* stack up in real life? What does the data say about unicorn founders?

Venture capitalist Ali Tamaseb's comprehensive study on US-based unicorns, Super Founders, found there's no disadvantage to being a non-technical CEO; and whilst the majority of unicorns have two or three co-founders, 20 percent have a solo founder at their helm.

Serial entrepreneurs have founded almost 60 percent of unicorns. A significant portion had their initial ventures fail, some even twice; but, as Ali Tamaseb discovered, those that went on to attain an annual revenue of over $10 million or an exit of more than $50 million were much more likely to build a unicorn. Ali calls these "Super Founders." Immad from Mercury, Chris from Ripple, Kevin from Eventbrite, and Dileep from Jeeves are a testament to this. Ali shares, "The best preparation to start a multibillion-dollar company is to start a $10 million company first, and the best preparation for that is to start something, anything." We saw this with the Venmo founders, Tom from Monzo, and Mario from Oscar, who all had limited success before founding their respective unicorns (although GoCardless would later cross the billion-dollar threshold). Indeed, those with past failures were still 1.6 times more likely to found a unicorn in Ali's analysis. SG from Toss took eight failures to hit gold on his ninth. Although 70 percent of unicorn CEOs have previously founded or worked at another startup, this proportion is significantly lower for the second-in-command.

Fifty percent of unicorn founders have over 10 years of experience; however, that past experience need not be in the same industry. In fact, most unicorn founders have not worked in their industry before. Real estate platforms Zillow and Trulia's founders began at various travel startups. Both were outsiders to real estate but had scaled marketplaces. Jack Dorsey founded the Twitter (now X) and then payments startup Square. David from Nubank was an outsider to Brazil.

Despite the majority of unicorn founders in this industry being male, leading figures such as Martha Lane Fox are quickly changing the landscape. There are numerous other examples. Shuo Wang is the Chief Revenue Officer and co-founder of decacorn Deel, an all-in-one HR and payroll platform for global teams. Shuo led the company in scaling from $1 million to $100 million in Annual Recurring Revenue (ARR) in under 20 months. Christina Cacioppo is the CEO and Founder of Vanta, a security and compliance platform valued at over $2.5 billion. Yada Piyajomkwan co-founded the Indonesian brokerage Ajaib; Tessa Wijaya co-founded the Southeast Asian payment infrastructure company Xendit; Julie Coin co-founded DriveWealth, which provides API-driven brokerage infrastructure. Talent investor Entrepreneur First, co-founded and led by Alice Bentinck, has helped seed a number of unicorns and is valued at over $500 million in its own right. Fern Mandelbaum, Managing Partner of Emerson Collective, suggests diverse entrepreneurs "turn [their] difference into an advantage," sharing the Eleanor Roosevelt quote, "You gain strength, courage, and confidence by every experience in which you really stop to look fear in the face. You must do the thing which you think you cannot do."

Being the first product on the market is not as important as once thought. According to Ali, over half of US-based unicorns were built in established markets dominated by several incumbents. In fact, this signaled that the opportunity was great and there were captive customers. Sixty-five percent of US-based unicorns sought to take market share from other players, often those who were established and outdated, rather than create a new market.

For aspiring founders, this data would suggest that finance revenue pools are still ripe for disruption.

The Future of Money

Fintech Has Come a Long Way

Technology has come a long way since the dotcom era.

To purchase deals on Lastminute.com, customers entered their credit card details into the website, assuming booking was a seamless experience. It wasn't. The information entered the Lastminute. com database and the team would quickly but *manually* fax details to the supplier.

So things could go wrong.

In co-founder Martha's words, "I remember losing bits of paper and booking the wrong hotels and things not existing when we thought they existed. This was all at the last minute. Right?" Now code and even AI automate many of these transactions.

Meanwhile, in the United States, as rival discount travel startup Hotwire began to gain traction among users, the team soon discovered a small percentage of underhand bookings. Co-founder Spencer Rascoff reveals, "A small to sometimes medium-sized problem [with early customers]... was prostitution rings booking hotel rooms using stolen credit cards." On Hotwire, customers could save a ton of money on bookings, but the hotel was not revealed until after purchase. These rings were booking five or so hotel rooms per night with stolen cards. Hotwire eventually solved the issue with fraud detection tools.

Back in 2014, the payments ecosystem was dominated by traditional point-of-sale (POS) systems like card terminals and paper-based business transactions. Digital innovations like mobile wallets and peer-to-peer (P2P) payments were just beginning to emerge.

Since then, digital challengers such as Nubank and Monzo have redefined banking with user-friendly, transparent services. The rise of e-commerce, driven by platforms such as PayPal, has created new livelihoods and expanded economic opportunities globally. Meanwhile, the widespread adoption of mobile wallets and real-time payment systems, particularly in emerging markets, has significantly increased financial inclusion, as seen with Alipay in China. Despite the hype, cryptocurrencies have yet to become mainstream in payments, but the foundational changes in infrastructure and digital tools have set the stage for future advances.

And yet, there are so many other inspiring and intriguing stories we could have delved into—Stripe, Simple Bank, Plaid, Chime, Shopify, Deel, Marcus by Goldman Sachs, Coinbase, Klarna, Ramp, Brex, Intuit, and more. They have reinvented payments, payroll, credit cards, banking data, and buy-now-pay-later credit.

Over the past decade, the fintech landscape has changed dramatically.

Fintech Futures

Looking ahead, the next decade promises even more transformation in fintech.

Instant payments are expected to become ubiquitous, offering diverse settlement options and transforming working capital management for businesses. The integration of enterprise resource planning (ERP) tools with bank accounts will break down silos between accounting systems and payments, enabling the seamless bookkeeping and tracking of transactions.

More and more companies will start to look and act like fintech companies. Embedded payments will permeate various industries, turning software platforms into financial operating systems that automate and optimize financial processes; in doing so, this will fulfill General Partner at a16z Angela Strange's prediction that every company will become a fintech company.

As the digital transformation expands into traditionally paper-based segments and underpenetrated regions, the total addressable market for fintech solutions will grow exponentially. Innovations in AI will enhance risk management and fraud detection, ensuring the security and efficiency of this rapidly evolving ecosystem. With these advancements, the value created in the fintech sector is poised to soar, promising a future where financial services are more inclusive, efficient, and integrated than ever before.

What will be the first trillion-dollar fintech company? Will Apple continue on its warpath developing Apple Wallet? Will Meta take a second shot at metaverse currencies? Will Nubank scale to a billion users? The decentralized cryptocurrency Bitcoin has already passed the trillion-dollar market cap threshold. Will Ethereum be next?

Despite the Ambition, Fintech is Still a Force for "Good"

In the grand narrative of ongoing fintech wars, technology's role as a force for good cannot be lost. Consider Kiva, a non-profit fintech providing microloans to entrepreneurs in developing regions. Kiva's peer-to-peer lending model has distributed over $2 billion in small investments, transforming lives, lifting families out of poverty, and spurring local economic growth.

Kiva is not just in the service of funding micro-entrepreneurs; it's about human connection. As co-founder Jessica Jackley shares, "The stories we tell about each other matter very much. The stories we tell ourselves about our own lives matter. And most of all, I think the way that we participate in each other's stories is of deep importance." This philosophy is embedded in Kiva's platform, which allows lenders to connect directly with borrowers, fostering a sense of global community and empathy.

Elsewhere, Remitly, a digital remittance service, helps millions of immigrants send money to their families worldwide. Bypassing the high fees and slow processing of traditional remittance, Remitly redistributes global wealth with technology.

Nova Credit enables immigrants, who lack local credit histories, to access credit. By translating international credit records for domestic lenders, Nova Credit smooths integration and promotes broader financial mobility.

Misha Esipov, Nova's founder (and a mentor to Spike in the early days of Newfront), shares that even with a strong mission, "entrepreneurship is hard and it doesn't get all that much easier eight years in. We entered this problem space with a lot of naive optimism believing that we could pull this off in a year or two; it took us a lot longer." Just as Nova found product-market fit, Misha had the "rug pulled out" from under him by the Covid-19 pandemic. Yet the team persevered. Fast forward—Nova has data on close to 4 billion people around the world. Misha suggests, "Anytime you feel lost around direction, the answer is always get closer to the customer." Nova supports people who are "pursuing the American dream, or the Canadian dream, or the British dream. [Nova's customers] come from all over the world to build a better life for themselves. [Nova] allows them to make that better life come a little faster. Capital accelerates time."

PayJoy addresses the digital divide. Using proprietary lock technology (locking devices if payments are missed), PayJoy enables individuals without credit histories to purchase smartphones on installment plans—increasing internet access in underserved populations and helping users build credit histories, the foundations for broader financial inclusion.

GiveDirectly connects charitable donors with individuals in extreme poverty. This giving approach cuts out middlemen, reduces overheads, and empowers recipients to decide how best to improve their lives. By combining the efficiency of digital payments with a trust in the agency of the poor, GiveDirectly challenges traditional aid models, making philanthropy more transparent and effective.

Carbon trading platforms leverage fintech to combat climate change, monetizing environmental stewardship and allowing companies to offset their emissions. By aligning economic incentives with ecological preservation, these marketplaces accelerate the global transition to low-carbon.

And in the next era of the internet, the transformative potential of blockchain and cryptocurrencies could be unlocked to bring all of these applications on-chain. By offering decentralized and transparent transaction methods, blockchain technology is paving the way for more secure and efficient financial systems, owned by individuals, not institutions.

Returning to the proverb offered to Capital One co-founder Nigel Morris by a friend—"The darkest time is just before the dawn"—we have seen the dark side of fintech. Sabotaged IPOs, mutinies that made unicorns, bank collapses, 1,000,000 percent returns, pseudonymous founders, lawsuits, missing billions, and jail time. Yet, out of startup wars and conflict come innovation and optimism.

And now we are looking into the dawn.

SOURCES

Introduction

Interview with Hans Morris, Managing Partner, Nyca Partners

Interview with Nigel Morris, Co-founder, Capital One

Boston Consulting Group (2023) *Global Fintech 2023—Reimagining the Future of Finance*, https://web-assets.bcg.com/69/51/ f9ce8b47419fb0bb9aeb50a77ee6/bcg-qed-global-fintech-report-2023-reimagining-the-future-of-finance-may-2023.pdf (archived at https://perma.cc/RM4G-6HAK)

Brynjolfsson, E., Rock, D., and Syverson, C. (2021) "The productivity J-curve: How intangibles complement general purpose technologies" *American Economic Journal: Macroeconomics*, 13(1), 333–72, DOI: 10.1257/mac.20180386

Buffett, W. E. (1987) "Chairman's Letter," https://www.berkshirehathaway.com/letters/1987.html (archived at https://perma.cc/V9CW-8PDY)

Capital One (2009) *Capital One Reports 2008 Net Loss*, https://investor.capitalone.com/static-files/dcc45bca-e3e7-407a-aae4-2f05c9f11647 (archived at https://perma.cc/C6SS-99Y4)

Da Costa, P. N. (2014) "Bernanke: 2008 Meltdown Was Worse Than Great Depression," *Wall Street Journal*, https://www.wsj.com/articles/BL-REB-27453 (archived at https://perma.cc/2RWX-T68H)

Encyclopedia.com (2024) International Directory of Company Histories, https://www.encyclopedia.com/books/politics-and-business-magazines/signet-banking-corporation (archived at https://perma.cc/3ZVB-ARZF)

Hackett, M. C. (2020) *The Capital One Story*, HarperCollins Leadership

ITU (2023) "Population of Global Offline Continues Steady Decline to 2.6 Billion People in 2023," *ITU*, https://www.itu.int/en/mediacentre/Pages/PR-2023-09-12-universal-and-meaningful-connectivity-by-2030.aspx (archived at https://perma.cc/2KF3-KLDY)

Kortina, A. (2024) "Origins of Venmo," https://kortina.nyc/essays/
origins-of-venmo (archived at https://perma.cc/G3FU-THJH)

Munger, C. (2011) *Poor Charlie's Almanack: The Wit and Wisdom of
Charles T. Munger*, Stripe Press

Rubinstein, M. (2023) "Capital One: Buffett's Latest Banking Pick,"
Net Interest, https://www.netinterest.co/p/capital-one-buffetts-latest-
banking (archived at https://perma.cc/Q86K-LJ77)

United States Securities And Exchange Commission (2024) "Nu
Holdings Ltd.," https://www.sec.gov/Archives/edgar/data/1691493/
000129281423001671/nuform20f_2022.htm (archived at
https://perma.cc/GB98-9UC5)

Chapter 1

Interview with Roelof Botha, Managing Partner, Sequoia Capital

Interview with Reid Hoffman, Co-founder, LinkedIn and Inflection AI,
former COO, PayPal

Interview with Keith Rabois, Co-founder, Opendoor and former COO,
PayPal

Cag, D. (2022) "The Story of PayPal: The World's Most Valuable Fintech
Firm," *FinTech Magazine*, https://fintechmagazine.com/digital-
payments/story-paypal-worlds-most-valuable-fintech-firm (archived at
https://perma.cc/N6LF-6SZM)

Cullen, A. (2024) "Commentary: Unicorns in Zoos: The Rise of Billion
Dollar Companies, Stanford Economic Review," *Stanford Economic
Review*, https://stanfordeconreview.com/2023/02/18/commentary-
unicorns-in-zoos-the-rise-of-billion-dollar-companies (archived at
https://perma.cc/3H7T-9Z4M)

Mangalindan, J. (2021) "eBay CEO: Why We're Spinning Off PayPal,"
Fortune, https://fortune.com/2014/09/30/ebay-ceo-why-were-
spinning-off-paypal/ (archived at https://perma.cc/T53Y-M4NY)

O'Brien, J. M. (2021) "The PayPal Mafia," *Fortune*, https://fortune.
com/2007/11/13/paypal-mafia/ (archived at https://perma.cc/Y2NX-
E77W)

Chapter 2

Interview with Bryan Johnson, Founder, Braintree

Interview with Sam Lessin, Co-founder, Slow Ventures

Interview with Bill Ready, CEO Pinterest and former CEO, Braintree

Interview with Iqram Magdon-Ismail and Andrew Kortina, Co-founders, Venmo

Interview with Andrew Staub, Dan Garfinkel and Jenny Stanchak, early Venmo employees

Attarbashi, B. H. (2022) "Andrew Kortina: How an Accident Inspired a Mobile Payment App," *LinkedIn*, https://www.linkedin.com/pulse/andrew-kortina-how-accident-inspired-mobile-payment-app-attarbashi/ (archived at https://perma.cc/9LZW-BMAU)

Burton, K. (2024) "Short Seller Hindenburg Nabs Tiny Gains Off $173 Billion Carnage," *Bloomberg.com*, https://www.bloomberg.com/news/features/2023-08-06/how-much-did-hindenburg-make-from-shorting-adani-dorsey-icahn?embedded-checkout=true+-+stock+price+fall (archived at https://perma.cc/K4NF-SGP9)

Gitnux (2024) "The Most Surprising Venmo Statistics and Trends in 2024," *GITNUX*, https://gitnux.org/venmo-statistics/ (archived at https://perma.cc/RWS7-LELQ)

Johnson, A. (2021) "Cash App is Culture," *Fintech Takes* https://newsletter.fintechtakes.com/p/cash-app?s=r (archived at https://perma.cc/ZPH6-G6UE)

Johnson, B. (2024) Blueprint, https://blueprint.bryanjohnson.com/ (archived at https://perma.cc/H7XH-HUEK)

Kortina, A. (2024) "Origins of Venmo," *kortina.nyc*, https://kortina.nyc/essays/origins-of-venmo (archived at https://perma.cc/G3FU-THJH)

Samaha, A. (2023) "Bob Lee's Murder Shook San Francisco. What Really Happened?," *Rolling Stone*, https://www.rollingstone.com/culture/culture-features/bob-lee-murder-cash-app-what-happened-1234852853/ (archived at https://perma.cc/2YPU-4LB6)

Self Financial (2023) "The Unbanked and Underbanked Population 2023," *Self Financial*, https://www.self.inc/info/unbanked-and-underbanked-population/ (archived at https://perma.cc/4B95-VX2G)

Chapter 3

Interview with Brian Wong, Former Vice President, Global Initiatives, Alibaba

Bloomberg UK (2014) "Tech Upstarts Paying 17 Times Interest Upset China Banks," https://www.bloomberg.com/news/articles/2014-01-13/tech-upstarts-paying-17-times-interest-upset-china-banks (archived at https://perma.cc/Y53M-MW7N)

CompaniesMarketCap.com (nd) Alibaba, https://companiesmarketcap.com/alibaba/marketcap (archived at https://perma.cc/M24E-PJCT)

He, L. (2023) "How Much Did Jack Ma's Speech Cost Ant Group? About $230 Billion," CNN, https://edition.cnn.com/2023/07/10/investing/china-ant-group-valuation-jack-ma-intl-hnk/index.html (archived at https://perma.cc/D36H-BXLK)

Kharpal, A. (2017) "Tencent Becomes First Asian Tech Firm to be Valued Over $500 Billion and is Now Closing In on Facebook," CNBC, https://www.cnbc.com/2017/11/20/tencent-first-asian-company-to-be-valued-over-500-billion.html (archived at https://perma.cc/C3LJ-RN4L)

Lashinsky, A. (2021) "Alibaba v. Tencent: The Battle for Supremacy in China," Fortune, https://fortune.com/longform/alibaba-tencent-china-internet/ (archived at https://perma.cc/PPA7-2REA)

Li, L. (2024) "WeChat pay vs Alipay: Which is Better for Expats in China?," Wise, https://wise.com/en-cn/blog/wechat-vs-alipay-for-expat-in-china (archived at https://perma.cc/DE2G-XHZS)

McDougall, M. (2018) "This South African Company Bet on Tencent in 2001. It Paid Off Massively," CNN Money, https://money.cnn.com/2018/07/30/investing/naspers-tencent-share-price/index.html (archived at https://perma.cc/2FRF-G3Q3)

Meixler, E. (2018) "Singles Day vs Black Friday: What's the Difference?," Time, https://time.com/5445756/singles-day-vs-black-friday (archived at https://perma.cc/ZB5V-W235)

Millward, S. (2015) "WeChat Users Sent Each Other 1 Billion Cash-Filled Red Envelopes Last Night," Tech in Asia, https://www.techinasia.com/wechat-1-billion-red-envelopes-chinese-new-year-2015 (archived at https://perma.cc/MZB7-AFXP)

National Bureau of Statistics of China (2019) "Gross Domestic Product, National Data," https://data.stats.gov.cn/english/easyquery. htm?cn=C01 (archived at https://perma.cc/S9FP-DEM8)

Pfanner, E. (2020) "SoftBank's Alibaba Alchemy: How to Turn $20 Million Into $50 Billion," *Wall Street Journal*, https://www.wsj.com/ articles/BL-DGB-37805 (archived at https://perma.cc/D7HQ-VQFZ)

Studio, S. (2024) "Hongbao: The Digital Red Envelope War in China," *Sekkei Digital Group*, https://sekkeidigitalgroup.com/digital-hongbao-war-china (archived at https://perma.cc/BER7-LNA5)

Taylor, C. (2023) "Jack Ma, Once Asia's Richest Person, Has Seen More Than Half of his $61 Billion Fortune Wiped Out in the Past 3 Years," *Fortune*, https://fortune.com/2023/07/12/jack-ma-alibaba-founder-asias-richest-person-net-worth-ant-group-crackdown/ (archived at https://perma.cc/U2ND-8EN8)

Tech Wire Asia (2017) "Chinese Tech Giants are Killing Small Business in Southeast Asia," *Tech Wire Asia*, https://techwireasia.com/09/2017/ chinese-tech-giants-killing-small-business-southeast-asia (archived at https://perma.cc/PCL6-Q5CA)

The Economist (2020) "Regulators Spoil Ant's Party Less than 48 hours Before it Starts Trading," https://www.economist.com/finance-and-economics/2020/11/03/regulators-spoil-ants-party-less-than-48-hours-before-it-starts-trading?ref=hackernoon.com (archived at https://perma.cc/D6Q2-WNDL)

Van Boom, D. (2016) "Why India Snubbed Facebook's Free Internet Offer," *CNET*, https://www.cnet.com/tech/tech-industry/why-india-doesnt-want-free-basics (archived at https://perma.cc/KD8F-2EF9)

Wang, H. H. (2012) "How eBay Failed in China," *Forbes*, https://www.forbes.com/sites/china/2010/09/12/how-ebay-failed-in-china/?sh=103daf1f5d57 (archived at https://perma.cc/3ZAB-KM6K)

Yang, J. and Wei, L. (2020) "China's President Xi Jinping Personally Scuttled Jack Ma's Ant IPO," *Wall Street Journal*, https://www.wsj.com/ articles/china-president-xi-jinping-halted-jack-ma-ant-ipo-11605203556 (archived at https://perma.cc/JLP7-3SGF)

Zucchi, K. (2023) "Top 10 Largest Global IPOs of all Time," *Investopedia*, https://www.investopedia.com/articles/investing/011215/ top-10-largest-global-ipos-all-time.asp (archived at https://perma.cc/ 5YYK-BNUT)

Chapter 4

Interviews with Nubank Co-founders, David Vélez, Edward Wible, Cristina Junqueira

Interview with former Nubank Vice President of Product, Hugh Strange

Interviews with early Nubank employees: Flávia Beatriz Cruz and Bruno Koba

Chapter 5

Interview with Immad Akhund, Co-founder, Mercury

Interview with Ian Brady, Co-founder, SoFi

Interview with Dileep Thazhmon, Co-founder, Jeeves

Interview with Maurice Werdegar, CEO, Western Technology Investment

Azevedo, M. A. (2023) "SVB's Collapse Drove 26K Customers to Mercury in 4 Months," *TechCrunch*, https://techcrunch.com/2023/07/07/mercury-says-it-gained-nearly-26k-new-customers-in-the-four-months-after-svbs-collapse (archived at https://perma.cc/2ZXZ-RQ49)

Azevedo, M. A. (2024) "Fintech Mercury, Whose B2B Business is Caught up in Regulatory Scrutiny Expands into Consumer Banking," *TechCrunch*, https://techcrunch.com/2024/04/17/fintech-banking-startup-mercury-is-expanding-into-consumer-banking (archived at https://perma.cc/Q5YC-3U3S)

Contrary Research (2024) "Mercury," https://research.contrary.com/reports/mercury (archived at https://perma.cc/E9ML-AMM8)

Crunchbase (2024) "Mercury," https://www.crunchbase.com/organization/mercury-technologies (archived at https://perma.cc/K468-EBKX)

Franceschi, P. (2023) "How Brex is Supporting SVB Customers and the Broader Startup Community," *Brex*, https://www.brex.com/journal/how-brex-is-supporting-svb-customers (archived at https://perma.cc/M6KN-A7UU)

Garfinkle, A. (2024) "Big Banks Have Seen The Most Deposits From Startups Since SVB's Collapse—But There's One Startup in the Mix," *Fortune*, https://fortune.com/2024/03/13/mercury-bank-startup-deposits (archived at https://perma.cc/WM9C-CV27)

Hayes, D. (2023) "SVB, Signature Racked Up Some High Rates of Uninsured Deposits," *S&P Global Homepage*, https://www.spglobal.com/marketintelligence/en/news-insights/latest-news-headlines/svb-signature-racked-up-some-high-rates-of-uninsured-deposits-74747639 (archived at https://perma.cc/99HU-YMQY)

Liu, H. and Staff in the Office of Technology (2021) "Online Student Loan Refinance Company SOFI Settles FTC Charges, Agrees to Stop Making False Claims About Loan Refinancing Savings," *Federal Trade Commission*, https://www.ftc.gov/news-events/news/press-releases/2018/10/online-student-loan-refinance-company-sofi-settles-ftc-charges-agrees-stop-making-false-claims-about (archived at https://perma.cc/82SE-HH2N)

SoFi (2024) "SOFI Surpasses $6 Billion in Funded Loans, Bolsters Leadership Team," *SoFi*, https://www.sofi.com/press/sofi-supasses-6-billion-in-loans (archived at https://perma.cc/F6LF-WTKH)

Surane, J. (2023) "SVB's Giant Treasury Book, Tech Focus Made it Uniquely Shaky," *Bloomberg Law*, https://news.bloomberglaw.com/mergers-and-acquisitions/svbs-giant-treasury-book-tech-focus-made-it-uniquely-shaky (archived at https://perma.cc/947E-KJL9)

Wile, R. (2023) "Silicon Valley Bank Shutdown: How it Happened and What Comes Next," *NBCNews.com*, https://www.nbcnews.com/business/business-news/silicon-valley-bank-collapse-news-updates-rcna74384 (archived at https://perma.cc/33RV-PFZD)

Chapter 6

Interview with Tom Blomfield OBE, Co-founder, Monzo and GoCardless

Interview with Chi-Hua Chien, Co-founder and Managing Partner, Goodwater Capital

Blomfield, T. (2022) "Monzo Growth", https://tomblomfield.com/ (archived at https://perma.cc/9NXS-SS9B)

Blomfield, T. (2022) "Five Unbreakable Rules for Startups", https://tomblomfield.com/ (archived at https://perma.cc/9NXS-SS9B)

Crowdcube (2018) "The Story of Monzo", https://www.crowdcube.com/explore/raising/success-stories/monzo (archived at https://perma.cc/2987-KCB2)

Kuckestein, J. (2018) "Monzo Staff Weekly Q&A – Jonas Huckestein (Co-Founder and CTO)," *Monzo Community*, https://community. monzo.com/t/monzo-staff-weekly-q-a-jonas-huckestein-Co-founderchief-technical-officer/40853/21 (archived at https://perma.cc/ 2UZSDSHN)

Mellino, E. (2019) "Revolut Insiders Reveal the Human Cost of a Fintech Unicorn's Wild Rise," *Wired*, https://www.wired.com/story/ revoluttrade-unions-labour-fintech-politics-storonsky (archived at https://perma.cc/NL83-HS52)

Mucklejohn, L. (2024) "Monzo Hits $5bn Valuation With New Funding Round Led by Capitalg," CityAM, https://www.cityam.com/ monzohits-5bn-valuation-with-new-funding-round-led-by-alphabet (archived at https://perma.cc/X6LQ-SGBG)

Smart Money People (2024) "British Bank Awards 2024," https://smartmoneypeople.com/british-bank-awards (archived at https://perma.cc/Q8GF-DPJD)

Taub, B. (2023) "How The Biggest Fraud in German History Unravelled," *The New Yorker*, https://www.newyorker.com/magazine/ 2023/03/06/how-the-biggest-fraud-in-german-historyunravelled (archived at https://perma.cc/QJ6Z-DYZZ)

Chapter 7

Interview with Alvan Chow, GameStop Trader

Interview with Jack Fuchs, Director of Principled Entrepreneurship at Stanford and Partner, Blackhorn Ventures

Interview with Nick Hungerford, Founder of Nutmeg

Interview with Andy Rachleff, Founder, Wealthfront and General Partner, Benchmark

Interview with Scott Sandell, Executive Chairman and CIO, NEA

Cagé, J. et al (2023) "Heroes and Villains: The Effects of Heroism on Autocratic Values and Nazi Collaboration in France," *American Economic Review*, 113 (7), pp 1888–932

Chaparro, F. (2020) "Robinhood's 17-hour Outage Reignites Debate Over a Controllable Rule that Reshaped the Stock Market," *The Block*, https://www.theblock.co/post/57587/robinhoods-17-hour-outage-reignites-debate-over-a-controversial-rule-that-reshaped-the-stock-market (archived at https://perma.cc/M8LZ-64QW)

Constine, J. (2017) "Robinhood Stock-Trading App Confirms $110M Raise at $1.3B Valuation," *TechCrunch*, https://techcrunch.com/2017/04/26/robincorn (archived at https://perma.cc/H2BL-78HA)

Curry, D. (2024) "Robinhood Revenue and Usage Statistics (2024)," *Business of Apps*, https://www.businessofapps.com/data/robinhood-statistics (archived at https://perma.cc/KNF5-L247)

Jha, S. (2013) "Trade, Institutions and Ethnic Tolerance: Evidence from South Asia," *American Political Science Review*, 107 (4), SSRN 2155918

Kelly, M. (2021) "Hill Report: Who Wants to Talk to Reddit?," *The Verge*, https://www.theverge.com/2021/2/18/22290110/house-financial-services-robinhood-gamestop-squeeze-roaringkitty-hearing (archived at https://perma.cc/9V8L-3GC7)

King, H. (2023) "Robinhood Co-founder Vlad Tenev Talks About What He Learned from GameStop Saga," *Axios*, https://www.axios.com/2023/12/20/robinhood-vlad-tenev-gamestop (archived at https://perma.cc/Z4E6-V2AF)

Richards, A. (2022) "What Happened to the Retail Investors in 'Eat the Rich: The GameStop Saga'?", *Netflix Tudum*, https://www.netflix.com/tudum/articles/gamestop-alvan-chow-interview (archived at https://perma.cc/QM5H-6NUS)

Surane, J., Massa, A. and Gittelsohn, J. (2020) "As Robinhood's Stock-trading App Failed, the Company was Maxing Out its Credit," *Los Angeles Times*, https://www.latimes.com/business/story/2020-03-10/robinhood-credit (archived at https://perma.cc/VHW9-9HQY)

Tenev, V. (2024) "Robinhood CEO Vlad Tenev on New Credit Card," *CNBC*, https://www.cnbc.com/video/2024/03/27/robinhood-ceo-vlad-tenev-on-new-credit-card-the-idea-is-to-add-more-things-to-robinhood-gold.html (archived at https://perma.cc/Q35L-DE58)

US Securities and Exchange Commission (2021) "Staff Report On Equity And Options Market Structure," *Sec.com*, https://www.sec.gov/files/staff-report-equity-options-market-struction-conditions-early-2021.pdf (archived at https://perma.cc/7M5L-V38Q)

US Securities and Exchange Commission (2021) "Robinhood Resale," *Sec.com*, https://s28.q4cdn.com/948876185/files/doc_downloads/Robinhood-Resale-S-1_opt.pdf (archived at https://perma.cc/BN2V-YHBY)

Chapter 8

Interview with Morgan Beller, Co-creator, Libra

Interview with Chris Dixon, Founding Partner, a16z Crypto

Interview with Devin Finzer, Co-founder, OpenSea

Interview with Chris Larsen, Co-founder, Ripple

Interview with David Marcus, Former president of PayPal and co-creator of Libra

Bambrough, B. (2024) "'The Dollar Will Be Worth Nothing' Elon Musk Issues Stark Fed Warning As 'Stealth Money Printing' Grinds Bitcoin, Ethereum and XRP Price Higher," *Forbes*, https://www.forbes.com/sites/digital-assets/2024/05/04/the-dollar-will-be-worth-nothing-elon-musk-issues-stark-fed-warning-as-stealth-money-printing-grinds-bitcoin-ethereum-and-xrp-price-higher (archived at https://perma.cc/FN29-6YP6)

Chang, S. (2018) "Facebook Aggressively Hiring Blockchain Devs, Discussed Launching Cryptocurrency: Report," *Yahoo!* https://au.lifestyle.yahoo.com/finance/news/facebook-aggressively-hiring-blockchain-devs-000137909.html (archived at https://perma.cc/867S-FXJG)

CNBCTV18 (2023) "Has Blur Already Displaced OpenSea as the Most Used NFT Marketplace? What Data Says on OpenSea vs Blur," *CNBCTV*, https://www.cnbctv18.com/cryptocurrency/has-blur-already-displaced-opensea-as-the-most-used-nft-marketplace-what-data-says-on-opensea-vs-blur-16780901.htm (archived at https://perma.cc/J82T-K62Y)

CoinCodex (2024) "Convert 10000 BTC to USD—Bitcoin to US Dollar Converter," https://coincodex.com/convert/bitcoin/usd/10000/ (archived at https://perma.cc/4FUR-5MAX)

Dixon, C. (2024) *Read Write Own: Building the Next Era of the Internet*, Penguin

Greig, J. (2024) "$112 Million Stolen From Founder of Ripple Cryptocurrency Platform," *The Record Cyber Security News*, https://therecord.media/xrp-theft-ripple-founder-account (archived at https://perma.cc/6EKU-VG3Q)

Hayes, A. (2024) "Who is Satoshi Nakamoto?," *Investopedia*, https://www.investopedia.com/terms/s/satoshi-nakamoto.asp (archived at https://perma.cc/BW4K-GRZ2)

Helmore, E. (2017) "Ripple: Cryptocurrency Enjoys End-of-Year Surge – But Will It Endure?," *The Guardian*, https://www.theguardian.com/technology/2017/dec/31/ripple-cryptocurrency-bitcoin-value (archived at https://perma.cc/F9LB-KUZ7)

Kharpal, A. and Browne, R. (2023) "Davos Crypto Crowd Distance Themselves From FTX and Sam Bankman-Fried: 'It's Fraud'," *CNBC*, https://www.cnbc.com/2023/01/19/davos-crypto-crowd-distance-themselves-from-ftx-and-sam-bankman-fried.html (archived at https://perma.cc/J82Z-89DP)

Leigh, D. (2023) "New Study Reveals 95% of NFTS Have a Market Cap of Zero," *TechRound*, https://techround.co.uk/news/new-study-reveals-95-of-nfts-have-a-market-cap-of-zero (archived at https://perma.cc/M2KZ-AEYS)

Meta (2020) "Coming in 2020: Calibra," https://about.fb.com/news/2019/06/coming-in-2020-calibra (archived at https://perma.cc/PUB9-Q5NZ)

McCall, M. (2020) A $200 Million Pizza! Here's How Bitcoin Made That Possible, *Nasdaq*, https://www.nasdaq.com/articles/a-$200-million-pizza-heres-how-bitcoin-made-that-possible-...-2020-12-02 (archived at https://perma.cc/U2PP-EW5S)

Murphy, H. and Stacey, K. (2022) "Facebook Libra: The Inside Story of How The Company's Cryptocurrency Dream Died," *Financial Times*, https://www.ft.com/content/a88fb591-72d5-4b6b-bb5d-223adfb893f3 (archived at https://perma.cc/GZT2-QM5A)

NFT Evening (2023) "OpenSea Drops Royalties, And Here's What Twitter Had to Say," https://nftevening.com/opensea-drops-royalties-and-heres-what-twitter-had-to-say (archived at https://perma.cc/X3ER-4SXP)

Orcutt, M. (2019) "The Radical Idea Hiding Inside Facebook's Digital Currency Proposal," *MIT Technology Review*, https://www.technologyreview.com/2019/06/25/800/how-facebooks-new-blockchain-might-revolutionize-our-digital-identities/ (archived at https://perma.cc/K68U-YWXS)

Shome, A. (2019) "PayPal Becomes The First to Withdraw from Libra Association, Finance Magnates," *Financial and Business News*, https://www.financemagnates.com/cryptocurrency/news/paypal-becomes-the-first-to-withdraw-from-libra-association (archived at https://perma.cc/YM67-58P9)

University of Birmingham (2022) "Where Next For Cryptocurrency After FTX Collapse?" https://www.birmingham.ac.uk/news/2022/where-next-for-cryptocurrency-after-ftx-collapse (archived at https://perma.cc/JZ8X-HSW2)

Wilson, T. (2019) Ahead of Libra, XRP Cryptocurrency Gains Toehold in Commerce, *Reuters*, https://www.reuters.com/article/idUSKBN1WP0R7 (archived at https://perma.cc/8G7B-RSRN)

Chapter 9

Interview with Peter Colis, Co-founder, Ethos Life
Interview with Scott Kupor, Managing Partner, Andreessen Horowitz
Interview with Spike Lipkin, Co-founder, Newfront
Interview with Alex Pall, The Chainsmokers and Mantis VC
Interview with Spencer Rascoff, Co-founder, Zillow
Interview with Mario Schlosser, Co-founder, Oscar Health
Interview with Professor Ilya A. Strebulaev, lecturer at Stanford Business School

Eldon, E. (2012) "Facebook in Brazil: A Big Ending to 2011 Finally Pushes It Past Orkut," *TechCrunch*, https://techcrunch.com/2012/01/17/facebook-in-brazil-a-big-ending-to-2011-finally-pushes-it-past-orkut (archived at https://perma.cc/ZY78-SUVN)

Ferowich, G. (2016) "Oscar's Ties To Trump Put It In Tricky Position," *Fierce Healthcare*, https://www.fiercehealthcare.com/payer/oscar-trump-admin-could-be-interesting-mix (archived at https://perma.cc/AE7C-BAJC)

Gee, S. E. (2023) Cryptocurrency Insurance: Protecting Crypto Assets After FTX Collapse, *Reed Smith*, https://www.reedsmith.com/en/perspectives/cyber-insurance-claims/2023/06/cryptocurrency-insurance-protecting-crypto-assets-after-ftx-collapse (archived at https://perma.cc/RQ6K-9MPW)

The Insurer TV (2023) "Newfront's Lipkin: AI is a 'Once-In-A-Generation Opportunity' to Reshape an Industry," *The Insurer TV*, https://www.theinsurertv.com/close-quarter/newfronts-lipkin-ai-is-a-once-in-a-generation-opportunity-to-reshape-an-industry (archived at https://perma.cc/9E3J-6JNV)

Onaizah, P. (2017) "Oscar Health—Revolutionizing Health Insurance Through Data Analytics," *Digital Innovation and Transformation*, https://d3.harvard.edu/platform-digit/submission/oscar-health-revolutionizing-health-insurance-through-data-analytics (archived at https://perma.cc/U4FN-73GU)

Orland, K. (2011) "Vostu Pays Undisclosed Sum to Zynga to Settle Copyright Infringement Lawsuit," *Venture Beat*, https://venturebeat.com/games/vostu-pays-undisclosed-sum-to-zynga-to-settle-copyright-infringement-lawsuit (archived at https://perma.cc/F8TY-2VZM)

Picchi, A. (2016) "The Billion-Dollar Obamacare Business with Trump Family Ties," *CBS News*, https://www.cbsnews.com/news/donald-trump-obamacare-josh-kushner-jared-kushner-oscar-insurance/ (archived at https://perma.cc/MD4V-XJ5X)

Rao, L. (2011) "Zynga, Vostu Settle Copyright Lawsuit; Brazilian Gaming Company to Pay Up," *TechCrunch*, https://techcrunch.com/2011/12/06/zynga-vostu-settle-copyright-lawsuit-brazilian-gaming-company-to-pay-up (archived at https://perma.cc/T7R7-4URF)

Renken, C. (2022) "Newfront Hits $2.2B Valuation with $200m Goldman Sachs Investment," *Built In SF*, https://www.builtinsf.com/articles/newfront-raises-200m-2b-valuation-goldman-sachs (archived at https://perma.cc/PG4N-8YDY)

Smarter Legal Research (2011) "Zynga, Inc. v. Vostu USA, Inc," https://casetext.com/case/zynga-inc-v-vostu-usa-inc (archived at https://perma.cc/72LA-W72F)

Chapter 10

Interview with Roelof Botha, Managing Partner, Sequoia Capital
Interview with Jeff Epstein, former CFO, Oracle
Interview with Pete Flint OBE, Co-founder, Trulia
Interview with Kevin Hartz, Co-founder, Eventbrite, Xoom
Interview with Reid Hoffman CBE, Co-founder, LinkedIn
Interview with Jessica Jackley, Co-founder, Kiva
Interview with Martha Lane-Fox CBE, Co-founder, Lastminute.com
Interview with Keith Rabois, Co-founder, Opendoor

Interview with Spencer Rascoff, Co-founder, Hotwire and Zillow

Interview with Ali Tamaseb, Author of Super Founders and General Partner, Data Collective

Ayas, R. (2022) "Who's The Next Paypal Mafia?," *Revelio Labs*, https://www.reveliolabs.com/news/tech/who-is-the-next-paypal-mafia (archived at https://perma.cc/25JZ-TX4Y)

Beer-Gabel, G. (2024) "Breeding Fintech Unicorns: The Surprising Drivers Behind Billion-Dollar Success," *Team8*, https://team8.vc/rethink/fintech/breeding-fintech-unicorns-the-surprising-drivers-behind-billion-dollar-success (archived at https://perma.cc/TGG7-6T7A)

Gilson, D. (2021) "What Makes Unicorns Special?," *Stanford Graduate School of Business*, https://www.gsb.stanford.edu/insights/what-makes-unicorns-special-these-numbers-may-hold-answers (archived at https://perma.cc/AX5Z-RBB9)

Hoffman, R. and Yeh, C. (2018) *Blitzscaling: The Lightning-Fast Path to Building Massively Valuable Businesses*, Harper Collins

Iuchanka, A. (2023) "Fintech Unicorns: Facts and Figures," *Vention*, https://ventionteams.com/fintech/unicorns (archived at https://perma.cc/SG2Q-GVSB)

NFX (2022) "70 Percent of Value in Tech is Driven by Network Effects," *NFX*, https://www.nfx.com/post/70-percent-value-network-effects (archived at https://perma.cc/S2E9-2N9B)

NFX (2023) "The Network Effects Manual: 16 Different Network Effects (and Counting)," https://www.nfx.com/post/network-effects-manual (archived at https://perma.cc/ZYX8-DZ74)

Tamaseb, A. (2021) "Land Of The 'Super Founders' - A Data-Driven Approach To Uncover The Secrets Of Billion Dollar Startups," *Medium*, https://alitamaseb.medium.com/land-of-the-super-founders-a-data-driven-approach-to-uncover-the-secrets-of-billion-dollar-a69ebe3f0f45 (archived at https://perma.cc/BC8T-8PQ9)

YouTube (2023) "Keith Rabois: Spotting Talent, Operating, and the PayPal Mafia," *YouTube*, https://www.youtube.com/watch?v=S9by0kQ12aI (archived at https://perma.cc/S2B5-EQ7W)

INDEX

Looking for another book?

Explore our award-winning
books from global business
experts in Digital and
Technology

Scan the code to browse

www.koganpage.com/digital-
technology

Also Available

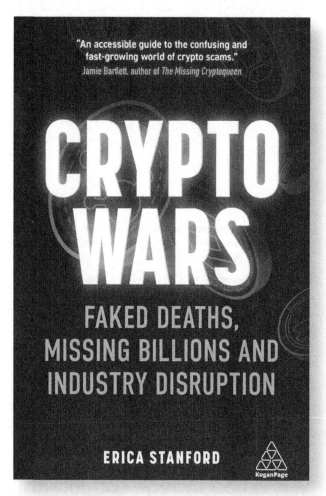

"An accessible guide to the confusing and fast-growing world of crypto scams."
Jamie Bartlett, author of *The Missing Cryptoqueen*

CRYPTO WARS

FAKED DEATHS, MISSING BILLIONS AND INDUSTRY DISRUPTION

ERICA STANFORD

KoganPage

ISBN: 9781398600683

www.koganpage.com

Printed in Great Britain
by Amazon

48815181R00155